After Meaning

ELGAR STUDIES IN LEGAL THEORY

Series Editor: Wojciech Sadurski, *Sydney Law School, University of Sydney, Australia*

Elgar Studies in Legal Theory is a series designed to cultivate and promote high quality works of scholarship on all aspects of legal theory. The focus of the series is on the development of original thinking in legal theory, with topics ranging from law and language, logic and legal reasoning, morality and the law, critical legal studies, and transnational law. Innovative work is encouraged from both established authors and the new generation of scholars.

Titles in this series include:

After Meaning
The Sovereignty of Forms in International Law

Jean d'Aspremont

Professor of International Law, Sciences Po Law School, France and Chair of Public International Law, University of Manchester, UK

ELGAR STUDIES IN LEGAL THEORY

Edward Elgar
PUBLISHING

Cheltenham, UK • Northampton, MA, USA

Published by
Edward Elgar Publishing Limited
The Lypiatts
15 Lansdown Road
Cheltenham
Glos GL50 2JA
UK

Edward Elgar Publishing, Inc.
William Pratt House
9 Dewey Court
Northampton
Massachusetts 01060
USA

Paperback edition 2023

A catalogue record for this book
is available from the British Library

Library of Congress Control Number: 2021947961

This book is available electronically in the **Elgar**online
Law subject collection
http://dx.doi.org/10.4337/9781802200928

ISBN 978 1 80220 091 1 (cased)
ISBN 978 1 80220 092 8 (eBook)
ISBN 978 1 0353 2038 7 (paperback)

Printed and bound by CPI Group (UK) Ltd, Croydon, CR0 4YY

Contents

Preface

After meaning. The international lawyer always arrives after meaning has already slipped away from the form. It is not that the international lawyer should have come earlier to have a chance to catch meaning. Meaning, as this book argues, never stays in the form, for it is always deferred. It is one of the main claims of this book that meaning is perpetually absent from the forms of the international legal discourse. In the absence of meaning, the international lawyer is left with forms, only forms.

To many, the claim made here will sound preposterous. After all, how can meaning possibly be absent from the forms of the international legal discourse whereas international legal thought and practice are almost entirely dedicated to determining, fathoming, evaluating, weighting, discussing, enforcing, scrutinizing, contesting, discrediting, or criticizing the meaning of the words, idioms, aphorisms, and texts of international law? Any possible resistance to this book's claim that meaning is absent from the forms of the international legal discourse would not be surprising. In fact, such resistance would be the manifestation of the very way of thinking that this book seeks to question, namely what it calls meaning-centrism. As will be demonstrated in the following chapters, international legal thought and practice have until today remained premised on the presupposition that words, idioms, aphorisms, and texts—thus the forms—of international law perform a signifying function whereby they mean a thing, an idea, a norm, a practice, a behaviour, an institution, a discourse, and so on. Notwithstanding the contemporary sensibility for indeterminacy and the performativity of texts, the words, idioms, aphorisms, and texts of the international legal discourse continue to be approached as standing for a thing, an idea, a norm, a practice, a behavior, an institution, a discourse, and so on. This book takes issue with this dominant meaning-centrism of international legal thought and practice. It argues that the international legal discourse is *a site of infinite meaning deferral* and shows that meaning, being perpetually deferred, is absent from the forms of the international legal discourse.

These few introductory considerations may not suffice to explain why I have chosen the recourse to "sovereignty" in the title of this book. In that respect, I must acknowledge that the recourse to that specific word proved no easy decision. I had long thought that I would never ever use the word "sovereignty" in my legal writing on international law, even less so on the cover of a book. For the past 15 years, I have consciously circumvented the use of that specific word, for I felt that never has a word that is so instrumental in the many paradigmatic necessities of the international legal discourse been so casually treated by the international lawyer. Actually, during all these years I consciously boycotted the word "sovereignty" as a reaction against what I perceived as deplorable discursive nonchalance in order to avoid being myself complicit therewith. That self-imposed embargo on the word "sovereignty" ended with this book. There are at least two reasons for me to be now using the word "sovereignty" which I have long resented. First, I came to realize that bemoaning the discursive nonchalance accompanying the use of sovereignty in the international legal discourse is unwarranted. It is not that I believe that sovereignty is used rigorously after all. I continue to think that such word is the beacon of a sloppy discursive practice. It is rather that, as I came to appreciate when writing this book, sovereignty is a form which, like all words, idioms, aphorisms, and texts, never carries and deliver meaning but points away to other words, idioms, aphorisms, and texts. In particular, sovereignty is a form of the international legal discourse that continuously points away to other forms and perpetually defers meaning, the latter being made indefinitely absent. The meaning which one envisages when invoking the form "sovereignty" is at best a hope at the moment that form is uttered or written but is always condemned to be absent. In that sense, there was no longer any reason for me to continue to lament the absence of meaning of that word in international legal thought and practice, for, as this book argues, *meaninglessness is the condition of any form*. Second, I have come to think that, if sovereignty can work as a useful shorthand in the international legal discourse, it is precisely to indicate that, in the absence of meaning, forms sovereignly reign over international legal thought and practice.[1]

In challenging the dominant meaning-centrism of the international legal discourse and shedding light on the sovereignty of forms, this book seeks to promote a new attitude towards textuality in international law. This new attitude to textuality, which includes a new take on interpretation, critique, history, comparison, translation, referencing, and so on, is sketched out in the last part of this book. At this introductory stage, I nonetheless deem it extremely important to emphasize that this book's contestation of the dominant meaning-centrism of international legal thought and practice should certainly not be construed as an invitation for passivity and complacency toward what the forms of the international legal discourse do horribly wrong

---

[1]   On the idea that divisible sovereignty is no longer sovereignty as it would otherwise not be sovereign, see Jacques Derrida, *The Beast and the Sovereign*, vol 1 (University of Chicago Press 2011) 57, 76–77. See also Jacques Derrida, *Papier Machine* (Galilée 2001) 345.

as well as all the discriminations and inequalities they are complicit with. It is quite the opposite. In my view, it is because the forms of the international legal discourse do all what they do without pre-existing meaning that they warrant the greatest scrutiny *as forms*. In that regard, I believe that the international lawyer too often banks on the decent meaning that the forms of the international legal discourse supposedly carry and deliver in order to confront the indecency, reactionary agendas, and discursive vandalism promoted by the many post-truth delinquents nowadays roaming our streets, institutions, and (social) medias.[2] If anything, this book shows that it is vain to wait for decency to be carried and delivered by the forms of the international legal discourse. Decency is neither the cause, the origin, nor the product of the forms of the international legal discourse. Decency is what one does with such forms, and especially what one does with the perpetual and indefinite deferral of meaning at work in the international legal discourse. In that sense, this book can also be read as inviting the international lawyer to fight for decency though her appreciation of the gigantic deferral of meaning by the forms of the international legal discourse rather than through a quest for an ever-absent meaning.[3]

This book comes ten years after *Formalism and the Sources of International Law* (hereafter FSIL),[4] which constituted my most articulate and comprehensive venture into the study of legal forms so far. And yet, although only ten years have passed, the distance traveled since then is cosmic. From the perspective developed in the chapters that follow, FSIL probably epitomizes the meaning-centric obsession of international legal thought and practice for origins and causes with which this current book takes issue. Although FSIL's main ambition back then was to uphold the possibility of reform of legal forms, it remained a heavily meaning-centric enterprise, one that presupposes that meaning is the cause and origin of forms and one that promotes the elucidation of such cause and origin. This book also comes nearly seven years after *Epistemic Forces in International Law* (EFIL)[5] and five years after

---

2   See gen. Bruno Latour, 'Why has Critique Run out of Steam? From Matters of Fact to Matters of Concern' (2004) 30 Critical Inquiry 225.

3   George Steiner once wrote the following: "I have had neither the compulsion nor the courage to enter politics. The sum of my politics is to try and support whatever social order is capable of reducing, even marginally, the aggregate of hatred and of pain in the human circumstances... I think of myself as Platonic anarchist." See George Steiner, *Errata: An Examined Life* (Weidenfeld and Nicholson 1997) 121.

4   Jean d'Aspremont, *Formalism and the Sources of International Law: A Theory of the Ascertainment of Legal Rules* (OUP 2011).

5   Jean d'Aspremont, *Epistemic Forces of International Law: Foundational Doctrines and Techniques of International Legal Argumentation* (Edward Elgar Publishing 2015).

International Law as a Belief System (ILBS).[6] What I have tried to show, albeit somewhat clumsily, in both EFIL and ILBS is that international law functions as a system of inscription that reflects the very specific material conditions of its production. In unearthing the material conditions of the production of such system of inscription, ILBS and EFIL particularly sought to show the contingency of forms and debunk some of the false necessities of the international legal discourse. Yet, just like FSIL, ILBS and EFIL constituted meaning-centric exercises, for they were built, like most of contemporary works on the contingency of international law, on the presupposition that forms are capable to carry and deliver meaning. If the reader were to seek a rupture between the present book and those earlier works, it certainly lies in the meaning-centrism that afflicted the latter.[7] And yet, there is nothing in the abovementioned books that I could regret, rebut, or contradict. It is not only that FSIL, ILBS, and EFIL were important milestones in my thought-forming and thought-changing journey.[8] It is more fundamentally that these books, just like any other text, are themselves caught in the indefinite process of deferral of meaning and, thus, never had any meaning which I could possibly regret, rebut, or contradict.[9] Meaning is always absent from texts. International law books are no exception.

---

[6]   Jean d'Aspremont, *International Law as a Belief System* (CUP 2017).

[7]   I believe that this charge of meaning-centrism similarly applies, albeit to a lesser extent, to my more recent *The Discourse on Customary International Law* (OUP 2021), which constitutes a sort of venture into structuralist poetics for the sake of studying the discursive performances that are required to generate an argument on customary international law. Although acknowledging that the meaning is absent from the omnipresent text, this recent book did not entirely exclude that meaning, in the form of a discursive performance, remains present, thereby upholding some kind of meaning-centrism. On the extent to which structuralist poetics upholds meaning-centrism, see Jonathan Culler, *Structuralist Poetics: Structuralism, Linguistics, and the Study of Literature* (2nd edn, Routledge 2002) 156–157. It should be emphasized here that the current book, while turning interpretation into an exercise of poetics rather than hermeneutics, stays away from a type of poetics that is structuralist, which is one of the ways in which it differs from my earlier *The Discourse on Customary International Law*. See Chapter 4, Section 1.

[8]   Michel Foucault, *L'archéologie du savoir* (Gallimard 1969) 29: "Ne me demandez pas qui je suis et ne me dites pas de rester le même: c'est une morale d'état civil; elle régit nos papiers. Qu'elle nous laisse libres quand il s'agit d'écrire." This has been translated as follows: "Don't ask me who I am and don't tell me to remain the same: leave it to our bureaucrats and our police to see that our papers are in order. At least spare us their morality when we write." See Michel Foucault, *The Archaeology of Knowledge* (Routledge 2002) 19.

[9]   Ludwig Wittgenstein once wrote: "I find it important in philosophizing to keep changing my posture, not to stand for too long on one leg, so as not to get stiff." See

Although I did not subject this book to prolonged public testing as I did with my previous monographs, the following chapters have benefited from the—direct and indirect as well as conscious and unconscious—input of many colleagues and friends. I wish to mention a few of them. Rich and regular exchanges with Pierre Legrand, Fuad Zarbiyev, and Vincent Forray on the work (and the life) of Jacques Derrida have been very instrumental in shaping some of the thoughts that appear in this book. As for many of my previous books, Akbar Rasulov, Sahib Singh, and John Haskell have been fantastic thinking companions and regularly accepted acting as sounding boards for half-baked ideas. I have also immensely benefited from conversations with Pierre Schlag, Samantha Besson, Christian Tams, Maiko Meguro, and Frédéric Audren. Mikhail Xifaras has regularly and generously provided me with reading recommendations over the last years, some of which proved absolutely decisive in my intellectual journey. I am grateful to Matilda Gillis and Anaïs Brucher for their editorial assistance. Ben Booth at Edward Elgar encouraged me to take the risk of this book and, once more, has been a very valuable guide in yet another of my attempts at thought-entrepreneurship. I wish to thank them all very warmly.

Paris, Rue de l'Université, June 2021

Ludwig Wittgenstein, *Culture and Value* (Peter Winch tr, University of Chicago Press 1980) 27.

1. Meaning and form in international law

International law's words, idioms, aphorisms, and texts—what are called here the forms of the international legal discourse—are commonly thought as representing and referring to some pre-existing meaning. Indeed, it is ordinary to bestow on the forms of the international legal discourse a signifying function whereby such words, idioms, aphorisms, and texts represent a thing, an idea, a norm, a practice, a behavior, an institution, a discourse, and so on. According to this dominant meaning-centric understanding, meaning necessarily pre-exists the form that is derived from it, for it is only if the meaning precedes the form that the form can come to represent that meaning. In short, in international legal thought and practice, meaning is deemed the cause and origin of forms.

This book challenges the meaning-centrism of international legal thought and practice. It argues that the forms of the international legal discourse cannot find their origin or cause in some pre-existing meaning, for the latter is always absent. This book particularly shows that meaning is nowhere to be found and always absent from the forms of the international legal discourse because it is constantly deferred by them. According to the argument developed in this book, the absence of meaning from the forms of the international legal discourse bears important consequences. Indeed, the forms of the international legal discourse, finding neither their cause nor origin in any preceding meaning, do not need meaning to do what they do but only need other forms. Forms are accordingly the real sovereign of international legal thought and practice. This book is a venture into the *sovereignty of forms* and its implications for international legal thought and practice.

This chapter starts by describing the dominant meaning-centric attitude witnessed in international legal thought and practice (1) as well as the three main modes of thinking associated with it (2). This chapter then spells out the main argument of this book, namely that the forms of the international legal discourse are sovereign in that they do not carry or delivery any pre-existing meaning but constantly defer meaning (3). Although this will be the object of the last part of the book, this chapter already sketches out some of the main implications of the sovereignty of forms for international legal thought and practice (4). This chapter ends with a few observations on the contents of this book as well as a few caveats about the argument developed therein (5).

Before elucidating the meaning-centrism of international legal thought and practice, a preliminary remark is in order. As it is understood here, the meaning-centrism of international legal thought and practice corresponds to a well-known and more general pattern of thought that is called logocentrism.[1] It should accordingly be no surprise that the following exposition of meaning-centrism of international legal thought and practice makes use of the categories that have been used to described logocentrism in literary theory and critical literature.

1.   MEANING-CENTRISM IN INTERNATIONAL LEGAL THOUGHT AND PRACTICE

In international legal thought and practice, any word (for example, immunity, aggression, reparation, torture, and so on), idiom (for example, *opinio juris, jus cogens*, force majeure, and so on), aphorism ("the parties aim to reach global peaking of greenhouse gas emissions as soon as possible," "every internationally wrongful act of a State entails the international responsibility of that State," and so on), or text (Article 53 of the Vienna Convention on the Law of Treaties, Article 38 of the Statute of the International Court of Justice, and so on) always stands for a thing, an idea, a norm, a practice, a behavior, an institution, a discourse, and so on. In that sense, the words, idioms, aphorisms, and texts of international law—what are called here the forms of the international legal discourse[2]—perform a signifying function whereby they represent

---

[1]   On the idea of logocentrism, see Jacques Derrida, *De la Grammatologie* (Editions de Minuit 1967), 13, 21–23 (hereafter Derrida, *Grammatologie*); Jacques Derrida, *L'Ecriture et la différence* (Editions du Seuil 1967) 23 (hereafter Derrida, *Ecriture*). Such pattern has also been referred to as the expression of a *metaphysics of presence* as signs are always calling on a pre-existing meaning which they make permanently present. See Derrida, *Grammatologie* (n 1) 103; Jacques Derrida, *Marges de la Philosophie* (Editions de Minuit 1972) 187–188 (hereafter Derrida, *Marges*). Such logocentrism of Western thought has also been captured through the idea of the eternal journey of the sign as a representative of what it is supposed to represent. See Catherine Malabou and Jacques Derrida, *La Contre-Allée* (La Quinzaine Littéraire 1999) 44–45 (hereafter Malabou and Derrida, *Contre-Allée*).

[2]   Forms should not be reduced to textual inscriptions. As far as legal forms are concerned, images, symbols, gestures, paintings, ceremonies, rituals, stained glass windows, and so on are also forms which defer meaning. Forms are also in the oral language. Yet, the following chapters primarily engage with those international forms that consist of textual inscriptions. On non-textual inscriptions, see Jacques Derrida, *Papier Machine* (Galilée 2001) 384 (hereafter Derrida, *Papier Machine*). On the idea that language, even oral language, is already a type of writing, see Malabou and Derrida, *Contre-Allée* (n 1) 73–75. See also the remarks of Peter Goodrich, 'Europe in America: Grammatology, Legal Studies, and the Politics of Transmission' (2001) 101 Columbia

a thing, an idea, a norm, a practice, a behavior, an institution, a discourse, and so on.

To appreciate how meaning-centrism works in international legal thought and practice, it matters to highlight that the signifying function bestowed upon the forms of the international legal discourse is only possible to the extent that such words, idioms, aphorisms, and texts of international law are distinct from the meaning they refer to, that is, from the thing, the idea, the norm, the practice, the behavior, the institution, the discourse, and so on that they represent. In fact, meaning can only be represented, carried, and delivered by the forms of the international legal discourse if it is strictly distinct from such forms. It could even be said that the distinction between meaning and form is a condition of the discourse on international law. It is only as long as the forms of the international legal discourse and the pre-existing meaning they carry and deliver are distinguished that it is possible to excavate an alleged pre-existing meaning and thus to carry out an interpretation of the forms of the international legal discourse. From this mainstream perspective, meaning is thus external to international law's words, idioms, aphorisms, and texts.[3]

The forms of the international legal discourse are not only distinct from (and external to) the meaning they carry and deliver. They are also secondary thereto and derived therefrom.[4] In fact, according to such dominant meaning-centrism, there would be no forms in the international legal discourse if there were no preexisting meaning to carry and deliver and from which forms could be derived. This is why pre-existing meaning comes to be held, according to such dominant approach, as the cause and origin of the forms of

---

Law Review 2033, 2069–2084 (hereafter Goodrich, 'Europe in America'). For a similar choice to limit one's inquiry about forms to textual inscriptions, see Ntina Tzouvala, *Capitalism as Civilisation: A History of International Law* (CUP 2020) 18–19 (hereafter Tzouvala, *Capitalism*).

[3] It is no coincidence that distinguishing the forms of the international legal discourse from the meaning they refer to and represent is probably one of the greatest achievements of modern legal thought as it consolidated itself in the 19th and 20th centuries. On the modern modes of representation, see gen. Timothy Mitchell, *Questions of Modernity* (University of Minnesota Press 2000) 17–18 (hereafter Mitchell, *Modernity*). See gen. Michel Foucault, *Les mots et les choses* (Gallimard 1966) 58, 70–72 (hereafter Foucault, *Mots*); Derrida, *Grammatologie* (n 1) 50; Bruno Latour, *Nous n'avons jamais été modernes. Essai d'anthropologie symétrique* (La Découverte 1997) 24 (hereafter Latour, *Jamais été modernes*); Emmanuel Levinas, *Altérité et transcendence* (Fata Morgana 1995) 17.

[4] On the idea of derivation of writing in Western thought, see Malabou and Derrida, *Contre-Allée* (n 1) 44–45.

the international legal discourse, such forms being always at the service of that
pre-existing meaning.[5]

An important caveat is warranted at this stage. That the forms of the international legal discourse are thought as secondary to meaning does not entail that
they have not required attention. Actually, it is to uphold the transcendence
of forms and the meaning they deliver, and thus to facilitate the excavation of
such pre-existing meaning from the forms of the international legal discourse,
that modern international legal thought and practice have shown unprecedented care for identifying, inventorying, distinguishing, mapping, deciphering, tracing, organizing, and breaking down international law's forms.[6] In that
regard, it is no surprise that some of the most refined and revered scholarly
works on international law pertain to the forms of the international legal
discourse and that the judgments of international courts and tribunals that
are deemed canonical and referenced the most are often those judgments that
raise questions of forms. It is for the same reason that legal education in international law is primarily focused on mastering the forms of the international
legal discourse.[7]

Another aspect of the dominant meaning-centrism of international legal
thought and practice must be elucidated. In the meaning-centric way of thinking presented here, it is usually expected that the meaning that the forms of
the international legal discourse carry and deliver is determined through difference between the form concerned and other forms in the international legal
discourse. In other words, the pre-existing meaning carried and delivered by
the forms of the international legal discourse is supposedly retrieved through
a system of differences[8] between forms themselves. It is thus by virtue of the
differences between forms that the specific meaning carried and delivered by
a form of the international legal discourse can be determined. For instance,

---

[5] On the traditional idea that the form is treated as weightless and inconsequential
and what matters is the substantive meaning, see Pierre Schlag, '"Le Hors de Texte,
C'est Moi". The Politics of Form and the Domestication of Deconstruction' (1990) 11
Cardozo Law Review 1631, 1633 (hereafter Schlag, 'The Politics of Form'). See also
Vincent Forray and Sébastien Pimont, *Décrire le droit … et le transformer. Essai sur la
décriture du droit* (Dalloz 2017) 104 (hereafter Forray and Pimont, *Décrire le droit*).

[6] On the idea that the disintegration of the sign is a modern achievement, see
Roland Barthes, *Le Bruissement de la langue: Essais critiques IV* (Seuil 1984) 187
(hereafter Barthes, *Essais critiques IV*).

[7] I have myself succumbed to such meaning-centric obsession in my past work,
which I have long moved away from. See Jean d'Aspremont, *Formalism and the
Sources of International Law* (OUP 2011) (hereafter, d'Aspremont, *Formalism*).

[8] On the idea of system of differences, see Derrida, *Ecriture* (n 1) 426. See also the
remarks of Jonathan Culler, *Structuralist Poetics: Structuralism, Linguistics, and the
Study of Literature* (2nd edn, Routledge 2002) 5–6.

custom means what it means because, as a form, it is distinct from the treaty; the doctrine of sources refers to what it refers to because, as a form, it is not the doctrine of interpretation; an armed attack represents what it represents because, as a form, it is different from the use of force; compensation entails what it entails in terms of reparation because, as a form, it cannot be conflated with satisfaction, and so on. From this dominant perspective, the differences between international law's words, idioms, aphorisms, and texts constitute what allows the allocation of a pre-existing meaning to each and every form of the international legal discourse.[9]

It must be acknowledged that, albeit dominant and generally unquestioned in international legal thought and practice, meaning-centrism as well as the reliance on the differences between forms to determine meaning have come under extensive scrutiny over the past decades, especially following what has been called the "linguistic turn" in international legal thought.[10]

The "linguistic turn" is a common shorthand that refers to a series of attitudes that include the questioning of the stability of the text,[11] the playing down of authorship of law,[12] the demonstration that language is a huge site of power,[13] the necessity to un-trivialize legal forms,[14] and so on.

In particular, the very possibility of extracting a fixed meaning from the forms of the international legal discourse has been severely challenged by some international legal scholars who, mobilizing tools from structuralism[15]

---

[9]   The determination of meaning through the differences between forms has been theorized in traditional structuralist linguistics, which has shown the extent to which the identity of the sign is relational and differential and can only be determined through differences with other signs. See gen. Ferdinand de Saussure, *Course in General Linguistics* (Charles Bally and Albert Sechehaye eds, Open Court 1986). On this aspect of the work of Saussure, see the remarks of Derrida, *Ecriture* (n 1) 427.

[10]   For some general observations on the "linguistic turn" in international legal thought, see Ingo Venzke, 'Contemporary Theories and International Lawmaking' in Catherine Brölmann and Yannick Radi (eds), *Research Handbook on the Theory and Practice of International Lawmaking* (Edward Elgar Publishing 2016) 66–84.

[11]   Peter Goodrich and others, 'Introduction: A Philosophy of Legal Enigmas' in Peter Goodrich and others (eds), *Derrida and Legal Philosophy* (Palgrave MacMillan 2008) 2 (hereafter Goodrich and others, 'Introduction').

[12]   Ibid.

[13]   The expression is from Goodrich, 'Europe in America' (n 2) 2043.

[14]   The expression is from Schlag, 'The Politics of Form' (n 5) 1633.

[15]   On the structuralist foundations of Martti Koskenniemi's account of international legal argumentation, see Akbar Rasulov, 'From Apology to Utopia and the Inner Life of International Law' (2016) 29 Leiden Journal of International Law 641 (hereafter Rasulov, 'Inner Life'); Sahib Singh, 'International Legal Positivism and New Approaches to International Law' in Jörg Kammerhofer and Jean d'Aspremont (eds), *International Legal Positivism in a Postmodern World* (CUP 2014) 291–316; Justin Desautels-Stein, 'International Legal Structuralism: A Primer'

and popularizing findings already made in the 1970s[16] and early 1980s[17] in literary and linguistic studies, have shed light on the constant mediation between the world that is perceived (concreteness) and the world that is wanted (normativity) in the process of delivery of meaning by forms.[18] Such works were later continued and supplemented by an examination of the structural biases, institutional strategies, and special ethos that inform the delivery of meaning by the forms of the international legal discourse.[19] Building on earlier works on the self-explanatory character of legal forms and their inventing and organizing of their own formation and functioning,[20] the international legal literature has also turned its attention to the self-referential dialectics at work in forms' system of differences and the material conditions of their productions.[21]

(2016) 8 International Theory 201 (hereafter Desautels-Stein, 'International Legal Structuralism'). Emmanuelle Jouannet comes with a similar but more nuanced account. See Emmanuelle Jouannet, 'A Critical Introduction' in Martti Koskenniemi (ed), *The Politics of International Law* (Hart Publishing 2011) 2, 7–12.

[16]   George Steiner, *After Babel: Aspects of Language and Translation* (OUP 1975).

[17]   Robert Cover, 'The Supreme Court, 1982 Term – Foreword: Nomos and Narrative' (1983) 97 *Harvard Law Review* 4, 9.

[18]   David Kennedy, *International Legal Structures* (Nomos 1987); Martti Koskenniemi, *From Apology to Utopia* (CUP 2005) (hereafter Koskenniemi, *From Apology to Utopia*); Martti Koskenniemi, 'The Fate of International Law: Between Technique and Politics' (2007) 70 Modern Law Review 1.

[19]   Martti Koskenniemi, 'The Politics of International Law – 20 Years Later' (2009) 20 European Journal of International Law 7–9 (hereafter Koskenniemi, 'The Politics'); David Kennedy, *A World of Struggle: How Power, Law, and Expertise Shape Global Political Economy* (Princeton University Press 2016).

[20]   See Pierre Schlag, 'Normativity and the Politics of Form' (1991) 139 University of Pennsylvania Law Review 801; Pierre Schlag, 'The Empty Circles of Liberal Justification' (1997) 96 Michigan Law Review 1. See also Pierre Bourdieu, 'The Force of Law: Toward a Sociology of the Juridical Field' (1987) 38 Hastings Law Journal 805, 849. This is what has sometimes been called self-transcendence ('auto-transcendence'). See François Ost, *Du Sinaï au Champ-de-Mars: L'autre et le même au fondement du droit* (Lessius 1999) 20ff. See gen. Niklas Luhmann, *Social Systems* (John Bednarz and Dirk Baecker trs, Stanford University Press 1995).

[21]   See Jean d'Aspremont, *International Law as a Belief System* (CUP 2017) (hereafter d'Aspremont, *Belief System*). See also Jean d'Aspremont, 'Three International Lawyers in a Hall of Mirrors' (2019) 32 Leiden Journal of International Law 367.

Mention must similarly be made of these abounding works that have compellingly exposed the ideological,[22] neo-colonizing,[23] and masculine[24] dimensions of the world-making performances of the forms of the international legal discourse and of their system of differences.[25]

---

[22] Tzouvala, *Capitalism* (n 2); China Miéville, *Between Equal Rights: A Marxist Theory of International Law* (Haymarket Books 2006) (hereafter Miéville, *Between Equal Rights*); Liliana Obregon, 'Empire, Racial Capitalism and International Law: The Case of Manumitted Haiti and the Recognition Debt' (2018) 31 Leiden Journal of International Law 597; Rose Parfitt, *The Process of International Legal Reproduction: Inequality, Historiography, Resistance* (CUP 2019) (hereafter Parfitt, *International Legal Reproduction*). For some observations on ideology critique in international law, see Walter Rech, 'Ideology' in Jean d'Aspremont and Sahib Singh (eds), *Concepts for International Law: Contributions to Disciplinary Thought* (Edward Elgar Publishing 2019).

[23] Nathaniel Berman, 'In the Wake of Empire' (1999) 14 American University International Law Review 1515; Makau Mutua, 'What is TWAIL?' (2000) 94 American Society of International Law Proceedings 31; Makau Mutua, 'Savages, Victims and Saviors: The Metaphor of Human Rights' (2001) 42 Harvard International Law Journal 201; Sundya Pahuja, 'The Postcoloniality of International Law' (2005) 46 Harvard International Law Journal 459; Antony Anghie, 'The Evolution of International Law: Colonial and Postcolonial Realities' (2006) 27 Third World Quarterly 740; Buhpinder Chimni, 'Third World Approaches to International Law: A Manifesto' (2006) 8 International Community Law Review 18; Sundya Pahuja, *Decolonising International Law: Development, Economic Growth and the Politics of Universality* (CUP 2011); Antony Anghie, *Imperialism, Sovereignty and the Making of International Law* (CUP 2012). On the narratival structure of the contemporary discourse on imperialism in international law, see Akbar Rasulov, 'Imperialism' in Jean d'Aspremont and Sahib Singh (eds), *Concepts for International Law: Contributions to Disciplinary Thought* (Edward Elgar Publishing 2019) 422.

[24] Hilary Charlesworth, Christine Chinkin and Shelly Wright, 'Feminist Approaches to International Law' (1991) 85 American Journal of International Law 613; Karen Knop, 'Borders of the Imagination: The State in Feminist International Law' (1994) 88 Proceedings of the ASIL Annual Meeting 14; Hilary Charlesworth, 'The Sex of the State in International Law' in Ngaire Naffine and Rosemary Owens (eds), *Sexing the Subject of Law* (LBC Information Services 1997); Hilary Charlesworth and Christine Chinkin, *The Boundaries of International Law: A Feminist Analysis* (Manchester University Press 2000); Hilary Charlesworth, 'Feminist Ambivalence about International Law' (2005) 11 International Legal Theory 1; Dianne Otto, 'Resisting the Heteronormative Imaginary of the Nation-state: Rethinking Kinship and Border Protection' in Dianne Otto (ed), *Queering International Law: Possibilities, Alliances, Complicities, Risks* (Routledge 2018); Hilary Charlesworth, 'Prefiguring Feminist Judgment in International Law' in Loveday Hodson and Troy Lavers (eds), *Feminist Judgments in International Law* (Hart Publishing 2019).

[25] Koskenniemi, 'The Politics' (n 19) 7–19; Sundhya Pahuja, 'Decolonization and the Eventness of International Law' in Fleur Johns, Richard Joyce and Sundhya Pahuja (eds), *Events: The Force of International Law* (Routledge 2011); Ingo Venzke, *How Interpretation Makes International Law: On Semantic Change and Normative*

There is little doubt that the abovementioned critical evaluations of forms' deeds and of the false necessities they induce, as well as the demonstration of their contingency, have fundamentally reshaped the ways in which many scholars approach the meaning allegedly carried and delivered by the forms of the international legal discourse. For instance, there is nowadays much greater sensibility of the international lawyer for the ways and strategies through which forms, and especially legal forms, govern, shape, dictate, and blur the minds, the imagination, and the world. Yet, it is submitted here that the critical engagements with the forms of the international legal discourse that have accompanied the "linguistic turn" and which have been mentioned here have continued to abide by the mainstream meaning-centrism described in this section.[26] Even unfixed, hidden, strategically and ideologically defined, the meaning that accompanies the forms of the international legal discourse has remained construed as the cause and origin of those forms as well as of what such forms do. What is more, the very idea that the forms of the international legal discourse carry and deliver meaning, even if that meaning is said to be created at the moment of its delivery, has not been contested. In particular, the dualism which such critiques have relied on, be it the concreteness and the normativity, the center and the periphery, the form and the content, the male and the female, the universal and the particular, and so on, all continue to presuppose the presence of some kind of transcendental meaning anterior to the dichotomy that is being mobilized.[27] Thus, the forms of the international

---

Twists (OUP 2012) (hereafter Venzke, *On Semantic Change*). On the success of the so-called constructivist approaches to world-making, see Nicholas Onuf, *World of Our Making: Rules and Rules in Social Theory and International Relations* (University of South Carolina Press 1989); Nicholas Onuf, 'The Constitution of International Society' (1994) 5 European Journal of International Law 1, 6; Jutta Brunnée and Stephen Toope, 'International Law and Constructivism: Elements of an International Theory of International Law' (2000) 39 Columbia Journal of Transnational Law 19; Jutta Brunnée and Stephen Toope, 'Constructivism and International Law' in Jeffrey L Dunoff and Mark A Pollack (eds) *Interdisciplinary Perspectives on International Law and International Relations: The State of the Art* (CUP 2012). For compilation of the concepts at work in world-making by international law, see Jean d'Aspremont and Sahib Singh (eds), *Concepts for International Law: Contributions to Disciplinary Thought* (Edward Elgar Publishing 2019). See also the general observations of Andrea Bianchi, *International Law Theories: An Inquiry into Different Ways of Thinking* (OUP 2016) 16–19.

[26] It must be acknowledged that departing from meaning-centrism was not necessary for these critical works to fulfil their ambitions. For instance, one does not need to de-necessitate meaning-centrism to show the false necessities which these forms induce and rely on or to shed light on their contingency.

[27] Jacques Derrida, *Positions* (Editions de Minuit 1972) 41 (hereafter Derrida, *Positions*); Maurice Merleau-Ponty, *Signes* (Gallimard 1960) 70–73 (hereafter Merleau-Ponty, *Signes*).

legal discourse—and all of what they do horribly wrong—have continued to be discussed in relation to the meaning that they carry and deliver. This meaning-centric feature of critical scholarship has already been acknowledged and discussed in the literature.[28] It is accordingly not necessary to expose it further. What matters to stress here is that the meaning-centrism dominating international legal thought and practice has never been seriously discontinued or contested.[29] Whilst copiously borrowing from structuralist modes of thinking,[30] the critical works that have been mentioned above have fallen short of realizing the post-structuralist[31] revolution in international legal thought and practice.[32]

---

[28] See eg the remarks of Parfitt, *International Legal Reproduction* (n 22) 21; Tzouvala, *Capitalism* (n 2) 38–40; Fuad Zarbiyev, *Le discours interprétatif en droit international* (Bruylant 2015) 109–118 (hereafter Zarbiyev, *Discours interprétatif*). See also the remarks of Akbar Rasulov who argues that Martti Koskenniemi's engagement with structuralism in *From Apology to Utopia* (Koskenniemi, *From Apology to Utopia* (n 18)) is much more on the side of traditional French(-speaking) structuralism and that it is more a structuralism *à la Saussure* (see Rasulov, 'Inner Life' (n 15)). Cf the remarks of China Miéville on the work of Martti Koskenniemi in Miéville, *Between Equal Rights* (n 22) 55–56. For a similar claim about the meaning-centric use of deconstruction in US legal scholarship, see Schlag, 'The Politics of Form' (n 5) 1643–1645.

[29] On how critique has remained attached to the modern distinction between the form and the world, see gen. Mitchell, *Modernity* (n 3) 20.

[30] For a very insightful overview of the merits of structuralism for international legal thought, see Desautels-Stein, 'International Legal Structuralism' (n 15); Justin Desautels-Stein, 'Structuralist Legal Histories' (2015) 78 Law and Contemporary Problems 37. See also the remarks of David Kennedy, 'Critical Theory, Structuralism and Contemporary Legal Scholarship' (1986) 21 New England Law Review 209 (hereafter Kennedy, 'Critical Theory'); Martti Koskenniemi, 'What Is Critical Research in International Law? Celebrating Structuralism' (2016) 29 Leiden Journal of International Law 727. On the unexploited potential of structuralism in international legal thought, see the remarks by Tzouvala, *Capitalism* (n 2) 5–7.

[31] On the various uses of structuralist semiology and the move from structuralism to post-structuralism, see Roland Barthes, *L'aventure sémiologique* (Seuil 1985) 9–14 (hereafter Barthes, *L'aventure sémiologique*). On the distinction between structuralism and post-structuralism, see Jonathan Culler, *On Deconstruction: Theory and Criticism after Structuralism* (Routledge 2008) 22–30 (hereafter Culler, *On Deconstruction*). Cf the idea of superstructuralism of Richard Harland to encapsulate the work of both structuralists and poststructuralists as well as to account for the work of those thinkers that do not really fit in either of these categories or have moved between them: see Richard Harland, *Superstructuralism: The Philosophy of Structuralism and Post-Structuralism* (Routledge 1987) (hereafter Harland, *Superstructuralism*).

[32] This affirmation will certainly prove polemical. This is why it must be complemented by a few observations. The point here is certainly not that the work of post-structuralist thinkers like Derrida has been overlooked by legal scholars, let alone by international legal scholars. For instance, David Kennedy has shown serious engagement with the work of Jacques Derrida in the 1980s (see eg Kennedy, 'Critical

2.   THE MAIN MODES OF THINKING ASSOCIATED WITH MEANING-CENTRISM

The meaning-centrism of international legal thought, according to which meaning necessarily pre-exists forms of which it is the cause and origin, manifests itself in myriads of ways. This book zeroes in on three main expressions of meaning-centrism, which it respectively calls *originist thinking, deliverability thinking*, and *reifying thinking*. Whilst Chapter 2 below illustrates the working of these three manifestations of meaning-centrism in contemporary international legal thought and practice, it is the aim of this section to provide a few definitional observations on how originist thinking, deliverability thinking, and reifying thinking bespeak, each in their own way, the idea that meaning pre-exists the forms of the international legal discourse, and thus the centrality of meaning.

Theory' (n 30) 284–287). For his part, Martti Koskenniemi has referred to Derrida in the first footnote of *From Apology to Utopia*, which he however deems "less accessible" (Koskenniemi, *From Apology to Utopia* (n 18) 6). Yet, the point made here is more that Derrida, contrary to Foucault, has never been very explicitly relied on—and "exploited," so to speak—in international legal literature. In this regard, see the remarks of Juan M Amaya-Castro and Hassan El Menyawi, 'Moving Away From Moving Away: A Conversation About Jacques Derrida and Legal Scholarship' (2005) 6 German Law Journal 101, 106–107 (hereafter Amaya-Castro and El Menyawi, 'Moving Away'). A possible explanation for this lack of explicit reliance on Derrida lies in the extent to which a great deal of post-structuralist thought has been obfuscated and hijacked by the debate on the merits of deconstruction (for some famous examples of a discussion of Derrida through the sole lens of deconstruction, see Jack M Balkin, 'Deconstructive Practice and Legal Theory' (1987) 96 Yale Law Journal 743 (hereafter Balkin, 'Deconstructive Practice'); Jack M Balkin, 'Deconstruction's Legal Career' (2005) 27 Cardozo Law Review 719. See the criticisms of Balkin's treatment of Deconstruction by Schlag, 'The Politics of Form' (n 5). On the claim that the attention in legal scholarship was deflected away from Derrida by virtue of the debate on deconstruction, see Goodrich, 'Europe in America' (n 2) 2037–2042. On the idea that Derrida's has been a fashionable label but was not really read, see Goodrich and others, 'Introduction' (n 11) 4, 7–10. On the idea that the reception of the work of Derrida and especially the main insights of Grammatology have yet to occur in legal academia, see Goodrich, 'Europe in America' (n 2) 2041–2042. See however the use of Derrida by Schlag, 'The Politics of Form' (n 5). For an account of the common themes and sensibilities shared by critical legal scholars and Derrida, see Serpil Tunç Utebay, *Justice en tant que loi, justice au-delà de la loi: Hobbes, Derrida et les Critical Legal Studies* (L'Harmattan 2017) 177–221 (hereafter Tunç Utebay, *Justice en tant que loi*). For an interesting rebuttal by Derrida himself of the uses of deconstruction in the United States, see Jacques Derrida, 'Letter to a Japanese Friend' in David Wood and Robert Bernasconi (eds), *Derrida and Différance* (Northwestern University Press 1988) 3 (hereafter Derrida, 'Letter to a Japanese Friend').

2.1   Originist Thinking

Originist thinking refers here to the common understanding of forms as necessarily having an origin, an author, and a context of making. Said differently, originist thinking corresponds to the experience of a necessity to search for an origin of the forms of the international legal discourse. From such perspective, international law's words, idioms, aphorisms, and texts are supposed to always have an origin, a source, an author, and a context that can, if needed, be unearthed, recorded, revived, or simply studied.[33] As is reflected in the amount of scholarly efforts spent on "finding" or "retrieving" the source, the authors, and the context of the forms of the international legal discourse,[34] it is fair to say that originist thinking is deeply entrenched in international legal thought and practice.

Originist thinking, as is understood here, is not only the expression of the appetite for genealogy of modern legal thought[35] but is more fundamentally a reflection of the meaning-centrism described above.[36] Indeed, as long as the forms of the international legal discourse are thought as having been caused by the pre-existing meaning that they are meant to carry and deliver, international legal thought and practice cannot turn a blind eye to the origin, source, actors, and context at work in the loading of that meaning onto the forms of the international legal discourse carrying and delivering them.[37] Such origin, and thus the source, the author, and the context of forms, is experienced as a necessity, for they are supposed to subsequently direct the functioning of the forms concerned and constitute their centre.[38]

---

[33]   Unearthing the sources and the authors of the forms of the international legal discourse has been the object of some of my earlier inquiries. See d'Aspremont, *Belief System* (n 21). See also d'Aspremont, *Formalism* (n 7).

[34]   On the complicity of source-discourse with originist thinking, see Derrida, *Marges* (n 1) 13; Barthes, *Essais critiques IV* (n 6) 63–69.

[35]   On the idea that the question of production of human artefacts and human discourses is very modern, see Michel de Certeau, *L'écriture de l'histoire* (Gallimard 1975) 27–28. See also Barthes, *Essais critiques IV* (n 6) 63–69.

[36]   See Chapter 1, Section 1.

[37]   For a traditional affirmation of such meaning-centric understanding of the context, see Quentin Skinner, *The Foundations of Modern Political Thought*, vol 1 (CUP 1998) ix, xiii.

[38]   On this traditional mode of thinking, see Derrida, *Ecriture* (n 1) 409–410; Jacques Derrida, *The Beast and the Sovereign*, vol 1 (University of Chicago Press 2011) 17 (hereafter Derrida, *The Beast and the Sovereign*, vol 1); Barthes, *Essais critiques IV* (n 6) 75, 139.

2.2   Deliverability Thinking

International legal thought and practice are also dominated by a meaning-centric leaning for what is called here deliverability thinking,[39] whereby forms—whether they are thought of as carrying pre-existing meaning loaded onto them or not—come to the point when they deliver meaning. [40] Deliverability thinking corresponds to the experience of a necessity to search for a content for the forms concerned.[41] The strong version of such deliverability thinking posits that the meaning loaded onto the forms of the international legal discourse is never found at the surface of the form and ready to be delivered but requires a careful process of extraction, the latter being commonly referred to as "interpretation." According to this strong version of deliverability thinking, interpretation refers to the process of extraction of the pre-existing meaning that has allegedly been loaded onto the forms of the international legal discourse and which the latter are supposed to carry and deliver. Although this strong version of deliverability thinking may not necessarily correspond to an actual belief and often amounts to a casual and inarticulate disciplinary narrative, it has been extensively debunked in international legal literature for several decades. Indeed, it is common to reduce the extraction of the meaning that is loaded onto international legal thought to a theatrical performance[42] and to claim that the interpretation of forms is always performative in that it constitutes the meaning thereof.[43] Likewise, approaches that emphasize the reader as well as the readership community[44] have gained popularity, thereby further discrediting the strong version of deliverability thinking.[45]

---

[39]   I have been tempted to call it "inventory thinking." On the idea of interpretation and the action of inventorying, see Merleau-Ponty, *Signes* (n 27) 260.

[40]   On the idea that law is not only a form of inscription but also a system of delivery, see Goodrich, 'Europe in America' (n 2) 2066.

[41]   Deliverability thinking often comes with a presumption of inconsequentiality and weightlessness of forms in the process of transmission of meaning. See Schlag, 'The Politics of Form' (n 5) 1633.

[42]   On the metaphor of the theater, see Stephen Humphreys, *Theatre of the Rule of Law: Transnational Legal Intervention in Theory and Practice* (CUP 2010).

[43]   See eg Venzke, *On Semantic Change* (n 25).

[44]   For a classic, see also Stanley Fish, *Is There a Text in This Class? The Authority of Interpretive Communities* (Harvard University Press 1980); Stanley Fish, 'Fish v. Fiss' (1984) 36 Stanford Law Review 1325.

[45]   See Andrea Bianchi, 'The Game of Interpretation in International Law: The Players, the Cards, and Why the Game is Worth the Candle' in Andrea Bianchi, Daniel Peat and Matthew Windsor (eds), *Interpretation in International Law* (OUP 2015); Andrea Bianchi, 'Textual Interpretation and (International) Law Reading: The Myth of (in) Determinacy and the Genealogy of Meaning' in Pieter Bekker (ed), *Making Transnational Law Work in the Global Economy – Essays in Honour*

Importantly, even if deliverability thinking has not survived in its strong version, the presupposition that the forms of the international legal discourse deliver meaning on which it is predicated has endured in international legal thought and practice. Indeed, notwithstanding the—nowadays rather mainstream—claims about indeterminacy, the performative effects of interpretation, and the primacy of the reader, the very postulation that the forms of the international legal discourse deliver meaning continues to be upheld across the board, for the form is still held as delivering meaning at one point or another. In that sense, international legal thought and practice, notwithstanding the common acceptance that meaning is created in the process of extraction, continues to be dominated by deliverability thinking by virtue of which the forms of the international legal discourse supposedly deliver meaning. Even the most critical takes on delivery thinking continue to be predicated on the idea that the forms of the international legal discourse simply mean.[46]

2.3   Reifying Thinking

Meaning-centrism similarly manifests itself in the presupposition that the pre-existing meaning which forms carry and deliver is anchored in a certain reality. This is what is called here reifying thinking. By virtue of reifying thinking, the thing, the idea, the norm, the practice, the behavior, the institution, the discourse, and so on which the forms of the international legal discourse represent are supposedly real. Said differently, reifying thinking entails that the forms of the international legal discourse are responding to certain facts. Reifying thinking thus corresponds to the experience of a necessity to search for a reality of forms. It is noteworthy that such reifying thinking, in a strong variant, sometimes goes as far as considering that forms themselves constitute a thing: words, idioms, aphorisms, and texts are often deemed to have a material actuality and to belong to the order of things. According to such strong variant, reifying thinking entails that in international legal thought and practice, forms are not only responses to facts and grounded in facts but they are also artefacts (about the facts they respond to and are grounded in).

---

of Detlev Vagts (CUP 2010) 35. This used to be my position too. See Jean d'Aspremont, *Epistemic Forces in International Law* (Edward Elgar 2016); Jean d'Aspremont, 'The Multidimensional Process of Interpretation: Content-Determination and Law-Ascertainment Distinguished' in Andrea Bianchi, Daniel Peat and Matthew Windsor (eds), *Interpretation in International Law* (OUP 2015) (hereafter d'Aspremont, 'The Multidimensional Process').

[46]   On the dominance of meaning as *vouloir-dire* in contemporary thought in general, see Derrida, *Positions* (n 27) 66–67.

3.   MOVING AWAY FROM MEANING-CENTRISM: THE SOVEREIGNTY OF FORMS

This book questions the meaning-centrism of international legal thought and practice, and the various manifestations thereof as they have been introduced in the previous section. This book demonstrates that the forms of the international legal discourse do not carry and deliver any pre-existing meaning and that meaning cannot be the cause and origin of such forms. This book particularly argues that the words, idioms, aphorisms, and texts of international law do not carry and deliver any pre-existing meaning but, instead, constantly postpone meaning, thereby condemning meaning to be permanently absent from forms. Indeed, according to the argument made here, when asked to signify a thing, an idea, a norm, a practice, a behavior, an institution, a discourse, and so on, the forms of the international legal discourse constantly pass on the job of signification to other forms. When these other forms to which signification is passed are, in turn, asked to signify, they will similarly point away to yet other forms. In other words, when asked to signify a thing, an idea, a norm, a practice, a behavior, an institution, a discourse, and so on, the forms of the international legal discourse permanently defer meaning to other forms without such deferral process ever being completed and meaning ever being pinned down. The signification of words, idioms, aphorisms, and texts of international law never closes or ends, remaining indefinitely caught in a chain of supplements.[47] As a result of it being constantly passed on to another legal form, meaning is permanently deferred[48] and condemned to be nomadic.[49] Being perpetually deferred, meaning is eternally absent and nowhere to be found in the forms of the international legal discourse of which it cannot be the cause or the origin.[50] By perpetually deferring meaning and ensuring its absence, the forms of the international legal discourse, as this book claims, can sovereignly reign over international legal thought and practice.[51]

Before developing this claim further in the ensuing chapters, it must be emphasized that deferring meaning, as the forms of the international legal dis-

---

[47]   Derrida, *Positions* (n 27) 54.

[48]   In the same vein, see Goodrich, 'Europe in America' (n 2) 2059.

[49]   The expression is from Pierre Legrand, '"Il n'y a pas de hors-texte": Intimations of Jacques Derrida as Comparatist-at-Law' in Peter Goodrich and others (eds), *Derrida and Legal Philosophy* (Palgrave MacMillan 2008) 131 (hereafter Legrand, 'Il n'y a pas de hors-texte').

[50]   In the same vein, Zarbiyev, *Discours interprétatif* (n 28) 37–45. See also Goodrich, 'Europe in America' (n 2) 2062.

[51]   Cf the idea that sign works 'despotically' by Harland, *Superstructuralism* (n 31) 124.

course do, is no deficiency that calls for fixing or mitigation. It is argued here that, quite the opposite, the deferral of meaning by forms is the very condition of forms. In that sense, the forms of the international legal discourse are bound to defer meaning for them to function as forms. Actually, in the presence of meaning, the forms of the international legal discourse would cease to be forms: they would be made redundant by the arrival of meaning.[52]

Two aspects of the sovereignty of forms, as is understood here, must now draw the attention. First, it must be shown that the deferral of meaning by the forms of the international legal discourse is not confined to a specific social or disciplinary space and that such deferral of meaning cannot be approached as a phenomenon, let alone a legal phenomenon (3.1). Second, and most importantly, the way in which the deferral of meaning by the forms of the international legal discourse plays out must be further elucidated. On that occasion, it will be demonstrated that the deferral of meaning is possible by virtue of each form's self-difference (3.2).

3.1   A Sovereignty Without Borders

Although the deferral of meaning by the forms of the international legal discourse is no material or natural phenomenon, let alone a phenomenon that can be ascribed to a specific location, an important remark is warranted as to the impossibility of assigning the deferral of meaning by the forms of the international legal discourse to a specific social or disciplinary space.

It must be acknowledged that the deferral of meaning by the forms of the international legal discourse is most visible between the forms of the international legal discourse themselves. For sure, for the international lawyer, the chain of supplements through which meaning is perpetually moving is most visibly composed of forms which she is trained to invoke and explicitly respond to. For instance, and without the following corresponding to any unique or fixed deferral process, custom possibly refers to practice, practice possibly refers to states, states possibly refer to state officials, and so on. To take but another example, the idiom of wrongful act possibly refers to breach, breach possibly refers to bindingness, bindingness possibly refers to sources, sources possibly refer to Article 38, and so on. Yet, it is of the utmost importance to stress that the deferral of meaning by the forms of the international legal discourse is not confined to any legal space. Actually, the deferral of meaning knows no border, let alone any social or disciplinary border, for any bordering of the deferral of meaning is itself caught in the deferral of meaning.

---

[52] See the analogy with theology and philosophy made by Peter Salmon, *An Event, Perhaps* (Verso 2020) 15 (hereafter Salmon, *An Event, Perhaps*).

In that sense, the deferral of meaning by the forms of the international legal discourse is out of any social or disciplinary space. To return to the abovementioned example, wrongful act possibly refers to the idea of wrong too; wrong possibly refers to the idea of inadmissible behavior; which in turns possibly refers to the idea of good; which then possibly mobilizes certain strategies of moral universalization; which possibly raises a question of hegemony, and so on. Likewise, custom possibly refers to social acceptability, which possibly refers to the idea of society or community, which possibly refers to a certain idea of the social contract, which in turn possibly makes modern mode of thinking surface, and all that comes with it.

That the deferral of meaning by the forms of the international legal discourse is out of space and knows no social or disciplinary border bears an important consequence that ought to be mentioned here. The sovereignty of forms in international law is not reserved to those forms which the international lawyer is specifically trained to invoke and respond to but is a privilege of all forms. Said differently, the deferral of meaning by the forms of the international legal discourse is neither *in* nor *out* of the "legal."[53] Actually, the very distinction between the "legal" and the "non-legal"—just like any social or disciplinary ordering[54]—is itself a form caught in a chain of supplements and whose meaning is perpetually deferred.[55] Claiming otherwise and, thus, reducing the deferral of meaning by the forms of the international legal discourse to a "legal" phenomenon taking place in a specific social or disciplinary space would presuppose a transcendental legal phenomenon, thereby perpetuating, rather than debunking, the dominant meaning-centrism of international legal thought and practice. The deferral of meaning by the forms of the international

---

[53]   In that regard, Pierre Legrand has claimed that the different discourses that are traditionally be said to be outside the law are not existing outside of it but are *of it*. See Pierre Legrand, 'Foreign Law: Understanding Understanding' (2011) 6 Journal of Comparative Law 67, 80–81 (hereafter Legrand, 'Understanding Understanding').

[54]   On the idea that distinctions, and especially disciplinary distinctions, are powerful modes of ordering, see Roland Barthes, *Leçon* (Seuil 1978) 12; Latour, *Jamais été modernes* (n 3) 68–69; Foucault, *Mots* (n 3) 68–69. For a specific discussion of such disciplinary ordering in relation to international law, see Jean d'Aspremont, 'International Law, Theory, and History: Ordering through Distinctions' in Jean d'Aspremont (ed), *The History and Theory of International Law,* vol 1 (Edward Elgar Publishing 2020) x.

[55]   For some remarks on the disciplinary pedigrees of concepts and forms, see Vidya Kumar, 'Revolutionaries' in Jean d'Aspremont and Sahib Singh (eds), *Concepts for International Law. Contributions to Disciplinary Thought* (Edward Elgar Publishing 2019) 773. See also Jean d'Aspremont, 'Legal Imagination and the Thinking of the Impossible', *Leiden Journal of International Law* (forthcoming).

legal discourse reminds us that the international legal discourse does not exist in isolation from other discourses.[56]

3.2 Sovereign Forms and Self-Difference

The claim that forms postpone meaning by perpetually deferring the latter and thereby leaving the process of signification eternally unachieved is no novel affirmation. It corresponds to a finding that has been compellingly theorized in post-structuralist philosophy and literary theory and which ought not to be recalled here.[57] Yet, what post-structuralist philosophy and literary theory can teach the international lawyer is that the abovementioned permanent deferral of meaning and thus the latter's perpetual absence entail neither the emptiness of forms nor a conflation between them. Indeed, it is possible for the forms of the international legal discourse to have an identity of their own short of any ingrained or assigned pre-existing meaning. In other words, the forms of the international legal discourse have a meaning-less identity, that is, an identity that cannot be reduced to any fixed or inherent meaning. The identity of forms, post-structuralist philosophy and literary theory, lies in the forms' *self-difference*.[58]

---

[56] Pierre Legrand, 'Siting Foreign Law: How Derrida Can Help' (2011) 21 Duke Journal of Comparative and International Law 595, 609 (Legrand, 'Siting Foreign Law').

[57] Derrida, *Grammatologie* (n 1) 11–126; Derrida, *Marges* (n 1) 1–29; Derrida, *Ecriture* (n 1) 411. On this aspect of the work of Derrida, see the remarks of Salmon, *An Event, Perhaps* (n 52) 12. See also Geoffrey Bennington, *Jacques Derrida* (Seuil 1991) 56 (hereafter Bennington, *Jacques Derrida*). Cf Barthes, *Essais critiques IV* (n 6); Roland Barthes, S/Z (Seuil 1970) 9–11 (hereafter Barthes, *S/Z*). On the idea that Derrida's Grammatology is predicated upon a Talmudic conception of an infinite text and belonged to a tradition of interpretation rooted in the pre-Christian world, see Goodrich, 'Europe in America' (n 2) 2033–2084. See also Jürgen Habermas, *The Philosophical Discourse of Modernity: Twelve Lectures* (Frederik Lawrence tr, Polity Press 1987) 165. Cf Gillian Rose, *The Dialectic of Nihilism: Post-Structuralism and Law* (Basil Blackwell 1984) 133–135. For a rejection by Derrida of any influence of the Talmudic tradition of commentary, see Derrida, *Papier Machine* (n 2) 373. For an earlier, albeit still meaning-centric, contestation of the idea that language is the instrument of a pre-existing thought, see Edward Sapir, *Language: An Introduction to the Study of Speech* (Ishi Press 2014) 14–17 (who claims that language performs a pre-rational function and that the thought and the words grow together in a dialectic manner).

[58] "Self-difference" is one of the ways in which Derrida's idea of *différance* has been translated in English. Simon Glendinning, *Derrida. A Very Short Introduction* (OUP 2011) 62. Cf the translation of différance as *spacing* by Culler, *On Deconstruction* (n 31) 97. On the concept of *différance*, see Derrida, *Marges* (n 1) 1–29; Derrida, *Positions* (n 27) 17, 37–41. See the application of the concept of *différance* by Derrida, *The Beast*

This possibility of upholding the identity of forms through self-difference is critical for the argument made here as it demonstrates that moving away from the meaning-centrism that dominates international legal thought and practice is not exclusive of each and every form of the international legal discourse having a distinct identity. In fact, although meaning is perpetually deferred by the forms of the international legal discourse, invalidity is not wrongfulness, general principles of law are not customary law, an armed attack is not a use of force, an injured state is not a non-injured state, responsibility is not liability, *jus cogens* is not *erga omnes*, and so on. Notwithstanding the perpetual deferral of meaning, the forms of the international legal discourse have their own distinct identity and can neither be deemed empty nor conflated with one another.

To appreciate how each and every form of the international legal discourse has an identity of its own despite it carrying and delivering no pre-existing meaning, two observations are warranted about what the identity of forms cannot possibly be. First, it should be repeated that the distinct identity of each and every form of the international legal discourse is not any kind of inherent meaning or meaning in disguise, for that would contradict the constant deferral of meaning and re-introduce the very meaning-centrism with which this book takes issue. Second, and more fundamentally, it must be emphasized that the distinct identity of the forms of the international legal discourse is not simply and mechanically constituted by the relationships of difference with other forms, for this would, once again, re-introduce a presupposition of a transcendental pre-existing meaning typical of meaning-centrism.[59]

If not from any inherent meaning, from some meaning in disguise, or from relationships of difference with other forms, what is it that makes a form what it is and not another form? In other words, what is the self-difference of forms if not some kind of inherent meaning, some meaning in disguise or the result of a system of differences *à la Saussure*? It is argued here that the difference with other forms is not *outside* the form concerned—that is, in its relationship of difference with other forms—but *within* each and every form. More specifically, each and every form differentiates itself from others by virtue of the

---

and the Sovereign, vol 1 (n 38). See the comments of Bennington, *Jacques Derrida* (n 57) 70–82. See also the comments of Salmon, *An Event, Perhaps* (n 52) 107. See also Tunç Utebay, *Justice en tant que loi* (n 32) 79–81. On the kinship between Derrida's *différance* and the work of Heidegger, see Walter A Brogan, 'The Original Difference' in David Wood and Robert Bernasconi (eds), *Derrida and Différance* (Northwestern University Press 1988) 31.

[59] This is the presupposition of what has been called the transcendental signified. See Derrida, *Grammatologie* (n 1) 24, 69–70; see also Derrida, *Positions* (n 27) 30. See also Merleau-Ponty, *Signes* (n 27) 70–73.

otherness *within itself*. To take but a few examples from the international legal discourse, it is by virtue of such self-difference that invalidity is not wrongfulness, general principles of law are not customary law, an armed attack is not a use of force, an injured state is not a non-injured state, responsibility is not liability, *jus cogens* is not *erga omnes*, and so on. Inhabited by what it is not, each and every form of the international legal discourse has an identity of its own.[60]

The difference within the selfsame which informs the work of self-difference is sometimes captured through the notion of *trace* which is said to haunt the form.[61] The trace is "the event of the other-in-the-law."[62] It indicates the vanishing presence of other forms of which it is a vestige.[63] The trace has already disappeared when it is noticed. It is thus absent too.[64] In that sense, the trace is a ghost of the other.[65] The trace is itself porous, always unfinished, and only traceable to other traces.[66] It can accordingly never be encountered as an object or as data,[67] let alone serve as a foundation[68] or context[69] of the form and of its self-difference. In other words, the trace is no surrogate for any pre-existing meaning, for it is always being induced and constructed in the process of

---

[60] For some illustrations of the work of self-difference in relation to legal texts, see Forray and Pimont, *Décrire le droit* (n 5) 219–222.

[61] On the notion of trace, see gen. Derrida, *Grammatologie* (n 1) 86–87. See also Bennington, *Jacques Derrida* (n 57) 73–75; Tunç Utebay, *Justice en tant que loi* (n 32) 81–82. On the idea that that trace haunts the text, see Jacques Derrida, *Spectres de Marx* (Galilée 1993) (hereafter Derrida, *Spectres de Marx*); Derrida, *Papier Machine* (n 2) 307. On this question of spectral dimension of legal texts, see Legrand, 'Siting Foreign Law' (n 56) 607. See also Legrand, 'Understanding Understanding' (n 53) 78.

[62] Legrand, 'Understanding Understanding' (n 53) 82.

[63] Legrand, 'Il n'y a pas de hors-texte' (n 49) 131. See also Legrand, 'Siting Foreign Law' (n 56) 607.

[64] Derrida claims that this self-difference is out of both the order of representation and the order of things and approaches "it" as neither a form nor a thing. Self-difference is out of space, temporality, causality, sensibility, as well as out of representation. See Derrida, *Marges* (n 1) 1–29. On the idea that the trace refers to the remnants of what is left, see Derrida, *Papier Machine* (n 2) 385. With a specific emphasis on legal studies, see the remarks of Legrand, 'Understanding Understanding' (n 53) 79. See also Tunç Utebay, *Justice en tant que loi* (n 32) 77–79.

[65] On the idea of ghost, see Legrand, 'Siting Foreign Law' (n 56) 607.

[66] Legrand, 'Understanding Understanding' (n 53) 79; Legrand, 'Il n'y a pas de hors-texte' (n 49) 131.

[67] Legrand, 'Understanding Understanding' (n 53) 82.

[68] In the same vein and in relation to legal studies, see Balkin, 'Deconstructive Practice' (n 32) 743.

[69] Legrand, 'Understanding Understanding' (n 53) 79.

deferral of meaning.[70] The notion of trace—which verbalizes the work of self-difference, that is, the difference within the selfsame—is helpful to understand how self-difference allows forms to have a distinct identity short of any pre-existing meaning and of a system of differences. Indeed, each form carries *the trace* of what it is not, that is, the mark of other forms which it is different from. It is the trace of other forms (which is a difference within the selfsame) that confers the identity to the form. As a result of this trace of what it is not, each and every form of the international legal discourse can be said to have a *divided identity*, such form being always already inhabited by other forms.

That the identity of forms is a divided identity by virtue of the trace of other forms calls for yet another important remark. Such divided identity cannot be a binary identity and the trace of the other cannot be the trace of an opposite.[71] For sure, a form of the international legal discourse is inhabited by the traces of other forms that seem at variance with—and which differ from—the form being inhabited. Yet, such difference ought not to be construed as an opposite, for doing so would reduce self-difference to meaning. Indeed, as long as the other that inhabits the form constitutes its opposite, there is a presupposition of a fixed meaning by virtue of which the opposition is constructed and apprehended. Said differently, construing self-difference as a binary identity, and thus understanding the trace of the other as a trace of the opposite, amounts to a meaning-centric move that empties the sovereignty of forms. The other within the selfsame is not the opposite other but only *an* other.[72]

As the foregoing should show, self-difference, difference within the selfsame, and trace, which are the notions that have been relied on here to shed light on the deferral of meaning by the forms of the international legal discourse and explain the sovereignty of forms, are themselves caught in a deferral of meaning together with the notion of deferral of meaning and that of the

---

[70] Derrida, *Positions* (n 27) 39. See Zarbiyev, *Discours interprétatif* (n 28) 43–45. For a discussion of this idea in relation to legal studies, see Legrand, 'Understanding Understanding' (n 53) 82; Legrand, 'Siting Foreign Law' (n 56) 609.

[71] Derrida himself may have proved rather ambiguous on this point. On the one hand, he claims that the work of self-identity is not binary (see Derrida, *Positions* (n 27) 39. See also Malabou and Derrida, *Contre-Allée* (n 1) 73). On the other hand, in a move that he tries to strip of its Hegelian overtones, he claims that deconstruction must reverse hierarchies. See Derrida, *Positions* (n 27) 56–61. On this latter aspect of Derrida, see Salmon, *An Event, Perhaps* (n 52) 81.

[72] Reducing the divided identity of forms to a binary identity has often been witnessed in critical legal scholarship. See eg Balkin, 'Deconstructive Practice' (n 32) 754. This is yet another reason why critical legal scholarship has remained very meaning-centric. It is a question to which the following chapter returns. See Chapter 2, Sections 2.2 and 2.3. See also Chapter 4, Sections 1 and 3.

sovereignty of forms.[73] In fact, forms' identity through self-difference whose work can be captured through the trace of others is part of the very sovereignty of forms and of their perpetual deferral of meaning.[74] Put simply, it could be said that self-difference, difference within the selfsame, trace, the deferral of meaning, and the sovereignty of forms simply hang together. On the one hand, identity through self-difference is the condition of possibility of the deferral of meaning, for, short of a distinct identity through self-difference, the forms of the international legal discourse could not defer meaning. On the other hand, deferral of meaning is what upholds the forms' identity, for it is the forms to which meaning is pushed back that inhabit the form concerned and provide the latter with an identity.

4. THE SOVEREIGNTY OF FORMS AND ITS IMPLICATIONS

From the perspective of the sovereignty of forms foregrounded here, the forms of the international legal discourse do not carry and deliver pre-existing meaning but, instead, perpetually defer meaning by virtue of their identity-constituting self-difference. Being constantly deferred, meaning is made perpetually absent and leaves the forms to sovereignly reign over international legal thought and practice.

Putting the emphasis on the sovereignty of forms bears major consequences for the three abovementioned meaning-centric modes of thinking witnessed in international legal thought and practice, namely originist thinking, deliverability thinking, and reifying thinking.[75] As was already said, it is the ambition of the final chapter of this book to elaborate on some of the consequences of the sovereignty of forms for the international legal discourse as a whole.[76] Yet, even at this introductory stage, mention must be made of three major implications of the sovereignty of forms. These three major implications correspond to the de-necessitating of three traditional necessitarian moves in international legal thought and practice, namely the necessity of the quest for an origin, the necessity of the quest for content, and the necessity of the quest for reality—

---

[73] On the idea that trace and *différance* and all the other notions that Derrida mobilizes let themselves be replaced by one another and are replaceable in a chain of substitution, see hereafter Derrida, 'Letter to a Japanese Friend' (n 32) 4–5.

[74] This is what justifies that Jacques Derrida deliberately misspelled 'différance' in French. Indeed, "différance" plays on the fact that the French word *différer* means both "to defer" and "to differ," the substitution of a to the e of difference referring to "differant" (deferring). See Derrida, *Marges* (n 1) 8–9; Derrida, *Positions* (n 27) 54.

[75] See Chapter 1, Section 2.

[76] See Chapter 4.

which respectively are the expression of originist thinking, deliverability thinking, and reifying thinking.

4.1   De-necessitating the Quest for Origin

The sovereignty of forms according to which the forms of the international legal discourse have no origin, no author, no context other than forms to which meaning is deferred, and of which they bear the trace, comes to seriously question what has been called here the originist thinking that informs international legal thought and practice. This can be explained as follows. From the perspective of the sovereignty of forms, those forms—that neither carry nor deliver any pre-existing meaning—are identified through self-difference—that is, the trace of other forms within the selfsame—rather than any pre-existing meaning.[77] By virtue of such divided identity, the sovereign forms of the international legal discourse already bear the trace of all the forms that preceded them. The origin, the author, and the context of forms already inhabit them. In that sense, the origin of forms is always a repetition of those forms.[78] One could even say that forms always begin before they begin.[79] In other words, the origin of forms always ensues from the forms themselves and thus cannot any longer be the origin of that form.[80] Thus, the supposed origin of a given form of the international legal discourse is always secondary to that form, thereby making that origin an impossibility—for someone or something cannot be the origin of what it is secondary to. As a result, it is never possible to pinpoint a making-moment or a making-event independent from forms, for that making-moment or making-event is itself already in the forms and caught in the deferral of meaning.

---

[77] Jacques Derrida, *Marges de la Philosophie* (Editions de Minuit 1972) 15.

[78] See Vincent Descombes, *Le Même et l'Autre. Quarante-cinq ans de philosophie française* (Editions de Minuit 1979) 171.

[79] On the idea that writing has no beginning, see Derrida, *Positions* (n 27) 23. See also Derrida, *Spectres de Marx* (n 61) 255–56.

[80] See Derrida, *Marges* (n 1) 12–17; Derrida, *Ecriture* (n 1) 410; Derrida, *Grammatologie* (n 1) 87. On this aspect of Derrida, see the remarks of Bennington, *Jacques Derrida* (n 57) 4; Salmon, *An Event, Perhaps* (n 52) 50–51. In rejecting the common claim of an origin of the sign as being outside the sign, Derrida transposed his criticism of Husserl's phenomenology as resting on preconceptual originary moment to his critique of structuralism. See Derrida's criticisms of Husserl in Derrida, *Marges* (n 1) 185–207; Jacques Derrida, *Le problème de la genèse dans la philosophie de Husserl* (PUF 2010); Jacques Derrida, *La voix et le phénomène: Introduction au problème du signe dans la phénoménologie de Husserl* (PUF 2016). On the absence of origin, see also Barthes, *Essais critiques IV* (n 6) 75.

The consequences of such de-necessitating of originist thinking are wide-ranging for international legal thought and practice. Without anticipating Chapter 4 below, two of these consequences can be mentioned at a very general and abstract level. First, such de-necessitating of originist thinking entails that the forms of the international legal discourse should not be approached as having a *source* or an *author*. Indeed, the source and the author of a form always follow—rather than precede—the form.[81] Second, there is not only nothing "prior" to forms but there is nothing "outside" the forms either. The "outside" of the forms of the international legal discourse is itself produced by forms and can thus not be outside it.[82] In other words, the forms of the international legal discourse have no *context*, whether the context of their making or the context of the reading or invocation of the forms. The forms of the international legal discourse have no outside, for this outside is already in the forms by virtue of the latter's self-difference. The outside of the form—and thus the so-called context—can never be autonomously delineated and thought independently from those forms.

4.2   De-necessitating the Quest for Content

The sovereignty of forms similarly bears important consequences for the very idea of content-determination and interpretation as they are commonly understood in international legal thought and practice, and, more fundamentally, for deliverability thinking. It is submitted here that whether in its strong or mild version, deliverability thinking cannot withstand the sovereignty of forms that is foregrounded here. Indeed, as has been repeatedly indicated in the previous sections, the sovereignty of forms is premised on the postulation that no meaning is delivered by the forms of the international legal discourse. The sovereign forms of the international legal discourse thus strip interpretation of its hermeneutic dimension,[83] a matter to which Chapter 4 returns.[84] Simply said,

---

[81]   On the death of the author, see Barthes, *Essais critiques IV* (n 6) 63–69. Jonathan Culler speaks of the text being orphaned. See Jonathan Culler, *Structuralist Poetics: Structuralism, Linguistics, and the Study of Literature* (Ithaca 1975) 133. See the critical observations of Stanley Fish, 'With the Compliments of the Author: Reflections on Austin and Derrida' (1982) 8 Critical Inquiry 693.

[82]   On Derrida's famous claim that there is nothing outside the text in Derrida, *Grammatologie* (n 1) 225–226. See also the remarks of Bennington, *Jacques Derrida* (n 57) 83; Salmon, *An Event, Perhaps* (n 52) 143. With an emphasis on legal studies, see the remarks of Legrand, 'Understanding Understanding' (n 53) 80.

[83]   Derrida, *Marges* (n 1) 17; Barthes, *Essais critiques IV* (n 6) 47. On the earlier idea that the language is not at the service of signification but is signification itself, see Merleau-Ponty, *Signes* (n 27) 68–69, 379–80.

[84]   See Chapter 4, Section 1.

any imputation of meaning is impossible.[85] For the same reason, the identity of forms never raises a question of determinacy or indeterminacy. Indeed, a form never has a determinate or indeterminate identity but only bears the—always vanishing—traces of other forms within it.

The claim made here, and according to which the forms of the international legal discourse strip interpretation of its hermeneutic dimension for lack of any meaning or content to be interpreted, calls for two brief observations. First, it must be emphasized that the sovereignty of forms does not entail that the search for the meaning of forms is simply supplanted by a search for the meaning of forms' self-difference. Indeed, as was already indicated above,[86] the forms' self-difference does not constitute yet another content that can possibly be extracted, interpreted, or created. Such traces of otherness within the selfsame are no surrogate for meaning. Actually, the moment that traces of the other forms come within purview, they are already caught in the deferral of meaning and have vanished. In that sense, the trace of otherness within the selfsame, that is self-difference, can never be apprehended, produced, given a content, and interpreted. The forms of the international legal discourse are at best a site of passage, that is, a place of perpetual transit.[87] Second, it is equally important to highlight that the forms of the international legal discourse, as a site of passage, are not empty corridors. On the contrary, the forms of the international legal discourse are always in a state of saturation because of the constant deferral of meaning: forms' self-difference ensures that forms are always saturated with traces of those other forms to which meaning is deferred.

4.3   De-necessitating the Quest for Reality

The sovereignty of forms severely puts into question the abovementioned reifying thinking that dominates international legal thought and practice whereby forms are supposed to respond to or be anchored in a certain reality. In fact, by virtue of the sovereignty of forms, what the forms of the international legal discourse are supposed to respond to or be anchored in does not have a material existence outside and independent from forms.[88] Said differently, the reality of forms, be it of the thing, the idea, the norm, the practice, the behavior, the institution, the discourse, and so on which the forms of the international legal

---

[85]   Legrand, 'Il n'y a pas de hors-texte' (n 49) 131.

[86]   See Chapter 1, Section 3.

[87]   Barthes, *S/Z* (n 57) 10–11; Barthes, *L'aventure sémiologique* (n 31) 13; Barthes, *Essais critiques IV* (n 6) 56, 73–75.

[88]   Cf the critique of reifying thinking in comparative law by Pierre Legrand, and especially of the postulation that the foreign exists positively apart from the discourse, see Legrand, 'Understanding Understanding' (n 53) 72–73.

discourse represent, are anchored in, or respond to are never external to (and independent from) forms. From the perspective of the sovereignty of forms advocated here, the forms of the international legal discourse and the deferral of meaning should be deemed out of the order of experience.[89]

5.   THIS BOOK

This book exposes the meaning-centrism of international legal thought and practice, sheds lights on the deferral of meaning by international legal forms, and elaborates on the implications of the sovereignty of forms. In doing so, this book ventures a new attitude toward textuality in international law. The discussion is organized as follows. Chapter 2 provides a series of illustrations of the main manifestations of meaning-centrism of international legal thought and practice, and especially of originist thinking, deliverability thinking, and reifying thinking that are witnessed therein. Chapter 3 illustrates how meaning is constantly deferred by the forms of the international legal discourse by virtue of their self-difference. Chapter 4 elaborates on the concrete implications of the sovereignty of forms and of the de-necessitating of meaning-centrism, especially with respect to interpretation, the international lawyer herself, the critical attitude, the study of history in international law, the exercise of comparison, the translation of international legal texts, and the practice of referencing.

At this preliminary stage, two caveats are warranted. First, this book, although it visibly draws on some post-structuralist thinkers, is no attempt to transpose the works of the latter in international legal thought. As will be further argued in Chapter 4, transposition is not a possibility.[90] In fact, the works of these post-structuralist thinkers are, like all texts, caught in the infinite deferral of meaning, and thus have no pre-existing meaning that could be mechanically transposed to international law. For the sake of this book, such post-structuralist texts are at best an event whose experience by the author of these lines is caught, like everything else in this book, in the indefinite deferral of meaning.[91]

---

[89]   See gen. Derrida, *Marges* (n 1) 1–29.

[90]   See the remarks of David Wood, 'Introduction' in David Wood and Robert Bernasconi (eds), *Derrida and Différance* (Northwestern University Press 1988) xi. On the idea that post-structuralist critique cannot just be applied or transposed to law, see Schlag, 'The Politics of Form' (n 5) 1657. For a logo-centric treatment of Jacques Derrida and an attempt to translate his work for legal studies, see Balkin, 'Deconstructive Practice' (n 32).

[91]   On the idea of texts as events and happenings, see Chapter 4, Section 1.

Second, it must be made clear that, whilst this book is an attempt to de-necessitate the dominant meaning-centrism of international legal thought and practice, this book itself cannot escape meaning-centrism.[92] De-necessitating the dominant meaning-centrism of international legal thought and practice does not entail a neutralization of meaning-centrism. Meaning-centrism remains at work throughout this book. For instance, the resort to notions of meaning, meaning-centrism, self-difference, trace, deferral of meaning, thinking, reader, interpreter, interpretation, international lawyer, international law, loyalty, and so on, although these words and idioms are themselves caught in meaning deferral, may denote a meaning-centric posture.[93] The many idioms of ordinary language that this book resorts to ("it is argued," "it is submitted," "needless to say," "in other words," "as was said," and so on) are equally premised on an assumption of a pre-existing meaning. Meaning-centrism could similarly be found in this book *as book*.[94] Indeed, a book inevitably presents itself as the neat, linear, totalizing, and systematic container of a pre-existing argument or thought which it is supposed to carry and deliver.[95] And yet, a book's ambition to carry and deliver meaning—one would say "thoughts"—is always defeated, for meaning is deferred and made perpetually absent. The considerations and developments populating the following chapters as well as the format of their presentation thus remain part of the meaning-centric tradition they contest. For this reason, this book can be scrutinized in the very same way as it scrutinizes the dominant meaning-centrism of international legal thought and practice.

---

[92]   Derrida, *Positions* (n 27) 35, 56. See also Derrida, *Ecriture* (n 1) 46. On the idea that recuperative powers of logocentrism in legal studies must not be underestimated, see Schlag, 'The Politics of Form' (n 5) 1649.

[93]   Even the mobilization of certain authors and certain pieces of work in the footnotes denotes such a meaning-centric move although such authors and works are themselves caught in the deferral of meaning. See gen. Peter Goodrich, 'J.D.' (2005) 6 German Law Journal 15. See also Pierre Schlag, 'My Dinner at Langdell's' (2004) 52 Buffalo Law Review 851.

[94]   For an attempt to escape the meaning-centrism of the book through disruptive typographies, see Jacques Derrida, *Glas* (Galilée 1974); Jacques Derrida, *La carte postale: De Socrate à Freud et au-delà* (Flammarion 1980). Cf the attempt to escape the meaning-centrism of the law article by Amaya-Castro and El Menyawi, 'Moving Away' (n 32).

[95]   For some general remarks on the meaning-centric closure of a book, see Derrida, *Positions* (n 27) 11; Derrida, *Grammatologie* (n 1) 30–31; Derrida, *Papier Machine* (n 2) 27. On the idea that Derrida's Grammatology is about the end of the book, see Goodrich, 'Europe in America' (n 2) 2042; Florian Hoffmann, 'Epilogue: In Lieu of Conclusion' (2005) 6 German Law Journal 197. On the idea that every piece of writing has unity, see Brian Dillon, *Essayism* (Fizcarraldo Editions 2017) 15. On the linearity of international law books, see the remarks of Parfitt, *International Legal Reproduction* (n 22) 15.

This is also why this book, like any other international law book, is condemned to be born-dead, only to resuscitate each time it is read by a living being.[96] And yet, notwithstanding the fact that de-necessitating the meaning-centrism of international legal thought and practice does not neutralize meaning-centrism, it is hoped that this book will be instrumental in breeding a new way of *reading* international law texts, one that ceases to consider them as a conveyer of pre-existing thoughts and arguments and that makes such works open spaces saturated with traces and where meaning is only passing, never stopping, and always vanishing.

---

[96] Jacques Derrida, *The Beast and the Sovereign*, vol 2 (University of Chicago Press 2011) 131.

2. Meaning-centrism in international law

International legal thought and practice are meaning-centric in that they are predicated on a distinction between meaning and form whereby the latter is supposed to represent the former. According to such dominant meaning-centrism, the words, idioms, aphorisms, and texts of international law—what are called here the forms of the international legal discourse—always stand for a pre-existing thing, idea, norm, practice, behavior, institution, discourse, and so on. It is in meaning such thing, idea, norm, practice, behavior, institution, discourse, and so on that forms carry out what is perceived as their function, namely signifying. In meaning-centric thought, forms are always held to be derived from meaning, the latter being the cause and origin of such forms. And, as was highlighted above, in such meaning-centric type of thinking, the meaning that the forms of the international legal discourse carry and deliver is determined through a system of differences between the forms of the international legal discourse themselves.[1]

This chapter provides a series of illustrations of how such meaning-centrism plays out in international legal thought and practice. It particularly focuses on some manifestations of the three main meaning-centric modes of thinking mentioned in the previous chapter, namely originist thinking (1), deliverability thinking (2), and reifying thinking (3).

1. ORIGINIST THINKING IN INTERNATIONAL LAW

As one of the main manifestations of meaning-centrism in international law, originist thinking consists of understanding forms as necessarily having an origin, an author, and a context of making which pre-exist them. As the forms of the international legal discourse are thought to be caused by the pre-existing meaning that they are meant to carry and deliver, finding the origin, source, actors, and context of making of the form is turned into a necessity whereby the origin, a source, an author, and a context must constantly be searched, recorded, revived, and studied.[2] The following sections focus on the manifesta-

---

[1] See Chapter 1.
[2] See Chapter 1, Section 2.

tions of originist thinking in relation to the idea of treaty (1.1), the grounding of customary international law in social reality (1.2), and the experience of a need to endow international law with a history (1.3).

1.1   The Treaty as an International Legal Instrument

Originist thinking informs the very common notion of international legal instrument. In fact, international legal instruments are commonly thought as forms that are filled with pre-existing meaning which they are supposed to carry and deliver. The meaning so carried and delivered by an international legal instrument is thus the origin and the cause of that international legal instrument, the latter being at the service of the meaning it carries and delivers and from which it is derived.

The most common international legal instrument so understood is the treaty. The treaty is thought of as a form that contains some pre-agreed substance.[3] In that regard, it is sometimes said that the treaty is an *instrumentum*[4] that carries a *negotium*.[5] Such distinction between the treaty as an instrument and

---

[3]   Paul Reuter, 'Traités et transactions. Réflexions sur l'identification de certains engagements conventionnels' in *International Law at the Time of Its Codification. Essays in Honour of Roberto Ago* (Giuffrè 1987) 402–403 (hereafter Reuter, 'Traités et transactions'); Kal Raustalia, 'Form and Substance in International Agreements' (2005) 99 American Journal of International Law 581 (hereafter Raustalia, 'Form and Substance'); Catherine Brölmann, 'Law-Making Treaties: Form and Function in International Law' (2005) 74 Nordic Journal of International Law 383. For a slightly different variant, see Gerald Fitzmaurice, 'Some Problems Regarding the Formal Sources of International Law' in Frederik Mari van Asbeck (ed), *Symbolae Verzijl, présentées au professeur J. H. W. Verzijl à l'occasion de son LXXX-ième anniversaire* (Martinus Nijhoff Publishers 1958) 158 (hereafter Fitzmaurice, 'Some Problems') ("the treaty may be an instrument in which the law is conveniently stated, and evidence of what it is, but it is still not itself the law—it is still formally not a source of law but only evidence of it"). This is also a common assumption of the International Court of Justice. See Aegean Sea Continental Shelf Case *(Greece v Turkey)* (Judgment) [1978] ICJ Rep 3 [96].

[4]   See eg Reuter, 'Traités et transactions' (n 3) 403; Raustalia, 'Form and Substance' (n 3). Such system of differences is also found in legal theory and jurisprudence. See Gerald J Postema, *Legal Philosophy in the Twentieth Century: The Common Law World* (Springer 2001) 390–393. See also Ronald Dworkin, *Law's Empire* (Harvard 1986) 65–67.

[5]   The normative content of the treaty—that is, the extent to which it prescribes standards of conduct to be adopted by the parties—is classically called the *negotium*. If they enshrine the norm in a written instrument, the act which enshrines the norm is classically called the *instrumentum*. In that sense, the *instrumentum* is the "container." Such a distinction was already made by Hans Kelsen, 'Théorie du droit international public' (1953) 84 Collected Courses of the Hague Academy of International

its content has many ramifications in the contemporary understanding of the treaty. For instance, it is commonly contended that the determination of the legal nature of the treaty is said to be a question of sources,[6] whilst the determination of the normative content of the treaty is meant to raise a question of interpretation. It is also contended that each of these two dimensions of the treaty is subject to different modes of interpretation.[7]

It must also be noted that, as an instrument, the treaty is supposed to be the product of a few personified authors, namely *the Parties*. The Parties—whose "will" is said to be meant by the treaty—refers to the idea of a unified and

---

Law 1, 136. This distinction was also made by Brierly, the ILC Special Rapporteur on the Law of Treaties. ILC, 'Memorandum présenté par le Secrétariat' (14 July 1950) UN Doc A/CN.4/32, para 30. See also ILC, 'Report by G.G. Fitzmaurice, Special Rapporteur' (14 March 1956) UN Doc A/CN.4/101, art 14 and comm 24. See also Ambatielos *(Greece v United Kingdom)* (Judgment, Preliminary Objection), Dissenting Opinion of Judge Basdevant [1952] ICJ Rep 28; Codification of the Harvard Research (1935) 29 American Journal of International Law Sup 690. Some authors have preferred the words *actum* and *actus* to draw such a distinction between the content of the act and the instrument where it is enshrined: see Jacques Dehaussy cited by Jean-Paul Jacqué, *Eléments pour une théorie de l'acte juridique en Droit international public* (Librairie générale de droit et de jurisprudence 1972) 52 (hereafter Jacqué, *Théorie de l'acte juridique*). Jacqué, however, draws a distinction between, on the one hand, the negotium–instrumentum dichotomy, which are two constitutive elements of the legal act, and the act–norm dichotomy on the other hand. See Jacqué, *Théorie de l'acte juridique* (n 5) 47–56.

[6]   The dominant position is that it is the animus contrahendi and thus the intention to be bound, rather than the content of the agreement, that determines the legal character of the latter. For a classical affirmation of that position see Jules Basdevant, 'Règles générales du droit de la paix' (1936) 58 Collected Courses of the Hague Academy of International Law 471; Charles Rousseau, *Principes généraux du droit international public*, vol 1 (Pedone 1944) 156–157; Paul Reuter, *Introduction au Droit des Traités* (3rd edn, Presses Universitaires de France 1995) 30ff. For a criticism of that conceptual construction according to which states, through the choice of instrumentum, can freely decide to activate or not activate international law, see Jan Klabbers, *The Concept of Treaty in International Law* (Kluwer Publishing 1996) (hereafter Klabbers, *The Concept of Treaty*) who argues that once states have reached agreement, international law will attach certain legal effects to such agreements without it being a matter of choice for the parties. More recently, see Jan Klabbers, 'Not Re-Visiting the Concept of Treaty' in Alexander Orakhelashvili and Sarah Williams (eds) *40 Years of the Vienna Convention on the Law of Treaties* (British Institute of International and Comparative Law 2010) (hereafter Klabbers, 'Not Re-Visiting the Concept').

[7]   Jean d'Aspremont, 'The Multidimensional Process of Interpretation: Content-Determination and Law-Ascertainment Distinguished' in Andrea Bianchi, Daniel Peat and Matthew Windsor (eds), *Interpretation in International Law* (OUP 2015).

mighty genitor that determined the content of the treaty.[8] Indeed, the Parties, as a cause of that form, are supposed to have controlled all the dimensions of the making of that treaty.[9] In that sense, treaties are always construed as the formal product of the Parties, which manifests the constant need for a cause and an origin.

Such originist mode of thinking is not only limited to the understanding of the making of the treaty. Indeed, having been deemed in control of the making of the treaty as instrument, the Parties are subsequently given control over the functioning of that instrument. Indeed, every now and then, the Parties are called back. The need to call back the Parties is particularly felt on two main occasions. First, those invoking the treaty will feel the need to refer to the Parties when the nature of the treaty as a treaty must be vindicated. In that case, one must attribute[10] an *animus contrahendi* to the Parties.[11] Second,

---

[8] Although the word "genitor" comes with a male pointer in British English, the term is used here without denoting any type of gender.

[9] In the same vein, Raustalia, 'Form and Substance' (n 3) 581; Hartmut Hillgenberg, 'A Fresh Look at Soft Law' (1999) 10 European Journal of International Law 499, 504–505. For a criticism of the correlative idea that states can freely decide to activate or not activate international law, see Klabbers, *The Concept of Treaty* (n 6) and Klabbers, 'Not Re-Visiting the Concept' (n 6). On the choice between law and non-law, see Jan Klabbers, 'The Commodification of International Law' in Hélène Ruiz Fabri, Emmanuelle Jouannet, and Vincent Tomkiewicz (eds), *Select Proceedings of the European Society of International Law*, vol 1 (Hart Publishing 2008) 341. See also the account of the cost and benefits of non-law by Charles Lipson, 'Why Are Some International Agreements Informal' (1991) 45 International Organization 495.

[10] For a review of all the numerous indicators used by the international lawyer to build this animus, see Anthony Aust, *Modern Treaty Law and Practice* (2nd edn, CUP 2007) 33–37 (hereafter Aust, *Modern Treaty Law*); Klabbers, *The Concept of Treaty* (n 6) 68–89; Oscar Schachter, 'The Twilight Existence of Nonbinding International Agreements' (1977) 71 American Journal of International Law 296–97 (hereafter Schachter, 'The Twilight Existence'). It has been noted that the finding of such animus remains a highly speculative operation: see Klabbers, *The Concept of Treaty* (n 6). See also the remarks of Gennadiĭ Mikhaĭlovich Danilenko, *Law-Making in the International Community* (Martinus Nijhoff Publishers 1993) 57. See also Christine Chinkin, 'A Mirage in the Sand? Distinguishing Binding and Non-Binding Relations Between States' (1997) 10 Leiden Journal of International Law 245–246 (hereafter Chinkin, 'A Mirage in the Sand?').

[11] On intent as the dominant treaty-ascertaining criterion, see Jacqué, *Théorie de l'acte juridique* (n 5) 121ff; Duncan Hollis, 'A Comparative Approach to Treaty Law and Practice' in Duncan Hollis et al (eds), *National Treaty Law and Practice* (Martinus Nijhoff Publishers 2005) 15; Aust, *Modern Treaty Law* (n 10) 20; Robert Jennings and Arthur Watts KCMG QCO (eds), *Oppenhein's International Law*, vol 1 (9th edn, Longman 1992) 1202; Klabbers, *The Concept of Treaty* (n 6) 68; Malgosia Fitzmaurice, 'The Identification and Character of Treaties and Treaty Obligations Between States in International Law' (2003) 73 British Yearbook of International Law 141, 145,

and most commonly, the Parties must also be called back when content must be given to the text of the treaty—an originist move that is accompanied by yet another meaning-centric move examined in the next section.[12] Whenever the Parties of the treaty are called back, a difficult exercise of reconstruction and personalization of the Parties is required. In fact, invoking the Parties of the treaty requires the invention of an intellectual creature, that of the mighty genitor. This is originist thinking at its best.

It must finally be emphasized that originist thinking about the treaty, as has been described here, is no simple way of thinking. Originist thinking about the treaty actually is in need of being supplemented by sophisticated constructions in order to sustain itself, for instance by finding foundations in a construction like *pacta sunt servanda*. That specific construction necessitates, in turn, additional moves,[13] like the resort to customary law,[14] jus cogens,[15] the idea of

---

165–166; Alexander Orakhelashvili, *The Interpretation of Acts and Rules in Public International Law* (OUP 2008) 59 (hereafter Orakhelashvili, *The Interpretation of Acts and Rules*). See also the general remarks of Ignaz Seidl-Hohenveldern, 'Hierarchy of Treaties' in Jan Klabbers and René Lefeber (eds), *Essays on the Law of Treaties: A Collection of Essays in Honour of Bert Vierdag* (Martinus Nijhoff Publishers 1998) 7; Jacqué, *Théorie de l'acte juridique* (n 5) 121; Chinkin, 'A Mirage in the Sand?' (n 10) 223; Kirsten Schmalenbach, 'Article 2' in Oliver Dörr and Kirsten Schmalenbach (eds), *Vienna Convention on the Law of Treaties. A Commentary* (Springer 2012) 39–40; Schachter, 'The Twilight Existence' (n 10) 296. Although the Vienna Convention is silent as to the decisive treaty-ascertainment criterion, it is uncontested in the view of the International Law Commission that the legal nature of an act hinges on the intent of the parties. Indeed, apart from Fitzmaurice who sought to make it an explicit crite- rion (ILC, 'Report of the International Law Commission covering the work of its eighth session' (23 April–4 July 1956) UN Doc A/3159, paras 34–37), the International Law Commission and its Special Rapporteurs took it for granted and did not deem it neces- sary to specify it in their definition of a treaty (ILC, 'Reports of the Commission to the General Assembly' (1996) UN Doc A/6309/Rev.1, pt I, s E, paras 11-12 and pt II, ch II, paras 9–38).

[12]   On the deliverability thinking at work in the interpretation of treaties, see Chapter 2, Section 2.1.

[13]   See Duncan Hollis, 'Introduction to the Oxford Guide to Treaties' in Duncan Hollis (ed), *The Oxford Guide to Treaties* (OUP 2012) 2 (hereafter Hollis, 'Introduction to the Oxford Guide'). On the idea that *pacta sunt servanda* cannot be a rule, let alone a source, see Hugh Thirlway, *The Sources of International Law* (OUP 2014) 32 (here- after Thirlway, *The Sources*).

[14]   On the idea that *pacta sunt servanda* is custom, see ILC, 'Report of the Special Rapporteur, Hersch Lauterpacht' (1953) UN Doc A/CN.4/63, 106; see also Andrew T Guzman, *How International Law Works: A Rational Choice Theory* (OUP 2008) 204–205.

[15]   On the idea that *pacta sunt servanda* is jus cogens, see Paolo Fois, cited in Thirlway, *The Sources* (n 13) 32.

inherent validity and natural law,[16] or the idea of a "rule of recognition"[17]—
which are moves that come to reinforce the originist thinking informing the
thinking of the treaty as an instrument.

1.2   The Custom-Making Moment

Dominant discourses on customary international law are also dominated by
originist thinking. Indeed, customary international law, as is commonly construed in international legal thought and practice, is supposed to be grounded
in a particular self-constituting social reality, one where the authors and the
addressees of the customary norm concerned are conflated.[18] In fact, the two
constitutive elements of customary international law, namely practice and
opinio juris, correspond to two sides of the pre-existing social reality which
customary international law is supposed to be grounded in and the reflection
of. Such grounding of customary international law in a social reality expressed
through practice and *opinio juris* epitomizes the ascribing of a cause and origin
to customary international law, which is characteristic of originist thinking.[19]

---

[16] On the idea of the inherent validity of *pacta sunt servanda* and its character as
natural law, see Fitzmaurice, 'Some Problems' (n 3) 164; Hollis, 'Introduction to the
Oxford Guide' (n 13) 2.

[17] For an illustration of the idea that *pacta sunt servanda* is rooted in a 'rule of recognition' of sorts, see Thomas Franck, *The Power of Legitimacy Among Nations* (OUP
1990) 187 and Junio Barberis, 'Le Concept de "traité international" et ses limites'
(1984) 30 Annuaire français de droit international 239, 268.

[18] See the remarks of Hugh Thirlway, *The Sources of International Law* (2nd edn,
OUP 2019) 61 (hereafter Thirlway, *The Sources*, 2nd edn).

[19] Even in the 19th century, where customary international law was thought to
be the product of tacit consent by states, customary international law was thought
along the same originist pattern of thought. For some illustrations of an understanding of custom built on tacit consent, as well as some remnants thereof, see
Triepel Heinrich, *Völkerrecht und Landesrecht* (Scientia Verlag 1899); John Westlake,
International Law (The University Press 1904) 14; Thomas Lawrence, *The Principles
of International Law* (7th edn, Heath & Co 1915); Karl Strupp, *Eléments du droit international public* (Rousseau & Co 1927); Dionisio Anzilotti, *Scritti di diritto internazionale pubblico* (Cedan Padova 1956) 1, 38, 95ff; Charles Chaumont, 'Cours général
de droit international public' (1970) 129 Collected Courses of the Hague Academy
of International Law 333, 440; Grigory Tunkin, *Theory of International Law* (HUP
1974) 124. For an attempt to modernise the consensual conception of customary international law, see Orakhelashvili, *The Interpretation of Acts and Rules* (n 11) 70–107;
Antony D'Amato, 'Treaties as a Source of General Rules of International Law' (1962)
3 Harvard International Law Journal 1. For an overview of 19th-century understanding
of customary law as tacit consent, see Anthony Carty, *The Decay of International Law:
A Reappraisal of the Limits of Legal Imagination in International Affairs* (Manchester
University Press 2019) 61–65 (hereafter Carty, *The Decay of International Law*). For

It is submitted here that, in the discourse on customary international law, the originist dimension probably comes to a head in the continuous postulation of a moment in the past where the social reality is supposed to have actually engendered the norm. For customary international law to be grounded in a pre-existing social reality, there must have been a moment in the past where customary international law was actually made. Yet, in international legal thought and practice, the actual moment where such pre-existing social reality has engendered a customary norm is never established but is always *presupposed*.[20] Such presumption of a custom-making moment that is necessary for customary international law to be deemed grounded in a pre-existing social reality can particularly be witnessed in the continuous setting aside, in international legal thought and practice, of the question of the duration of practice.[21] In the same vein, such presumption of a custom-making moment can similarly be observed in relation to domestic and international courts' locating the practice and *opinio juris in the present*,[22] thereby constantly avoiding the

---

an illustration of the resilience of the association between custom and consent in international legal thought, see John Tasioulas, 'Custom, Jus Cogens, and Human Rights' in Curtis Bradley (ed), *Custom's Future: International Law in a Changing World* (CUP 2016); Niels Petersen, 'The Role of Consent and Uncertainty in the Formation of Customary International Law' in Brian D Lepard (ed), *Reexamining Customary International Law* (CUP 2017).

[20] On the idea of an illusory historicism in customary international law, see Carty, *The Decay of International Law* (n 19) 59–80. See also Anthony Carty, 'The Need to be Rid of the Idea of General Customary Law' (2018) 112 American Journal of International Law Unbound 319, 321 ("CIL is merely the lens whereby lawyers choose to describe that society, which Chimni generously recognizes in citing me. By this I mean that within the field of international legal jurisprudence, the international lawyer came to talk of States as having a collective *opinio juris*, but as Guggenheim and Ago have already shown, this is an illusion of historicism. Since the international system is still broadly based upon nation States that are aggressively distrustful of others, there is simply no possibility of any CIL of significance emerging"). See however the understanding of customary international law as a rule short of a law-making fact defended by Roberto Ago. See Roberto Ago, 'Positive Law and International Law' (1957) 51 American Journal of International Law 691, 723 ("... those so-called elements of custom ... are nothing but the external data by which the existence and efficacy of a customary norm can be recognized"). In the same vein as Ago, see Brigitte Stern, 'Custom at the Heart of International Law' (2001) 11 Duke Journal of Comparative and International Law 89, 93.

[21] See Conclusion 8.1 in ILC, 'Draft Conclusions on Identification of Customary International Law, with Commentaries' (2018) UN Doc A/73/10, pt II; North Sea Continental Shelf *(Federal Republic of Germany v Denmark; Federal Republic of Germany v Netherlands)* (Judgment) [1969] ICJ Rep 3 [74]. See also Thirlway, *The Sources*, 2nd edn (n 18) 74.

[22] Military and Paramilitary Activities in and against Nicaragua *(Nicaragua v United States of America)* (Merits) [1986] ICJ Rep 14 [184]: "The Court must satisfy

establishment of a custom-making moment in the past. It is by virtue of the same necessity to ground customary international law in a pre-existing social practice that the International Law Commission, in its work on the identification of customary international law, decided not to look into the establishment of the custom-making moment, thereby enabling that such a custom-making moment is simply presumed. Indeed, as it stated in the commentaries to its 2018 conclusions:

> Dealing as they do with the identification of rules of customary international law, the draft conclusions do not address, directly, the processes by which customary international law develops over time. Yet in practice identification cannot always be considered in isolation from formation; the identification of the existence and content of a rule of customary international law may well involve consideration of the processes by which it has developed. The draft conclusions thus inevitably refer in places to the formation of rules of customary international law. They do not, however, deal systematically with how such rules emerge, change, or terminate.[23]

It is submitted here that the International Law Commission's choice to evade the question of the establishment of the custom-making moment was not simply informed by the material impossibility to track down the formation of customary international law but by the requirement that customary international law be grounded in a pre-existing social reality. Indeed, if the moment custom is made in the past were not presumed, it would not be possible to meet the necessity to ascribe an origin, a cause, and a source to customary international law. The presumption of a custom-making moment is thus not a move of convenience to bypass difficult methodological and evidentiary obstacles but a necessity to allow customary international law to be grounded in a pre-existing social reality, as is prescribed by the originist thinking that dominates international legal thought and practice on customary international law.

1.3   A History for International Law

Originist thinking is not only witnessed in relation to specific doctrinal constructions like those examined in the previous sections. It is also at work at the level of the discipline as a whole. It is submitted here that it has long been

---

itself that the existence of the rule in the *opinio juris* of States is confirmed by practice." This is also the case of the more rigorous ascertainment of practice and *opinio juris*. See Jurisdictional Immunities of the State *(Germany v Italy)* (Judgment) [2012] ICJ Rep 99 [64]–[78].

[23]   ILC, 'Draft Conclusions on Identification of Customary International Law, with Commentaries' (2018) UN Doc A/73/10, pt II, 124.

thought that international law, in order to constitute a discipline proper, needs an origin, a tradition that it continues, some founding events, as well as some forebears. Said differently, the consolidation of international law as a discipline is often construed as requiring a history. According to the argument made in this section, the experience of a need for a history of international law for the constitution of the latter as a discipline proper is itself a manifestation of the originist thinking discussed here.

Providing international law with such an origin has been the conscious endeavor of scholars in the second half of the 19th century and the beginning of the 20th century.[24] For them, designing an origin to international law proved a way to affirm international law's status as a discipline,[25] as well as the

---

[24] For a famous manifestation of this need for a disciplinary history, see Lassa Oppenheim, 'The Science of International Law: Its Task and Method' (1908) 2 American Journal of International Law 313, 316 (hereafter Oppenheim, 'Task and Method'). For a discussion of Oppenheim's claim, see Amanda Perreau-Saussine, 'A Case Study on Jurisprudence as a Source of International Law: Oppenheim's Influence' in Matthew Craven, Malgosia Fitzmaurice, and Maria Vogiatzi (eds), *Time, History and International Law* (Brill 2007). See also Mónica García-Salmones Rovira, *The Project of Positivism in International Law* (OUP 2013) (hereafter García-Salmones Rovira, *The Project of Positivism*). On this quest for a history, see gen. the remarks of Martti Koskenniemi, 'A History of International Law Histories' in Bardo Fassbender and Anne Peters (eds), *Oxford Handbook on the History of International Law* (OUP 2012); Martti Koskenniemi, 'Histories of International Law: Significance and Problems for a Critical View' (2013) 27 Temple International and Comparative Law Journal 215, 220 (hereafter Koskenniemi, 'Histories of International Law'). On the self-consciousness of the international lawyer, see Matthew Craven, 'The Invention of a Tradition: Westlake, The Berlin Conference and the Historicisation of International Law' in Luigi Nuzzo and Miloš Vec, *Constructing International Law: The Birth of a Discipline* (Klostermann 2012) (hereafter Craven, 'The Invention of a Tradition'). See also Benjamin Allen Coates, *Legalist Empire: International Law and American Foreign Relations in the Early Twentieth Century* (OUP 2016) 18–19 (hereafter Coates, *Legalist Empire*).

[25] Craven, 'The Invention of a Tradition' (n 24) 36. Describing this historical self-consciousness is one of the main purposes of Martti Koskenniemi, *The Gentle Civilizer of Nations: The Rise and Fall of International Law 1870–1960* (CUP 2001) (hereafter Koskenniemi, *The Gentle Civilizer*).

respectability,[26] the identity,[27] and the scientificity of the latter.[28] It is against this backdrop of this search for an origin that the works of Henry Wheaton,[29] François Laurent,[30] and Ernest Nys[31] and James Brown Scott[32] should be read.

---

[26] Liliana Obregón Tarazona, 'Writing International Legal History: An Overview' (2015) 7 Monde(s) 95, 110 (hereafter Obregón Tarazona, 'Writing International Legal History').

[27] Thomas Kleinlein, 'International Legal Thought: Creation of a Tradition and the Potential of Disciplinary Self-Reflection' in Giuliana Ziccardi Capaldo, *The Global Community: Yearbook of International Law and Jurisprudence 2016* (OUP 2016) 812 (hereafter Kleinlein, 'International Legal Thought').

[28] For some critical remarks, see Anne Orford, 'Scientific Reason and the Discipline of International Law' (2014) 25 European Journal of International Law 369 (hereafter Orford, 'Scientific Reason'). See also Luigi Nuzzo, 'The Birth of an Imperial Location: Comparative Perspectives on Western Colonialism in China' (2018) 31 Leiden Journal of International Law 569, 596 (hereafter Nuzzo, 'The Birth of an Imperial Location').

[29] Henry Wheaton worked extensively on the history of the law of nations and produced *Histoire des Progrès du Droit des Gens en Europe et en Amérique Depuis la Paix de Westphalie jusqu'à nos Jours* (Brockhaus 1841), later translated as *A History of the Law of Nations in Europe and America from the Earliest Times to the Treaty of Washington* (Gould, Banks & Co 1845). On the ambitions behind Wheaton's writing of a history of international law, see Obregón Tarazona, 'Writing International Legal History' (n 26) 103–105.

[30] François Laurent, *Histoires du droit des gens et des relations internationales* (Hebbelynck 1850). On the context in which Laurent embarked on the writing of his colossal work: Obregón Tarazona, 'Writing International Legal History' (n 26) 105–106.

[31] Ernest Nys, *Les origines du droit international* (Castaigne 1894). On the very rich work of Ernest Nys, see Henri Rolin, 'Notice sur Ernest Nys: bibliographie' (1951) 4 Revue de l'Université de Bruxelles 349. See also Jean Salmon, 'Notice Ernest Nys' (2007) 9 Nouvelle biographie nationale 283. Nys is said to have been one of the first to put emphasis on Vitoria's writing and elevate him to a founding father of the discipline. See Obregón Tarazona, 'Writing International Legal History' (n 26) 110.

[32] On James Brown Scott's efforts to build a history of the discipline, see Coates, *Legalist Empire* (n 24) 68–71. It is well known that Scott took a dim view of the status accorded Grotius in dominant European disciplinary histories and he sought to put the emphasis instead on Grotius's predecessors. For some critical remarks on the disciplinary history championed by Scott and his emphasis on Vitoria, Suarez, Baltasar de Ayala, and Alberico Gentili, see Randall Lesaffer, 'The Classical Law of Nations (1500–1800)' in Alexander Orakhelashvili (ed), *Research Handbook on the Theory and History of International Law* (Edward Elgar Publishing 2011); Stephen C Neff, *Justice Among Nations* (Harvard University Press 2014) 381; Kleinlein, 'International Legal Thought' (n 27) 816; Jose-Manuel Barreto, 'Cerberus: Rethinking Grotius and the Westphalian System' in Martti Koskenniemi, Walter Rech and Manuel Jiménez Fonseca (eds), *International Law and Empire: Historical Explorations* (OUP 2017) 153. The emphasis on Vitoria by Scott famously led Antony Anghie to show how the violence in Vitoria played out in American legal thought. See Anthony Anghie, 'Francisco De Vitoria and the Colonial Origins of International Law' (1996) 5 Social

Their ambition was to provide international law with an origin, thereby facilitating its consolidation as a discipline.

When embarking on the creation of a history in the 19th and 20th centuries those scholars obviously came to choose specific forebears, markers, periodizations, and causalities.[33] It is not necessary to recall the main choices made back then. It suffices to say that such choices were certainly not benign.[34] For instance, they espoused the modern idea of the social contract by finding some consensual and conventional causes to international law.[35] They also

---

and Legal Studies 321; Antony Anghie, *Imperialism, Sovereignty and the Making of International Law* (CUP 2004) 14 (hereafter Anghie, *Imperialism*).

[33]   For instance, there seems to be no doubt that Lauterpacht wrote the 'Grotian Tradition' with an acute historical self-consciousness and the ambition of writing disciplinary history. Martti Koskenniemi writes: 'Lauterpacht's oeuvre and career constitute a striking illustration of an international legal consciousness that sought to resuscitate the rationalism of the nineteenth century in the aftermath of the First World War but used up its emancipatory potential in the doctrinal struggles of the 1930s' (Martti Koskenniemi, 'Lauterpacht: The Victorian Tradition in International Law' (1997) 2 European Journal of International Law 215, 261). In the same sense, see Oona A Hathaway and Scott J Shapiro, *The Internationalists: How a Radical Plan to Outlaw War Remade the World* (Simon & Schuster 2017) 300.

[34]   Various explanations have been provided as to why Grotius was preferred to other writers. See eg Martti Koskenniemi, who has referred to his 'naturalist, scientifically-orientated way to look at the universe' as being instrumental in his success in the 19th and 20th centuries. See Koskenniemi, 'Histories of International Law' (n 24) 217. For Alain Wijffels, the success of Gentili and Grotius can be explained because their work could be read as 'general handbooks of the law of nations in the modern sense', thereby making international law a specialized branch of the law in its own right. They were the first authors to deal comprehensively with the law of nations. See Alain Wijffels, 'Early-Modern Scholarship on International Law' in Alexander Orakhelashvili (ed), *Research Handbook on the Theory and History of International Law* (Edward Elgar Publishing 2011) 42–44. Michael Lobban has argued that making Grotius and Vattel a central marker was a way to respond to the attack of Austin against international law: see Michael Lobban, 'English Approaches to International Law in the Nineteenth Century' in Matthew Craven, Malgosia Fitzmaurice and Maria Vogiatzi (eds), *Time, History and International Law* (Brill 2007) 80. On the reasons why Grotius was elected the father of international law in the context of the professionalization of the discipline, see Coates, *Legalist Empire* (n 24) 18.

[35]   On the choice of 1648 as a key marker of the history of international law, see Matthew Craven, 'Introduction: International Law and Its Histories' in Matthew Craven, Malgosia Fitzmaurice, and Maria Vogiatzi (eds), *Time, History and International Law* (Brill 2007) 8 (hereafter Craven, 'Introduction'). See also Bardo Fassbender, 'Peace of Westphalia (1648)' *Max Planck Encyclopedia of Public International Law* (2011) para. 7, 18-19. For Andreas Osiander the choice of 1648 should be traced back to the work of Nys (see Andreas Osiander, 'Sovereignty, International Relations, and the Westphalian Myth' (2001) 55 International Organization 251). For José-Manuel Barreto the origin of this periodization goes back as early as 1845 with Henry Wheaton (see José-Manuel

chose events conspicuously located in Europe,[36] thereby making the history of international law a part of the history of Western civilization and vice-versa.[37]

Shedding light on the agendas and ideologies informing the choices made in this quest for an origin has been at the heart of a scholarly sensibility that is nowadays referred to as the "historical turn."[38] In fact, taking issue with the agenda and ideologies of the traditional history of international law led to charges against narratives of progress informing the common history of international law[39] and its obfuscation of the wrong that international law is associated with.[40] The very linear character of the common history similarly came under attack as it was claimed that the history of international law should rather have been told as "pockmarked by a series of catastrophes and mutations."[41] Likewise, some of the fundamental markers of the discipline

---

Barreto, 'Cerberus: Rethinking Grotius and the Westphalian System' in Martti Koskenniemi, Walter Rech, and Manuel Jimenez Fonseca (eds), *International Law and Empire* (OUP 2017) 159–160). For the claim that the myth of Westphalia was created by Leo Gross in the middle of the 20th century, see Luis Eslava, Michael Fakhri, and Vasuki Nesiah, *Bandung, Global History and International Law: Critical Pasts and Pending Futures* (CUP 2017) 15 (referring to Leo Gross, 'The Peace of Westphalia, 1648–1948' (1948) 42 American Journal of International Law 29).

[36]   On the idea that 1648 makes the history of international law so European and Northern and pushes to the margins of the experience of African, Asian, or South American societies, Craven, 'Introduction' (n 35) 8.

[37]   For an illustration of the claim that history of international law is a branch of the history of Western civilization, see Oppenheim, 'Task and Method' (n 24) 317.

[38]   On the turn to history in contemporary international legal scholarship, see Matthew Craven, 'Theorizing the Turn to History in International Law' in Anne Orford and Florian Hoffmann (eds), *The Oxford Handbook of the Theory of International Law* (OUP 2016). See also George Galindo, 'Martti Koskenniemi and the Historiographical Turn in International Law' (2005) 16 European Journal of International Law 539. On the idea that the historical turn is better understood as a historiographical turn, see Jean d'Aspremont, 'Turntablism in the History of International Law' (2020) 22 Journal of the History of International Law 472.

[39]   Matthew Craven, 'Introduction: International Law and Its Histories' in Matthew Craven, Malgosia Fitzmaurice, and Maria Vogiatzi (eds), *Time, History and International Law* (Brill 2007), 9; Deborah Z Cass, 'Navigating the Newstream: Recent Critical Scholarship in International Law' (1996) 65 Nordic Journal of International Law 341.

[40]   Nuzzo, 'The Birth of an Imperial Location' (n 28) 596.

[41]   Nathaniel Berman, 'In the Wake of Empire' (1999) 14 American University International Law Review 1515, 1523: 'The genealogical approach rejects this account of international legal history as an ever-advancing dialectic of restatement and renewal. It views international legal history as pockmarked by a series of catastrophes and mutations, as rocked by the countless forms of colonial conquest and anti-colonial resistance.' At page 1524, he writes: "International legal genealogy rejects linear accounts of the origins and progress of the international community. It recounts the forging of that

came to be questioned, including, for instance, the fatherhood of Grotius,[42] the canonical status of his work,[43] and the cosmopolitan project associated there-with.[44] The extent to which the traditional forebears, markers, periodizations,

---

community through acts of unholy matrimony, through liaisons mostly asymmetrical, even when consensual, and all-too-often irreversibly coercive and massively violent – and usually constructing the power of some patriarch or other." See also John Haskell, 'The Traditions of Modernity within International Law and Governance: Christianity, Liberalism, and Marxism' (2014) 6 Human Rights and Globalization Law Review 29, 37 (discussing the kinship between modernity and linear history as well as the Christian heritage).

[42] For a plea to study the precursors of Grotius as Grotius is the heir of a tradition, see Randall Lesaffer, 'International Law and Its History: The Story of an Unrequited Love' in Matthew Craven, Malgosia Fitzmaurice, and Maria Vogiatzi (eds), *Time, History and International Law* (Brill 2007) 40. See also José-Manuel Barreto, 'Cerberus: Rethinking Grotius and the Westphalian System' in Martti Koskenniemi, Walter Rech, and Manuel Jimenez Fonseca (eds), *International Law and Empire* (OUP 2017) 154.

[43] As was discussed by Simpson, the earlier work by Grotius, and especially *De Jure Praedae*, seem to point in the exact opposite direction of the 20th-century progressive narrative which it is supposed to have engendered. In *De Jure Praedae*, Grotius distinguishes between dates on the basis of their internal politics and moral characteristics. See Gerry Simpson, *Great Powers and Outlaw States: Unequal Sovereigns in their International Legal Order* (CUP 2004) 4. See also the idea that the modernity of international law started with the Spanish age defended by Bardo Fassbender, 'Westphalia, Peace of (1648)' in Rüdiger Wolfrum (ed), *The Max Planck Encyclopedia of Public International Law* (OUP 2012) para 19. See also the remarks of John D Haskell, 'Hugo Grotius in the Contemporary Memory of International Law: Secularism, Liberalism, and the Politics of Restatement and Denial' in José María Beneyto and David Kennedy (eds), *New Approaches to International Law: The European and the American Experiences* (Asser Press 2012).

[44] On the idea of Dutch imperialism in the work of Grotius, see José-Manuel Barreto, 'Cerberus: Rethinking Grotius and the Westphalian System' in Martti Koskenniemi, Walter Rech, and Manuel Jimenez Fonseca (eds), *International Law and Empire* (OUP 2017) 158 ("Grotius has not lost his place between the founding fathers of modern international law. He remains inhabiting such an Olympus, yet in another sense or for different reasons. It has been made clear that Grotius is not the founder of international law defined as a system that regulates the affaires between equal and sovereign states. Together with Vitoria, Grotius remains in the selected group of the 'early parents of modern international law', a legal regime that is understood as emerging out of imperialism's needs for legitimation, and that regulated the relations between its subjects, including early modern companies"). On the idea that the writing of Grotius, like that of Gentili and Vattel, is construed as justifying "imperial activities of their clients," see Martti Koskenniemi, 'Introduction: International Law and Empire—Aspects and Approaches' in Martti Koskenniemi, Walter Rech, and Manuel Jimenez Fonseca (eds), *International Law and Empire* (OUP 2017) 4 (citing Jonathan Israel, *Dutch Primacy in World Trade 1585–1740* (Clarendon 1989) 16–17 and 69–73). For some critique of Grotius as serving the VOC, see Benjamin Straumann, '"Ancient Caesarean

and causalities of the history of international law work as a justification for Western hegemony and the universalization of global capitalism has similarly been extensively scrutinized.[45]

It is of no avail to elaborate on the abundant—and very compelling—manifestations of the "historical turn" here. It only matters to highlight that the growing historiographical sensibility that arose on that occasion did not discontinue the originist thinking informing the discourse on the history of international law. In fact, and as has been shown elsewhere already,[46] such

---

Lawyers" in a State of Nature: Roman Tradition and Natural Rights in Hugo Grotius's "De iure praedae"' (2006) 34 Political Theory 328; Renee Jeffery, *Hugo Grotius in International Thought* (Palgrave Macmillan 2006) 6–7; Tarik Kochi, *The Other's War: Recognition and the Violence of Ethics* (Birkbeck Law Press 2009) 59–60. On Grotius and mercantile capitalism, see Martti Koskenniemi, 'International Law and the Emergence of Mercantile Capitalism: Grotius to Smith' in Pierre-Mary Dupuy and Vincent Chetail (eds), *The Roots of International Law: Liber Amicorum Peter Haggenmacher* (Martinus Nijhoff Publishers 2014) 3. On the criticisms of Grotius for its neo-liberalism, see García-Salmones Rovira, *The Project of Positivism* (n 24).

[45] Among others, see Sundhya Pahuja, 'The Postcoloniality of International Law' (2005) 46 Harvard International Law Journal 459 (hereafter Pahuja, 'Postcoloniality'); China Miéville, *Between Equal Rights: A Marxist Theory of International Law* (Haymarket Books 2006) (hereafter Miéville, *Between Equal Rights*); Koskenniemi, *The Gentle Civilizer* (n 25); Martti Koskenniemi, 'Empire and International Law: The Real Spanish Contribution' (2011) 61 University of Toronto Law Journal 1. See also Makau Mutua, 'What is TWAIL?' (2000) 94 American Society of International Law Proceedings 31 (hereafter Mutua, 'TWAIL'); Makau Mutua, 'Savages, Victims and Saviors: The Metaphor of Human Rights' (2001) 42 Harvard International Law Journal 201 (hereafter Mutua, 'Savages, Victims and Saviors'); Antony Anghie, *Imperialism, Sovereignty, and the Making of International Law* (CUP 2005); Antony Anghie, 'The Evolution of International Law: Colonial and Postcolonial Realities'(2006) 27 Third World Quarterly 740 (hereafter Anghie, 'The Evolution of International Law'); Buhpinder Chimni, 'Third World Approaches to International Law: A Manifesto' (2006) 8 International Community Law Review 18 (hereafter Chimni, 'Third World Approaches'); Juan Pablo Scarfi, *The Hidden History of International Law in the Americas. Empire and Legal Networks* (OUP 2017); Antony Anghie, 'Domination' in Jean d'Aspremont and Sahib Singh (eds), *Concepts for International Law: Contributions to Disciplinary Thought* (Edward Elgar Publishing 2019) 222. For one of the foundational works of TWAIL, see Edward Said, *Orientalism* (Routledge 1978). The critique of law and empire has itself been the object of counter-critique. See eg Shotaro Hamamoto, 'A propos de deux clichés sur l'histoire du droit international en Asie de l'Est: une reconsidération de l'ordre mondial chinois et du discours de traités inégaux' in Pierre-Marie Dupuy and Vincent Chetail (eds), *The Roots of International Law: Liber Amicorum Peter Haggenmacher* (Martinus Nijhoff Publishers 2014).

[46] This is a claim already made in the literature. See eg Rose Parfitt, 'The Spectre of Sources' (2014) 25 European Journal of International Law 297, 304. A somewhat similar claim has already been made by Anne Orford who contends that such critical histories reinforce the power of discplinary history-writing dedicated to the creation of

critical works on the history of international law did not come to displace the originist thinking that was dominating the traditional discourse on the history of international law. It must be acknowledged that this continuous attachment to originist thinking is not entirely surprising, for scrutinizing the origin is a common move of critical thought.[47] Yet, the resilience of originist thinking after the "historical turn" confirms the dominance of meaning-centrism of international legal thought and practice, of which originist thinking is only a manifestation.

2.   DELIVERABILITY THINKING IN INTERNATIONAL LAW

Deliverability thinking constitutes another manifestation of the dominant meaning-centrism of international legal thought and practice. Deliverability thinking refers to the presupposition that the forms of the international legal discourse deliver content and that this content must be searched for. In other words, deliverability thinking presupposes that *forms mean*. This is a mode of thinking that even permeates those works that seek to unearth hidden meaning or those that demonstrate that meaning is not loaded onto the form and carried by it but simply created at the moment of its delivery.[48] In fact, in international legal thought and practice, deliverability thinking permeates the whole scholarly spectrum that stretches between attitudes associated with an hermeneutic of recovery and those attitudes reflecting an hermeneutic of suspicion.[49]

---

an "effet du réel." See Anne Orford, 'International Law and the Limits of History' in Wouter Werner, Marieke de Hoon, and Alexis Galán (eds), *The Law of International Lawyers: Reading Martti Koskenniemi* (CUP 2015) 308: "In performing these 'more or less confident acts of historicization', these 'critical' histories ironically shored up the status of history as a master discipline dedicated to producing the objective truth about the past. Even as these histories reveal the constructed nature of the disciplines they were critiquing, they reaffirmed 'the power of history as a disciplinary practice'." I have made a similar claim in relation to Martti Koskenniemi, *To the Uttermost Parts of the Earth: Legal Imagination and International Power 1300–1870* (CUP 2021) and argued that in this book Martti Koskenniemi presuppose a transcendental legal phenomenon which all the vocabularies deployed by the protagonist of his book originate in and can belong to. See my remarks in Jean d'Aspremont, 'Legal Imagination and the Thinking of the Impossible', Leiden Journal of International Law (forthcoming).

[47]   See Chapter 4, Section 4.
[48]   See Chapter 1, Section 2.2.
[49]   The distinction between a hermeneutic of recovery and a hermeneutic of suspicion is from Jonathan Culler, *Literary Theory: A Very Short Introduction* (OUP 1997) 68–69. For some critical remarks on the attitude associated with hermeneutics of suspicion in legal studies, see Duncan Kennedy, 'The Hermeneutic of Suspicion in Contemporary American Legal Thought Law' (2014) 25 Critique 91.

The following sections provide three illustrations of how deliverability thinking plays out in contemporary international legal thought and practice. Particular heed is first paid to the most common approaches to the interpretation of treaties (2.1). This section then elaborates on those scholarly works that scrutinize the world-making roles of forms and shows that such works also remain premised on the idea that the forms of the international legal discourse deliver meaning (2.2). Finally, this section turns to methodological debates about international law and demonstrates that international legal methods are commonly construed as modes of delivery of pre-existing naturalistic or discursive realities (2.3).

2.1   The Interpretation of Treaties

In international legal thought and practice, the doctrine of interpretation,[50] as it has been formalized in the Vienna Convention on the Law of Treaties,[51] is commonly approached—and criticized—as an extracting device whose

---

[50]   On the concept of doctrine, see Peter Goodrich, 'Law and Modernity' (1986) 49 The Modern Law Review 545, 556 ('doctrine is a way of administering and teaching discourse which consistently presents the doctrinal teaching in the form of a monologue, as the elaboration of a scientifically established and so incontestable authority, as the exegesis of a primary text'). See also Jean d'Aspremont, *International Law as a Belief System* (CUP 2017) 31–36 (hereafter d'Aspremont, *Belief System*).

[51]   On the alleged customary nature of these rules, see Richard Gardiner, *Treaty Interpretation* (2nd edn, OUP 2017) (hereafter Gardiner, *Treaty Interpretation*). See gen. Marc Eugen Villiger, *Customary International Law and Treaties: A Study of their Interactions and Interrelations with Special Consideration of the 1969 Vienna Convention on the Law of Treaties* (Martinus Nijhoff Publishers 1985) 334ff; Jean-Marc Sorel, 'Article 31' in Pierre Klein and Oliver Corten, *Les Conventions de Vienne sur le Droit des Traités. Commentaire article par article* (Bruylant 2006). See also Territorial Dispute *(Libyan Arab Jamahiriya v Chad)* (Judgment) [1994] ICJ Rep 6; Kasikili/Sedudu Island *(Botswana v Namibia)* (Judgment) [1999] ICJ Rep 1045; LaGrand *(Germany v United States of America)* (Judgment) [2001] ICJ Rep 501, para 99; *Legal Consequences of the Construction of a Wall in the Occupied Palestinian Territory* (Advisory Opinion) [2004] ICJ Rep 136, para. 94. See also *Arbitration regarding the Iron Rhine Railway (Belgium v Netherlands)* (2005) ICGJ 373, para 45. See also WTO, *United States—Standards for Reformulated and Conventional Gasoline* (29 April 1996) WT/DS2/AB/R [16]–[17]; WTO, *Japan–Taxes on Alcoholic Beverages* (4 October 1996) WT/DS8,10-11/AB/R [10]–[12]. See also *Golder v United Kingdom*, App no 4451/70, 21 February 1975, para 32. For an attempt to question the customary character of the rules on interpretation, see Jean d'Aspremont, 'Sources in Legal-Formalist Theories' in Samantha Besson and Jean d'Aspremont (eds), *The Oxford Handbook on the Sources of International Law* (OUP 2017) (hereafter d'Aspremont, 'Sources in Legal-Formalist Theories').

function is to enable the delivery of the meaning of the provisions of treaties.[52] Whether it is deemed a decently functioning doctrine,[53] a faulty construction,[54] or a deceitful smokescreen,[55] the doctrine of interpretation is constantly understood, discussed, or charged as a mechanism geared toward the delivery of the meaning carried by the forms constituting the treaty.

That the doctrine of interpretation is premised on deliverability thinking is probably not controversial. After all, the very wording of Article 31 of the Vienna Convention on the Law of Treaties makes explicit that interpretation is about extracting the meaning that the provision being interpreted is supposed to deliver.[56] In that regard, treaty interpretation can probably be considered the most obvious expression of deliverability thinking in international legal thought and practice.

Albeit very mundane, deliverability thinking requires some sophisticated constructions and moves that ought to be mentioned here. Actually, as is understood in international legal thought and practice, the very possibility of delivering of meaning comes as a multi-step and multidimensional process

---

[52]   On how interpretation and treaties are married in international legal thought, see Duncan Hollis, 'Interpretation' in Jean d'Aspremont and Sahib Singh (eds), *Concepts for International Law: Contributions to Disciplinary Thought* (Edward Elgar Publishing 2019) 549.

[53]   Gardiner, *Treaty Interpretation* (n 51). See also Tarcisio Gazzini, *Interpretation of International Investment Treaties* (Hart Publishing 2016).

[54]   Andrea Bianchi, 'Textual Interpretation and (International) Law Reading: The Myth of (in) Determinacy and the Genealogy of Meaning' in Pieter Bekker (ed), *Making Transnational Law Work in the Global Economy: Essays in Honour of Detlev Vagts* (CUP 2010) 35 (hereafter Bianchi, 'Textual Interpretation'); Jan Klabbers, 'Virtuous Interpretation' in Malgosia Fitzmaurice, Olufemi Elias, and Panos Merkouris (eds), *Treaty Interpretation and the Vienna Convention on the Law of Treaties: 30 Years On*, vol 1 (Martinus Nijhoff Publishers 2010) 17; Andrea Bianchi, 'The Game of Interpretation in International Law: The Players, the Cards, and Why the Game is Worth the Candle' in Andrea Bianchi, Daniel Peat and Matthew Windsor (eds), *Interpretation in International Law* (OUP 2015) (hereafter Bianchi, 'The Game of Interpretation').

[55]   George Letsas, 'Strasbourg's Interpretive Ethic: Lessons for the International Lawyer' (2010) 21 European Journal of International Law 535; Ingo Venzke, *How Interpretation Makes International Law. On Semantic Change and Normative Twists* (OUP 2012) (hereafter Venzke, *On Semantic Change*); d'Aspremont, 'Sources in Legal-Formalist Theories' (n 51). See gen. Duncan Kennedy, 'A Left Phenomenological Critique of the Hart/Kelsen Theory of Legal Interpretation' in Duncan Kennedy, *Legal Reasoning, Collected Essays* (The Davies Book Publishers 2008).

[56]   Article 31, para 1 reads: "A treaty shall be interpreted in good faith in accordance with the ordinary meaning to be given to the terms of the treaty in their context and in the light of its object and purpose."

and is anything but a "single combined operation."[57] In fact, the delivery of meaning by a treaty is particularly thought as entailing three distinct moves, each of these moves having attracted most of the attention in scholarship and case-law.[58] The first move in the delivery of meaning is what is called here *total interpretation*.[59] This is the interpretation whereby the treaty is interpreted as eligible for invocation.[60] This interpretation is "total" because it is what determines whether a treaty belongs to the totality of international law. By virtue of such total interpretation, the words of the treaty, the piece of paper, even the webpage, and all the components of the artefact become a text that possibly exists for the sake of international law and can possibly be known to international law. Short of this specific interpretive moment, the treaty would simply be left out of the totality of international law.[61] Total interpretation, as is understood here, precedes all the other steps in the delivery of meaning. It is only once the treaty has been interpreted as endowed with a legal character that can be known to international law that invocation of the treaty becomes possible and that delivery can take place.

In the process of delivering meaning, total interpretation, according to mainstream international legal thought and practice, is then followed by an interpretation of the very formal constraints that are meant to guide the interpretation of a treaty, namely those prescribed by Article 31 of the Vienna Convention on the Law of Treaties.[62] The interpretation of the formal constraints on interpre-

---

[57] ILC, 'Draft Conclusions on Identification of Customary International Law, with Commentaries' (2018) UN Doc A/73/10, 21. See also ILC, 'Reports of the Commission to the General Assembly' (1996) UN Doc A/6309/Rev.1, pt 3, section 3, para 8.

[58] I have examined these three moves in greater depth elsewhere. See Jean d'Aspremont, 'Current Theorizations about the Treaty in International Law' in Duncan Hollis (ed), *The Oxford Guide to Treaties* (2nd edn, OUP 2020) 53–55.

[59] This interpretive moment relates to what Duncan Hollis has called "existential interpretation." See Duncan Hollis, 'The Existential Function of Interpretation' in Andrea Bianchi, Daniel Peat and Matthew Windsor (eds), *International Law in Interpretation in International Law* (OUP 2014).

[60] On the idea that treaty-ascertainment entails an act of interpretation, see Michel Virally, 'Sur la notion d'accord' in Emanuel Diez (ed), *Festschrift für Rudolf Bindschedler* (Staempfli & Cie 1980).

[61] Theodor Adorno speaks about the voracity of any concept as it comes to create a totality which draws everything into it, tolerates nothing outside its domain, and translates everything into its own terms, even contradictions to it. See Theodor W Adorno, *Negative Dialectics* (EB Ashton tr, Routledge 1973). On this aspect of Adorno's work, see also the remarks of Frederic Jameson, *Late Marxism: Adorno or the Persistence of the Dialectic* (Verso 2007) 20–21, 25–34.

[62] On the question of the format and nature of these constraints as well as the question whether they are rules properly so-called, see gen. Richard Gardiner, 'The Vienna Convention Rules on Treaty Interpretation' in Duncan Hollis (ed), *The Oxford Guide to Treaties* (2nd edn, OUP 2020) 464–476; d'Aspremont, *Belief System* (n 50)

tation is what is called here *calibrating interpretation*. Calibrating interpretation is conducted independently from the text of the treaty and relates only to the very interpretive yardsticks that will subsequently be applied to the treaty to enable the delivering of meaning.[63] The bulk of the literature produced on treaty interpretation pertains to calibrating interpretation.[64]

Once calibrating interpretation has been conducted, the interpretation meant to extract the very content allegedly carried by the treaty, and thus the interpretation that leads to the delivery of meaning, can be initiated. This third step in the process of delivery of meaning is what is here called *operational interpretation*.[65] Operational interpretation consists of the application to the treaty of the constraints produced by the prior calibrating interpretation with a view to extracting an operational meaning from the treaty for the sake of delivering meaning.

Total interpretation, calibrating interpretation, and operational interpretation constitute the main moves around which deliverability thinking in relation to treaty interpretation is organized in contemporary international legal thought and practice. As has been shown here, deliverability thinking in relation to treaty interpretation is no simple affair.

37–39; d'Aspremont, 'The Multidimensional Process' (n 7); Bianchi, 'The Game of Interpretation' (n 54); Bianchi, 'Textual Interpretation' (n 54) 35.

[63]   It is interesting to note that the International Law Commission, despite explicitly recognizing that criteria of interpretation ought to be organized and weighted against one another, denies that this calibration constitutes an act of interpretation: see ILC, 'Draft Conclusions on Identification of Customary International Law, with Commentaries' (2018) UN Doc A/73/10, paras 4–5. See also Conclusion 9 at 70–71.

[64]   See the literature cited by Daniel Peat and Matthew Windsor, 'Playing the Game of Interpretation: On Meaning and Metaphor in International Law' in Andrea Bianchi, Daniel Peat, and Matthew Windsor, *Interpretation in International Law* (OUP 2015). See also the literature cited by Michael Waibel, 'Demystifying the Art of Interpretation' (2011) 22 European Journal of International Law 571. See also ILC, 'Draft Conclusions on Identification of Customary International Law, with Commentaries' (2018) UN Doc A/73/10. See also Panos Merkouris and others, 'Final Report of the ILA Study Group on Content and Evolution of the Rules of Interpretation' in International Law Association Report of the Seventy-Ninth Biennial Conference (Kyoto 2020) (International Law Association, Kyoto 2020).

[65]   This is what I have called elsewhere "content-determination" interpretation: see d'Aspremont, 'Sources in Legal-Formalist Theories' (n 51). This terminology has been taken over by the International Law Association Study Group on the Content and Evolution of the Rules of Interpretation, 'Final Report' (29 November–13 December 2020) <www.ila-hq.org> accessed 27 May 2021.

2.2   Discourses on the World-Making Performances of Forms

Another expression of deliverability thinking is found in the sophisticated accounts of forms' world-making performances that populate international legal literature.[66] Indeed, it is now common for the international lawyer to engage with the way in which the forms of the international legal discourse shape unitary spaces, experiences, and conflicts,[67] as well as with how they contribute and define the unequal character,[68] coloniality,[69] and masculinity[70] of the world. All those ventures in the performativity of forms are premised on the idea that the world is molded by the meaning delivered by these forms and, thus, that the forms of the international legal discourse deliver meaning.

---

[66]   This is an idea that I have myself extensively explored and defended in a series of essays published in Jean d'Aspremont, *Epistemic Forces in International Law: Foundational Doctrines and Techniques of International Legal Argumentation* (Edward Elgar Publishing 2015). For compilation of the concepts at work in world-making by international law, see Jean d'Aspremont and Sahib Singh (eds), *Concepts for International Law: Contributions to Disciplinary Thought* (Edward Elgar Publishing 2019). See also the general observations of Andrea Bianchi, *International Law Theories: An Inquiry into Different Ways of Thinking* (OUP 2016) 16–19 (hereafter Bianchi, *International Law Theories*).

[67]   See eg Martti Koskenniemi, 'The Politics of International Law—20 Years Later' (2009) 20 European Journal of International Law 7–19; Sundhya Pahuja, 'Decolonization and the Eventness of International Law' in Fleur Johns, Richard Joyce, and Sundhya Pahuja (eds), *Events: The Force of International Law* (Routledge 2011); Venzke, *On Semantic Change* (n 55); David Kennedy, *A World of Struggle: How Power, Law, and Expertise Shape Global Political Economy* (Princeton University Press 2016); Monica Hakimi, 'The Work of International Law' (2017) 58 Harvard International Law Journal 1.

[68]   See eg Miéville, *Between Equal Rights* (n 45); Emmanuelle Jouannet, 'Universalism and Imperialism: The True–False Paradox of International Law?' (2007) 18 European Journal of International Law 379; Pahuja, 'Postcoloniality' (n 45) 459; Liliana Obregon, 'Empire, Racial Capitalism and International Law: The Case of Manumitted Haiti and the Recognition Debt' (2018) 31 Leiden Journal of International Law 597.

[69]   See Anghie, *Imperialism* (n 32) 197; Mutua, 'TWAIL' (n 45); Anghie, 'The Evolution of International Law' (n 45) 740; Chimni, 'Third World Approaches' (n 45); Mutua, 'Savages, Victims and Saviors' (n 45); Pahuja, 'Postcoloniality' (n 45) 461–462.

[70]   Hilary Charlesworth, Christine Chinkin and Shelly Wright, 'Feminist Approaches to International Law' (1991) 85 American Journal of International Law 613; Hilary Charlesworth and Christine Chinkin, *The Boundaries of International Law: A Feminist Analysis* (Manchester University Press 2000); Hilary Charlesworth, 'Feminist Ambivalence about International Law' (2005) 11 International Legal Theory 1.

The international lawyer's engagement with the performativity of forms can be of different types, and thus so is the deliverability thinking witnessed on that occasion. Some of the facets of that engagement must be mentioned here, for they shed light on the ways in which deliverability thinking manifests itself in those scholarly works on the performativity of forms and their world-making capacity.

In some works, the world-making capacity of the forms of the international legal discourse entails that the forms of the international legal discourse pave the world with spatial, historical, and material continuities that pre-determine the phenomenality within that world.[71] From this perspective, anything that is perceived, felt, or seen is so within, through, and thanks to the repertoire of possible worlds and possible perceptions prescribed by forms' pre-discursive categories and intelligibility frameworks.[72] In other words, there is little to perceive outside the pre-discursive categories and intelligibility frameworks of forms. Having been naturalized[73] in advance by forms' pre-discursive categories and intelligibility frameworks, all pandemics, humanitarian disasters, cyber incidents, outer space discoveries, human-made environmental threats, or terror in relation to which international legal texts are invoked will be experienced as natural.[74]

In other works, the claim that the forms of the international legal discourse make the world entails that there is no worldly phenomenality that is foreign to forms' pre-discursive categories and intelligibility frameworks. Having made the world it applies to, the forms of the international legal discourse can be mobilized in relation to basically anything in the world, with the consequence that the world is always perceived in a way that is intelligible for the international lawyer.[75] As a result, there is, for example, no space, no phenomenon, no pandemic, no humanitarian disaster, no cyber incident, no outer space galaxy, no human-made environmental threat, or no terror that cannot be related back

---

[71]   Bruno Latour, *An Inquiry into Modes of Existence: An Anthropology of the Moderns* (Harvard University Press 2013).

[72]   cf the idea that law can do anything with anything of Laurent De Sutter, *Hors La Loi: Théorie de l'anarchie juridique* (Les Liens qui Libèrent 2021) 68–69.

[73]   On the ideas of naturalistic necessities and naturalized knowledge, see Judith Butler, *Gender Trouble: Feminism and the Subversion of Identify* (2nd edn, Routledge 1990) 45. See also Judith Butler, *Notes toward a Performative Theory of Assembly* (Harvard University Press 2018) 5, 40–41.

[74]   For an illustration of such performativity in relation to the ideas and experiences of nation and nationalism see Benedict Anderson, *Imagined Communities: Reflections on the Origin and Spread of Nationalism* (Verso 2016).

[75]   On the idea that concepts are deployed as identity checks, see Theodor W Adorno, *Negative Dialectics* (EB Ashton tr, Routledge 1973) 5. See also Henri Bergson, *La pensée et le mouvant* (Flammarion 2014) 229, 240.

to forms' pre-discursive categories and intelligibility frameworks.[76] Although the world may sometimes seem to resist the pre-discursive categories and intelligibility frameworks of forms, such resistance is itself the expression of the world being squeezed in forms' pre-discursive categories and intelligibility frameworks.[77]

Finally, the world-making capacity of forms which is being scrutinized in the literature can refer to forms' organization of conflicts and divergences in the experiences and perceptions of the world, as made by the forms of the international legal discourse.[78] These conflicts (e.g. practice vs absence of practice; compliant behavior vs non-compliant behavior; effective control vs absence of effective control; endangered species vs non-endangered species; causation vs non-causation; contribution to injury vs absence of contribution to injury; impact vs no impact; influence vs no influence) are never accidental or fortuitous, as they mechanically and neatly mirror forms' pre-discursive categories and intelligibility frameworks.[79] In other words, world-making also means that the conflicts about how the world, as made by the forms of the international legal discourse, is experienced and perceived constitute organized dissonance within the pre-discursive categories and intelligibility frameworks of forms.[80]

It would be of no relevance to further elucidate the various dimensions of the world-making capacity of the forms of the international legal discourse as they have been scrutinized in the literature. What matters is that, when the international lawyer studies the way in which the forms of the international legal discourse shape the world in any of the dimensions mentioned in the previous paragraphs, she postulates that the forms of the international legal discourse deliver meaning and that it is such a meaning that shapes the world.[81] This is yet another manifestation of deliverability thinking as it is understood here.

---

[76] What cannot be related back to international law is declared monstrous or ignored. On this question, see gen. Jacques Derrida, *De la Grammatologie* (Editions de Minuit 1967) 14.

[77] On the idea that theory cannot do its work on the phenomenal without resistance and that theory is itself this resistance, see Paul de Man, *The Resistance to Theory* (University of Minnesota Press 1986) 12–19 (hereafter de Man, *The Resistance to Theory*).

[78] On this idea, see Jean-François Lyotard, *Le Différend* (Editions de Minuit 1983).

[79] See Michel Foucault, 'Politics and the Study of Discourse' in Graham Burchell, Colin Gordon and Peter Miller (eds), *The Foucault Effect: Studies in Governmentality* (University of Chicago Press 1991) 58–59.

[80] Michel Foucault, *Les mots et les choses* (Gallimard 1966) 66–69; Jean-François Lyotard, *La Condition Postmoderne* (Editions de Minuit 1979) 17.

[81] On the dependence of performativity on "as if" postures, see Jacques Derrida, *L'Université sans condition* (Galilé 2001) 41, 73–74.

2.3   Methodological Debates about International Law

It is submitted here that deliverability thinking also permeates methodological debates about international law, for international legal methods are often construed as modes of delivery of pre-existing naturalistic or discursive realities.[82] Indeed, in the international legal literature, international legal methods are commonly associated with the project[83] of finding and knowing international legal practices and their contexts, the role of international legal methods being to deliver such practices and contexts.[84] More specifically, international legal methods are commonly construed in the international legal scholarship as *modes of delivery of meaning* in that they constitute formalistic devices deployed to deliver meaning about facts, rules, institutions, legal discourses, theories, interests, agendas, and so on.[85] Such a common approach to international legal methods, it is argued here, is yet another expression of delivera-

---

[82]   On the idea of naturalistic necessity, see Judith Butler, *Gender Trouble* (2nd edn, Routledge 2007) 45.

[83]   On this project, see gen. Orford, 'Scientific Reason' (n 28). See also the remarks of Anthony Carty, 'International Law and Nervous States in the Age of Anger, the Collapse of Legal Formalism and a Return to Natural Law' in Rossana Deplano and Nicholas Tsagourias, *Research Methods in International Law* (Edward Elgar Publishing 2021) 181 (hereafter Carty, 'International Law and Nervous States').

[84]   For an old expression of that idea, see Oppenheim, 'Task and Method' (n 24) 313. More recently, see Gregory Shaffer and Tom Ginsburg, 'The Empirical Turn in International Legal Scholarship' (2012) 106 American Journal of International Law 1 (hereafter Shaffer and Ginsburg, 'The Empirical Turn'). For an illustration, see Pierre-Hugues Verdier and Erik Voeten, 'How Does Customary International Law Change? The Case of State Immunity' (2015) 59 International Studies Quarterly (2015) 209 (hereafter Verdier and Voeten, 'The Case of State Immunity'). See also Jakob VH Holtermann and Mikael Rask Madsen, 'Toleration, Synthesis or Replacement? The "Empirical Turn" and Its Consequences for the Science of International Law' (2016) 29 Leiden Journal of International Law 1001 (hereafter Holtermann and Masden, 'Toleration, Synthesis or Replacement?'). It must also be noted that such a turn to empirical studies of international law is not completely unprecedented. See eg the work of the New Haven School and in particular that of Myres S McDougal, 'Law and Power' (1952) 46 American Journal of International Law 102. See also the work of the legal process school, as illustrated by Abram Chayes and Antonia Handler Chayes, *The New Sovereignty: Compliance with International Regulatory Agreements* (Harvard University Press 1995). For a claim about the virtuosity of empirical sensitivity, see Jorge E Vinuales, 'On Legal Inquiry' in Denis Alland and others (eds), *Unity and Diversity of International Law: Essays in Honour of Professor Pierre-Marie Dupuy* (Martinus Nijhoff Publishers 2014) 72–75.

[85]   Philip Allott understands methods as the structure of legal argument and the logic of discourse. See Philip Allott, 'Language, Method and the Nature of International Law' (1971) 45 British Yearbook of International Law 79.

bility thinking whereby pre-existing realities are expected to be extracted and delivered by forms.

Interestingly, the understanding of international legal methods as modes of delivery of meaning is not confined to doctrinal studies and orthodox juris-prudential works. Critical works similarly resort to such modes of delivery of meaning—although they may be averse to designating them as methods[86]—by virtue of their use, for instance, of structuralist modes of discursive analysis to make binary structures of discourses collapse in a way that reveals their project of ordering.[87] As is argued below, binary structures and modes of scrutiny based on opposites remain informed by a meaning-centric posture, one that presupposes that a form delivers meaning, albeit the opposite of what it claims.[88]

As modes of delivery of meaning, international legal methods can be as diverse as including the resort to qualitative or quantitative methods to measure the conditions under which international law is formed and produces effects on its addressees,[89] the use of modes of inquiry developed in interna-tional relations or in economics with a view to shedding light on an unexplored level of complexity of the environment in which law operates,[90] the recourse to computer-generated data about citation patterns in judicial practice or in scholarship,[91] the use of narratology to discover the techniques of narration at work in international legal scholarship,[92] the already mentioned reliance on

---

[86]   See gen. Martti Koskenniemi, 'Letter to the Editors of the Symposium' (1999) 93 American Journal of International Law 351.

[87]   On the idea that critique cannot abandon the geometry of structuralism, see Jacques Derrida, *L'écriture et la différence* (Editions du Seuil 1967) 47.

[88]   See Chapter 4, Sections 1 and 3.

[89]   See Shaffer and Ginsburg, 'The Empirical Turn' (n 84); Verdier and Voeten, 'The Case of State Immunity' (n 84). See also Holtermann and Masden, 'Toleration, Synthesis or Replacement?' (n 84).

[90]   See eg Jeffrey L Dunoff and Mark A Pollack (eds), *Interdisciplinary Perspectives on International Law and International Relations: The State of the Art* (CUP 2013).

[91]   See eg Niccolò Ridi, 'The Shape and Structure of the "Usable Past": An Empirical Analysis of the Use of Precedent in International Adjudication' (2019) 10 Journal of International Dispute Settlement 200. See also Niccolò Ridi, 'Doing Things with International Precedents: The Use and Authority of Previous Decisions in International Adjudication' (PhD thesis, King's College London) (on file with the author).

[92]   Matthew Windsor, 'Narrative Kill or Capture: Unreliable Narration in International Law' (2015) 28 Leiden Journal of International Law 743; Gerry Simpson, 'The Sentimental Life of International Law' (2015) 3 London Review of International Law 3; Walter Rech, 'International Law, Empire, and the Relative Indeterminacy of Narrative' in Martti Koskenniemi, Walter Rech and Manuel Jiménez Fonseca (eds), *International Law and Empire: Historical Explorations* (OUP 2017).

structuralist modes of scrutiny to unveil how international legal practice and international legal thought are articulated around opposites and allowing political and socio-economical preferences to steer legal discourses,[93] the design and use of new models of authority in global governance,[94] the mobilization of sociological tools to produce sociological insights about the functioning of international law,[95] the invocation of a specific "concept of law" to determine the content and contours of a study or a discourse,[96] and so on. The resort to heuristics as a critical device can also qualify as a mode of delivery of meaning.[97] So does the persistent and seemingly invincible resort to so-called positivist methods—a common shorthand to refer to the use of the doctrine of sources and the doctrine of interpretation with a view to discovering a meaning presumedly out there and knowable and allowing its delivery.[98] It is argued here that, in all the variants and uses mentioned here, international legal methods work as modes of delivery of meaning in that they are formalistic devices that are expected to carry and deliver meaning about certain realities, which is yet another expression of the deliverability thinking that dominates international legal thought and practice.

---

[93]   On the use of structuralist modes of scrutiny by the critical international lawyer, see Sahib Singh, 'International Legal Positivism and New Approaches to International Law' in Jörg Kammerhofer and Jean d'Aspremont (eds), *International Legal Positivism in a Post-Modern World* (CUP 2014) 291.

[94]   Nico Krisch, *Beyond Constitutionalism: The Pluralistic Structure of Postnational Law* (OUP 2010); Markus Jachtenfuchs and Nico Krisch, 'Subsidiarity in Global Governance' (2016) 79 Law and Contemporary Problems 1. See also Eyal Benvenisti and George W Downs, 'The Empire's New Clothes: Political Economy and the Fragmentation of International Law' (2007) 60 Stanford Law Review 59; Eyal Benvenisti, *The Law of Global Governance* (Brill 2014).

[95]   Moshe Hirsch, *Invitation to the Sociology of International Law* (OUP 2015) (hereafter Hirsch, *Invitation to the Sociology*). See also Jean d'Aspremont and others (eds), *International Law as a Profession* (CUP 2017).

[96]   Benedict Kingsbury, 'The Concept of "Law" in Global Administrative Law' (2009) 20 European Journal of International Law 23.

[97]   For a useful definition of heuristic methods of inquiry in international legal studies, see Cédric Dupont and Thomas Schultz, 'Towards a New Heuristic Model: Investment Arbitration as a Political System' (2016) 7 Journal of International Dispute Settlement 3.

[98]   Bruno Simma and Andreas L Paulus, 'The Responsibility of Individuals for Human Rights Abuses in Internal Conflicts: A Positivist View' (1999) 93 American Journal of International Law 302.

3. REIFYING THINKING IN INTERNATIONAL LAW

The third manifestation of meaning-centrism in international legal thought and practice which this chapter seeks to expose is what has been called here reifying thinking. According to reifying thinking as is understood here, the forms of the international legal discourse are supposed to be anchored in a certain reality which pre-exists them and which they are, in one way or another, responding to. More specifically, by virtue of reifying thinking, the thing, the idea, the norm, the practice, the behavior, the institution, the discourse, and so on which the forms of the international legal discourse represent are supposedly a reality external to and independent from the forms that represent them.

This section provides two illustrations of how reifying thinking, as is construed here, surfaces in international legal thought and practice. It first shows how the necessity to ground international law in the world, and especially in practice, constitutes an expression of reifying thinking (3.1). Second, it turns attention to the idea of rule of recognition that has recurrently informed the way in which the sources of international law are conceptualized, which similarly denotes reifying thinking (3.2).

3.1 The Role of Practice in the International Legal Discourse

A first illustration of reifying thinking is found in the common necessity to ground the forms of the international legal discourse in the actual world.[99] Grounding the forms of the international legal discourse in the actual world is one of the most central discursive necessities of the contemporary international legal discourse. In fact, a statement can hardly be "truth-claiming" for the sake of the international legal discourse if, in one way or another, it is not grounded in the actual world and responding to it.[100] The necessity to ground claims and arguments under the international legal discourse in the actual world certainly

---

[99] This necessity to speak the real is what Martti Koskenniemi has referred to as the requirement of 'concreteness' of international legal argument. See Martti Koskenniemi, *From Apology to Utopia* (CUP 2005) 17–23 (hereafter Koskenniemi, *From Apology to Utopia*). See also the remarks of Simon Chesterman, 'Herding Schrödinger's Cats: The Limits of the Social Science Approach to International Law' (2021) 22 Chicago Journal of International Law 1.

[100] The invocation of 'nature' as the ultimate truth-claiming criteria is a common feature of technical discourses. See gen. Bruno Latour, *Science in Action: How to Follow Scientists and Engineers Through Society* (Harvard University Press 1987).

perpetuates originist thinking as it was discussed above.[101] It also, as is argued in this section, constitutes a manifestation of reifying thinking.

Although the necessity to ground the forms of the international legal discourse in the actual world is not unheard of in pre-classical international legal thought,[102] it is in classical international legal thought—and especially in the work of Vattel and Martens—that it was first systematized.[103] For the authors of that period, the actual world meant the will of states. The need to ground the forms of the international legal discourse in the actual world, understood as the will of states, gained further currency in the first major treatises of the 19th century,[104] and it was in the following decades that it became one of the most central discursive necessities in international legal thought.[105] The necessity to ground the forms of the international legal discourse in the actual world was

---

[101]   See Chapter 1, Section 1.

[102]   Indeed, authors from the 17th and 18th centuries, while prioritizing moral needs in international legal discourses, recognized that international law could partly be an emanation of the actual world. See Samuel Pufendorf, *On the Law of Nature and of Nations* (Charles Henry Oldfather and William Abbott Oldfather trs, Clarendon Press 1934). See Christian Wolff, *Law of Nations Treated According to a Scientific Method* (Joseph H Drake tr, Clarendon Press 1934).

[103]   The 1758 work of Emmerich de Vattel, while perpetuating some of the assumptions of his predecessors regarding the necessity of natural law, made the need to ground international law in the actual world—which he reduced to the will of the states—the main cause of international law. Even more decisive was Georg Friedrich von Martens' radical move away from the moral necessities of natural law and the systematization of international law through treaty and custom *fondé sur les traités et l'usage*. With Martens the need to ground international law in the actual world became the exclusive cause of international law, the latter being turned into a discourse necessarily and exclusively articulated around the necessity to ground international law in the actual world. See Emmerich de Vattel, *The Law of Nations* (Charles G Fenwick tr, Carnegie Institution of Washington 1916); Georg Friedrich von Martens, *Précis du droit des gens moderne de l'Europe fondé sur les traités et l'usage* (Dieterich 1789).

[104]   See eg Henry Wheaton, *Elements of International Law* (Carey, Lea & Blanchard 1836); Robert Phillimore, *Commentaries upon International Law*, 4 vols (William Benning & Son 1854–61); Theodore D Woolsey, *Introduction to the Study of International Law* (4th edn, Scribnerm Amstrong & Co 1877). It should be noted that some of them, whilst making the need to ground international law in the actual world very central, continued to accommodate the idea that the international legal discourse must respond to reason or natural law, or sometimes the will of God.

[105]   It has been claimed that the necessity to ground international law in the actual world that arose in the 19th century was part of an overarching dialectical mode of argumentation that simultaneously required the espousal of some utopian principles. It was also said that, for 19th-century authors, responding to the actual world was a strategy to avoid being utopian. This is the thesis defended by Koskenniemi, *From Apology to Utopia* (n 99) 71–157.

perpetuated in the 20th century. It still governs international legal thought and practice today.[106]

Although in the 20th and 21st centuries international legal thought and practice have upheld the necessity to ground the forms of the international legal discourse in the actual world, the way in which the actual world is understood has undergone some significant developments. Indeed, the actual world in which claims or arguments under the international legal discourse must be grounded has ceased to be reduced to the will of the state and has come to include all kinds of new deeds and realities.[107] It is this expanded and renewed notion of the actual world that the 20th-century international lawyer generalized under the idea of *practice*, which any international legal claim or argument is now expected to draw on and respond to.

It is also noteworthy that this necessity to ground the forms of the international legal discourse in the actual world—now called "practice"—has also been extended to modes of study of the forms of the international legal discourse. For instance, the New Haven School in the 1950s and in the 1960s can be read as an attempt to ensure that the study of forms was better grounded in the actual world.[108] Studies on the legitimacy of the forms of the international

---

[106] Some 20th-century authors claimed that departure from the 19th century's need to ground international law in the actual world ought to be the main project of the 20th century. This is very apparent in Hersch Lauterpacht, *Private Law Sources and Analogies of International Law (with Special Reference to International Arbitration)* (Lawbook Exchange 2002, originally published by Longmans 1927); Hersch Lauterpacht, *The Function of Law in the International Community* (2nd edn, OUP 2011). Hans Kelsen's theorization of international law could also be read as countering this generalization of the need to ground international law in the actual world. Indeed, Kelsen's famous purification of international law was meant to make scholarly discourses autonomous from both crude facts and moral values. It must be acknowledged that Kelsen's charge against the need to ground international law in the actual world remained limited to scholarly discourses. Kelsen continued to construe international law as a product of factual—which he called political—phenomena, and thus as a set of rules grounded in the actual world. See eg Hans Kelsen, 'Law, State and Justice in the Pure Theory of Law' (1948) 57 Yale Law Journal 377, 383–384. For a similar reading, Jochen von Bernstorff, *The Public International Law Theory of Hans Kelsen: Believing in Universal Law* (CUP 2010) 2–3, 13, 44–48, 53.

[107] For a contestation of the 19th-century consensual basis of international obligations, see James Leslie Brierly, 'The Basis of Obligation in International Law' in Hersch Lauterpacht (ed), *The Basis of Obligation in International Law and Other Papers* (Scientia Verlag Aalen 1977). More recently, see Carty, 'International Law and Nervous States' (n 83) 181.

[108] See gen. W Michael Reisman, 'The View from the New Haven School of International Law' (1992) 86 Proceedings of the ASIL Annual Meeting 118; W Michael Reisman, Siegfried Wiessner and Andrew Willard, 'The New Haven School:

legal discourse in the 1990s[109] similarly sought to finetune the focus of international legal studies on the actual world with a view to better understanding
compliance dynamics.[110] In recent years, the necessity for studies of the forms
of the international legal discourse to be grounded in the actual world has
continued to thrive unabated, be it through the rise of a new legal realism in
international law[111] or the vindication, under the banner of a "new empirical
turn," of a more organized and systematized use of empirical data to study the
practical conditions under which international law is formed and has effects.[112]

It must be acknowledged that toward the end of the 20th century and at
the beginning of the 21st century the international lawyer, taking her cue
from, for example, works in literary theory, linguistics, moral theory, and
critical sociology,[113] came to acknowledge that the actual world—and thus the
practice—in which she grounds the forms of the international legal discourse
does not reveal itself to her, but is always mediated and constructed through
a wide range of mental, social, and cultural pre-discursive categories and intelligibility frameworks, which are themselves part of an ideological system of

---

A Brief Introduction' (2007) 32 Yale Journal of International Law 576. For a similar
reading of the New Haven approach, see Orford, 'Scientific Reason' (n 28) 381–382.

[109] See Thomas Franck, *Fairness in International Law and Institutions* (Clarendon
Press 1995) 6.

[110] On this aspect of the turn to legitimacy, see David Bederman, *The Spirit of
International Law* (Georgia University Press 2002). On the Manhattan School of inter-
national law and especially Tom Franck's school, see the 'Symposium on Thomas M.
Franck's Fairness in International Law and Institutions (1995)' (2002) 13 European
Journal of International Law 901. See also David Kennedy, 'Tom Franck and the
Manhattan School' (2003) 35 New York University Journal of International Law and
Politics 397.

[111] See gen. Howard Erlanger and others, 'New Legal Realism Symposium: Is
it Time for a New Legal Realism?' (2005) 2 Wisconsin Law Review 335; Stewart
Macaulay, 'The New Versus the Old Legal Realism: Things Ain't What They Used
to Be' (2005) 2 Wisconsin Law Review 365, 375; Gregory Shaffer, 'A New Legal
Realism: Method in International Economic Law Scholarship' in Colin B Picker,
Isabella Bunn, and Douglas Arner (eds), *International Economic Law—The State and
Future of the Discipline* (Hart Publishing 2008); Victoria Nourse and Gregory Shaffer,
'Varieties of New Legal Realism: Can A New World Order Prompt A New Legal
Theory' (2009) 95 Cornell Law Review 61.

[112] Shaffer and Ginsburg, 'The Empirical Turn' (n 84). See also Holtermann and
Masden, 'Toleration, Synthesis or Replacement?' (n 84).

[113] Nelson Goodman, *Ways of Worldmaking* (Hackett Publishing 1978); Pierre
Bourdieu, 'The Force of Law: Toward a Sociology of the Juridical Field' (1987) 38
Hastings Law Journal 805; Alasdair MacIntyre, *Whose Justice? Which Rationality?*
(Duckworth 1988) 352–353, 367; Stanley Fish, *Doing What Comes Naturally* (Duke
University Press 1989) 157; George Steiner, *Errata: An Examined Life* (Weidenfeld
and Nicholson 1997) 86–87.

representation.[114] Since then, sophisticated examinations of the ways in which the actual world is constructed, cognized, captured, and perceived have started to populate the international legal literature.[115] Yet, this greater awareness of the ways in which pre-discursive categories and intelligibility frameworks constitute the actual world has not sufficed to de-necessitize the grounding of any argument or claim under the international legal discourse in practice.[116]

There is no need to explore further the discursive necessity to ground the forms of the international legal discourse in the actual world—now commonly construed as practice. What must warrant attention for the argument made here is that this world in which the forms of the international legal discourse are grounded and to which they must respond is always approached as a thing having a meaning in itself independently from the form. Indeed, whether for law-ascertainment or hermeneutic purposes, to provide theoretical foundations to forms, to evaluate forms' societal relevance, or to study the practical conditions under which forms are formed or bear effects, and so on, the forms of the international legal discourse, in the common understanding that has been described in this section, must always be grounded in a worldly actuality, historicity, and materiality which has a meaning external to and independent from forms, which is an expression of reifying thinking.

3.2   Discourses on an International Rule of Recognition

Another illustration of reifying thinking can be found in the way in which the international lawyer has resorted to the idea of a rule of recognition,[117] a concept which she has borrowed from British analytical jurisprudence.[118] The rule of recognition constitutes a common narrative in international legal schol-

---

[114] On ideology as a system of representation, see Louis Althusser, *For Marx* (Ben Brewster tr, Verso 2006). For Paul de Man, the correspondence between linguistic categories and natural reality is what we should construe as the work of ideology. See de Man, *The Resistance to Theory* (n 77) 11.

[115] See eg Hirsch, *Invitation to the Sociology* (n 95); Andrea Bianchi, 'Reflexive Butterfly Catching: Insights from a Situated Catcher' in Joost Pauwelyn and others (eds), *Informal International Lawmaking* (OUP 2012); Andrea Bianchi, 'Epistemic Communities' in Jean d'Aspremont and Sahib Singh (eds), *Concepts for International Law: Contributions to Disciplinary Thought* (Edward Elgar Publishing 2019) 251–266; Bianchi, *International Law Theories* (n 66) 7–9, 17–18.

[116] See also Chapter 1, Section 2.2.

[117] See gen. Herbert LA Hart, *The Concept of Law* (2nd edn, OUP 1997) 144–50 (hereafter Hart, *The Concept of Law*).

[118] I have looked at the way in which the international lawyer uses the idea of secondary rules, including the rule of recognition, elsewhere. See Jean d'Aspremont, 'The Idea of "Rules" in the Sources of International Law' (2014) 84 British Yearbook of International Law 103. For a recent discussion, see Richard Collins, 'Taking Legal

arship, one which international legal scholars, legal advisers, counsels, judges, and teachers constantly rely on and perpetuate, especially in connection with the sources of international law which they specifically portray as constituting a (set of) rule(s) of recognition.[119] According to such popular construction, a more or less convergent practice by the so-called law-applying authorities is constitutive of the forms of the discourse on the sources to which it gives a meaning. From that perspective, the rule of recognition provides an alleged social foundation to the forms of the international legal discourse that pertain to law-ascertainment.

The point that must be made here is that the resort to the rule of recognition makes way for reifying thinking as it is understood here. Indeed, according to the idea of rule of recognition as it has been commonly adhered to, the latter exists as a matter of social fact, for it is derived from the practice conceived in terms of convergent behaviors and agreements in judgments among those deemed to be law-applying authorities.[120] The idea of rule of recognition thus

---

Positivism Beyond the State: Finding Secondary Rules?' in Luca Siliquini-Cinelli (ed), *Legal Positivism in a Global and Transnational Age* (Springer 2019) 65–91.

[119] See eg Anthony D'Amato, 'The Neo-Positivist Concept of International Law' (1965) 59 American Journal of International Law 321; Godefridus JH Van Hoof, *Rethinking the Sources of International Law* (Kluwer Publishing 1983) 288; Samantha Besson, 'Theorizing the Sources of International Law' in Samantha Besson and John Tasioulas (eds), *The Philosophy of International Law* (OUP 2010) 180–181; Keith Culver and Michael Giudice, *Legality's Borders: An Essay in General Jurisprudence* (OUP 2010); Diego Mejía-Lemos, 'On Self-Reflectivity, Performativity and Conditions for Existence of Sources of Law in International Law' (2014) 57 German Yearbook of International Law 289; Luka Burazin, 'The Rule of Recognition and the Emergence of a Legal System' (2015) 27 Revus 115. In my earlier work, I also defended a certain idea of the sources of international law along the lines of a rule of recognition grounded in social practice. See Jean d'Aspremont, *Formalism and the Sources of International Law* (OUP 2011). For some older account that comes very close to the idea of a rule of recognition, see Fitzmaurice, 'Some Problems' (n 3) 164. In contrast, for Ian Brownlie, there is not such a thing as a "neat ultimate rule of recognition which provides an intellectual basis for a system of rules but a complex state of political fact": Ian Brownlie, 'International Law at the Fiftieth Anniversary of the United Nations: General Course on Public International Law' (1995) 255 Collected Courses of the Hague Academy of International Law 9, 24. For another rejection of Hart and the defense of a Kelsenian understanding of international law, see Jörg Kammerhofer, 'Uncertainty in the Formal Sources of International Law: Customary International Law and Some of Its Problems' (2004) 15 European Journal of International Law 523, esp. 543–547; Jörg Kammerhofer, *Uncertainty in International Law: A Kelsenian Perspective* (Routledge 2010) 205ff, 224ff.

[120] Herbert LA Hart's chapter 'Jhering's Heaven of Concepts and Modern Analytical Jurisprudence' reproduced in Herbert LA Hart, *Essays in Jurisprudence and Philosophy* (Clarendon Press 1983) 277. See in particular Hart, *The Concept of Law* (n 117) 116–117. Cf Joseph Raz, *The Authority of Law: Essays on Law and Morality*

presupposes a certain law-ascertainment reality external to the forms of the discourse on the sources which give those forms a content, and from which these forms are derived and respond to.[121] The popular construction of the rule of recognition accordingly constitutes a very elaborated type of reifying thinking.

(Clarendon Press 1983) 200. According to Tamanaha, the social practice on which the rule of recognition is based must, accordingly, not be restricted to strictly defined law-applying officials but must include a wide variety of social actors. See Brian Z Tamanaha, *A General Jurisprudence of Law and Society* (OUP 2001) 159–166. It must be noted that John William Salmond, prefiguring Hart, had long contended that the validity of law is strictly a function of judicial recognition and this recognition is a matter of social fact. For him, the ultimate rule of validation is not derived or postulated but lies in the facts of the unified recognitional practice of courts. See John W Salmond, *First Principles of Jurisprudence* (Stevens and Haynes 1893) 83; John W Salmond, *Jurisprudence: or the Theory of the Law* (7th edn, Sweet and Maxwell 1924) 49–54.

[121] This point has been made by Sahib Singh, 'International Law as a Technical Discipline: Critical Perspectives on the Narrative Structure of a Theory' in Jean d'Aspremont, *Formalism and the Sources of International Law: A Theory of the Ascertainment of Legal Rules* (OUP 2013).

3. Deferral of meaning in international law

While the previous chapter has provided some illustrations of the various types of meaning-centrism dominating international legal thought and practice, this chapter shows how such meaning-centrism is always defeated by the perpetual deferral of meaning by the forms of the international legal discourse. This chapter particularly sheds light on how the forms of the international legal discourse always point away to other forms, thereby making meaning eternally absent. In doing so, this chapter will illustrate the work of self-difference and how the latter enables the deferral of meaning. As is understood in this book, self-difference is the trace of other forms in each form of the international legal discourse, that is, the trace of what that form is not. Inhabited by what it is not, each and every form of the international legal discourse has a divided identity enabling that form to do what it does. Importantly, as this chapter will show, such self-difference—and thus the trace of the other—never constitutes a binary identity. The other whose trace inhabits the form is not the opposite other but is only *an* other.[1]

At this stage, it is important to stress once more that the work of self-difference can never be anticipated or predicted, let alone fixed or captured. The deferral of meaning is always different from one reader of the forms of the international legal discourse to the other and from one moment to the next.[2] Examples of the work of self-difference are infinite, always changing, and never fixed. What is more, any account of the work of self-difference is itself always caught in self-difference. This is why one can never provide a snapshot of the work of self-difference without returning to meaning-centrism. Yet, and without the following constituting anything like a snapshot of a fixed state of the deferral of meaning, this chapter provides but a few illustrations of how, in the international legal discourse, the self-difference of forms *could* possibly operate in a way that allows the perpetual deferral of meaning and the eternal absence of the latter.

---

[1] See Chapter 1.
[2] On the idea that the reader is always a writer and that the writer is always a reader, see the remarks of Richard Harland, *Superstructuralism: The Philosophy of Structuralism and Post-Structuralism* (Routledge 1987) 132.

Attention turns first to the discourse on the law of statehood, as the latter provides a very plain illustration of deferral of meaning (1). The chapter then pays heed to the way in which self-difference plays out in the relation between the sources of international law and the modes of decision-making of the International Court of Justice as envisaged by Article 38 of the Statute of the International Court of Justice (2) as well as in the discourse on the law of international responsibility (3). Finally, this chapter shows that self-difference, and thus the constant deferral of meaning, similarly informs the way in which the forms of the international legal discourse interact with the practice which they are supposedly grounded in, shaping, and responding to (4).

1. SELF-DIFFERENCE AND THE LAW OF STATEHOOD

This section argues that it is possible to read the discourse on the law of statehood as a constellation of meaning-deferring forms that support and mediate one another while making the meaning of these forms permanently absent. In this section the forms of the discourse on the law of statehood are deemed meaning-deferring because they always point away to other meaning-deferring forms, whose meaning is equally deferred to other forms, and so on. As is shown in this section, the discourse on the law of statehood is nothing more and nothing less than forms that defer meaning to other forms through their self-difference.

The meaning-deferring forms around which the discourse on the law of statehood is commonly organized are key concepts whose distinct facets are constantly emphasized, over-emphasized, and de-emphasized. It suffices here to give a few examples of these meaning-deferring forms that populate and constitute the discourse on the law of statehood.

The *law of statehood* itself is commonly construed as a discourse built on mutually referring—and sometimes mutually excluding—principles such as self-determination and territorial integrity,[3] the principles of *ex iniuria ius non*

3   Jure Vidmar, 'Remedial Secession in International Law: Theory and (Lack of) Practice' (2010) 6 St Antony's International Review 37 (hereafter Vidmar, 'Remedial Secession'); Christian Walter and Antje von Ungern-Sternberg, 'Self-Determination and Secession in International Law: Perspectives and Trends with Particular Focus on the Commonwealth of Independent States' in Christian Walter, Antje van Ungern-Sternberg and Kavus Abuschov (eds), *Self-Determination and Secession in International Law* (OUP 2014) 1–2 (hereafter Walter and von Ungern-Sternberg, 'Self-Determination and Secession'); Jure Vidmar, 'The Concept of the State and its Right of Existence' (2015) 4 Cambridge Journal of International and Comparative Law 547 (hereafter Vidmar, 'The Concept of State'); Theodore Christakis, 'Self-Determination, Territorial Integrity, and Fait Accompli in the Case of Crimea' (2015) 75 ZaöRV/Heidelberg

oritur and *interest reipublicae ut sit finis litium*,[4] the principles of *uti possidetis* and effectiveness,[5] or the principle of self-determination and the neutrality of international law toward secession.[6]

The *state* in the discourse on the law of statehood is similarly conceptualized as meaning-deferring form. In fact, the concept of the state is now commonly construed in a way that mediates between the facticist position that the state is a fact[7] and the legalist position that the state is a legal construction.[8] In fact, it is often said that state creation is a factual process,[9] but that the state itself is a legal construct or a legal status.[10] From this dominant perspective, the state

---

Journal of International Law 75 (hereafter Christakis, 'The Case of Crimea'); Jure Vidmar, 'The Annexation of Crimea and the Boundaries of the Will of the People' (2015) 16 German Law Journal 365 (hereafter Vidmar, 'The Annexation of Crimea').

⁴   Christakis, 'The Case of Crimea' (n 3); Théodore Christakis, 'The State as a "Primary Fact": Some Thoughts on the Principle of Effectiveness' in Marcelo Kohen (ed), *Secession: International Law Perspectives* (CUP 2006) (hereafter Christakis, 'The State as a "Primary Fact"').

⁵   Christakis, 'The State as a "Primary Fact"' (n 4).

⁶   Olivier Corten, 'Are There Gaps in the International Law of Secession?' in Marcelo Kohen (ed), *Secession: International Law Perspectives* (CUP 2006) (hereafter Corten, 'Are There Gaps').

⁷   Lassa Oppenheim, *International Law*, vol 1 (1st edn, Longmans 1912) 264, para 209; Dionisio Anzilotti, *Corso di Diritto Internazionale*, vol 1 (Athenaeum 1928) 154–155; Gaetano Arangio-Ruiz, *L'Etat dans le sens du droit des gens et la notion de droit international* (Cooperativa Libraria Universitaria 1975); 'Opinion No 1 of the Badinter Commission of 29 November 1991' reprinted in Alain Pellet, 'The Opinions of the Badinter Arbitration Committee. A Second Breath for the Self-Determination of Peoples' (1992) 3 European Journal of International Law 178, 182 (hereafter Pellet, 'The Opinions of the Badinter Arbitration Committee'); James Crawford, *The Creation of States in International Law* (2nd edn, OUP 2006) 23 (hereafter Crawford, *The Creation of States*).

⁸   Hans Kelsen, *General Theory of Law and State* (Harvard University Press 1945); ILC, 'Second report on State responsibility, by Mr. James Crawford, Special Rapporteur' (17 March, 1 and 30 April, 19 July 1999) UN Doc A/CN.4/498; Anne Peters, 'Statehood after 1989: "Effectivités" between Legality and Virtuality' in James Crawford and Sarah Nouwen (eds), *Proceedings of the European Society of International Law*, vol 3 (Hart Publishing 2012) (hereafter Peters, 'Statehood after 1989').

⁹   See also Charles de Visscher, *Les effectivités du droit international public* (Pedone 1967) 34; Georges Abi-Saab, 'Cours général de droit international public' (1987) 207 Collected Courses of the Hague Academy of International Law 9, 68; Crawford, *The Creation of States* (n 7); 'Opinion No 1 of the Badinter Commission of 29 November 1991' reprinted in Pellet, 'The Opinions of the Badinter Arbitration Committee' (n 7) 182.

¹⁰   See Peters, 'Statehood after 1989' (n 8); Jure Vidmar, *Democratic Statehood in International Law* (Hart Publishing 2013) 49 (hereafter Vidmar, *Democratic Statehood*); Crawford, *The Creation of States* (n 7) 5.

is construed as having first emerged as a social reality before being apprehended by the law.[11] Such conceptions of the state lead many commentators to claim that facts and law are constantly intertwined and referring to one another in the discourse on the law of statehood,[12] which expresses the work of self-difference. The same self-difference is found in the more recent concepts of *de facto* states, illegal states, and *de facto* regimes.[13]

Secession is another meaning-deferring form found in the discourse on the law of statehood which denotes the work of self-difference. On the one hand, there is a great consensus in the literature that secession constitutes a factual phenomenon to which international law is blind, the latter neither authorizing nor prohibiting secession.[14] This is the so-called neutrality of the law of statehood toward secession.[15] On the other hand, the same authors claim that

---

[11]   Mathias Forteau, 'L'Etat selon le droit international: une figure à géométrie variable' (2007) 111 Revue Générale de Droit International Public 737, 739. For a historical overview of the state as social reality, see Antonio Cassese, 'States: Rise and Decline of the Primary Subjects of the International Community' in Bardo Fassbender and Anne Peters (eds), *Oxford Handbook on the History of International Law* (OUP 2012).

[12]   Christakis, 'The State as a "Primary Fact"' (n 4).

[13]   See gen. Nina Caspersen and Gareth Stansfield (eds), *Unrecognized States in the International System* (Routledge 2011); Jochen A Frowein, 'De Facto Regime' in Rüdiger Wolfrum (ed), *Max Planck Encyclopedia of Public International Law* (online edn, OUP 2013); Martin Riegl and Doboš Bohumil (eds), *Unrecognized States and Secession in the 21st Century* (Springer 2017). For some remarks on the idea of illegal states, Vidmar, 'The Concept of State' (n 3).

[14]   See contra Alexander Orakhelashvili, 'Statehood, Recognition and the United Nations System: A Unilateral Declaration of Independence in Kosovo' (2009) 12 Max Planck Yearbook of United Nations Law 1, 13.

[15]   *Accordance with International Law of the Unilateral Declaration of Independence in Respect of Kosovo* (Advisory Opinion) [2010] ICJ Rep 403 [84]. See also *Accordance with International Law of the Unilateral Declaration of Independence in Respect of Kosovo* (Advisory Opinion) oral proceedings of 10 December 2009, CR 2009/32, 47 [6] and oral proceedings of 4 December 2009, CR 2009/28, 27 [31]. See also Rosalyn Higgins, *Problems and Process: International Law and How We Use It* (OUP 1994) 125; Théodore Christakis, *Le droit à l'autodétermination en dehors des situations de décolonisation* (La Documentation Francaise 1999) 74 (hereafter Christakis, *Le droit à l'autodétermination*); John Dugard and David Raič, 'The Role of Recognition in the Law and Practice of Secession' in Marcelo Kohen (ed), *Secession: International Law Perspectives* (CUP 2006) 102 (hereafter Dugard and Raič, 'The Role of Recognition'); Christopher J Borgen, 'The Language of Law and the Practice of Politics: Great Powers and the Rhetoric of Self-Determination in the Cases of Kosovo and South Ossetia' (2009) 10 Chicago Journal of International Law 1, 8 (hereafter Borgen, 'The Language of Law'); Jure Vidmar, 'Explaining the Legal Effects of Recognition' (2012) 61 International and Comparative Law Quarterly 361 (hereafter Vidmar, 'Legal Effects of Recognition'); Crawford, *The Creation of States* (n 7) 267, 374, 390; Vidmar, 'The

international law disfavors secession[16] or provides for a presumption against secession,[17] thereby making the idea of secession a legal form that is dependent on the meaning of other forms themselves void of meaning because dependent on yet other forms. Alternatively, it is said that secession is "a legally neutral act whose consequences are regulated internationally,"[18] which also reflects the work of self-difference.

Recognition is a form of the discourse on the law of statehood that similarly exhibits a strong self-difference. For instance, it is common to understand recognition as a political (or sometimes a legal) act[19] that is discretionary but nonetheless calibrated through an obligation not to recognize,[20] or, albeit more

---

Annexation of Crimea' (n 3); Vidmar, 'The Concept of State' (n 3); Walter and von Ungern-Sternberg, 'Self-Determination and Secession' (n 3) 3; Corten, 'Are There Gaps' (n 6) 233; Stefan Oeter, 'The Role of Recognition and Non-Recognition with Regard to Secession' in Christian Walter, Antje van Ungern-Sternberg and Kavus Abuschov (eds), *Self-Determination and Secession in International Law* (OUP 2014) 45, 50 (hereafter Oeter, 'The Role of Recognition').

[16]   Christakis, 'The Case of Crimea' (n 3); Borgen, 'The Language of Law' (n 15) 8; Vidmar, 'The Annexation of Crimea' (n 3); Walter and von Ungern-Sternberg, 'Self-Determination and Secession' (n 3) 3; Daniel Turp, 'Le droit de sécession en droit international public' (1982) 20 Canadian Yearbook of International Law 24; Marc Weller, 'The International Response to the Dissolution of the Socialist Federal Republic of Yugoslavia' (1992) 86 American Journal of International Law 569, 606; Christian Tomuschat, 'Self-Determination in a Post-Colonial World' in Christian Tomuschat (ed), *Modern Law of Self-Determination* (Martinus Nijhoff Publishers 1993) 8; Robert McCorquodale, 'Self-Determination: A Human Rights Approach' (1994) 43 International and Comparative Law Quarterly 24; Pieter H Kooijmans, 'Tolerance, Sovereignty and Self-Determination' (1996) 43 Netherlands International Law Review 211, 215–16; René Lefeber and David Raič, 'Frontiers of International Law Part One: The Chechen People' (1996) 9 Leiden Journal of International Law 1; Christakis, *Le droit à l'autodétermination* (n 15) 314–15; Corten, 'Are There Gaps' (n 6) 235. On the idea that secession must meet certain legal conditions, see Anne Peters, 'The Crimean Vote of March 2014 as an Abuse of the Institution of the Territorial Referendum' in Christian Calliess (ed), *Liber Amicorum für Torsten Stein* (Nomos Verlag 2015) 261; Dugard and Raič, 'The Role of Recognition' (n 15) 106. On the idea that secession is prohibited in case of violation of jus cogens, see Christakis, 'The Case of Crimea' (n 3).

[17]   Christakis, 'The Case of Crimea' (n 3).

[18]   Oeter, 'The Role of Recognition' (n 15) 45, 51.

[19]   Ibid, 66.

[20]   See ILC, 'Draft Articles on Responsibility of States for Internationally Wrongful Act' (2001) II Yearbook of International Law Commission 26, arts 40–41. See gen. Stefan Talmon, 'The Duty Not to "Recognize As Lawful" a Situation Created by the Illegal Use of Force or Other Serious Breaches of a Jus Cogens Obligation: An Obligation Without Real Substance?' in Christian Tomuschat and Jean-Marc Thouvenin (eds), *The Fundamental Rules of the International Legal Order: Jus Cogens and Obligations Erga Omnes* (Martinus Nijhoff Publishers 2006); Anne Lagerwall,

controversially, through an obligation to recognize.[21] In the same vein, it is commonly argued that recognition is not a formal requirement of statehood but significantly impacts the statehood of an entity.[22] Others say that recognition, although primarily declarative,[23] occasionally has constitutive effects,[24] for instance in cases of unilateral secession and territorial illegality.[25]

The same deferral of meaning is witnessed in the ways in which the principle of *self-determination* is conceptualized. Self-determination is said to be a two-faceted concept, having an internal and external dimension.[26] The self-difference of the concept of self-determination is sometimes ascribed to

---

'The Duty Not to Recognise Unlawful Territorial Situations and the European Court of Human Rights' in Christina Binder and Konrad Lachmayer (eds), *European Court of Human Rights and Public International Law: Fragmentation or Unity?* (Nomos 2014) 11–39; Vidmar, *Democratic Statehood* (n 10) 54–61. The practice commonly associated with the obligation not to recognize includes resolutions on the TRNC: UNSC Res 541 (18 November 1983); Southern Rhodesia: UNGA Res 1747 (XVI) (27 June 1962), UNSC Res 202 (6 May 1965), UNGA Res 2022 (XX) (5 November 1965), UNGA Res 2024 (XX) (11 November 1965), UNSC Res 216 (12 November 1965), UNSC Res 217 (20 November 1965) and UNSC Res 277 (18 March 1970); and the South African Homelands: UNGA Res 2671F (8 December 1970), UNGA Res 2775 (29 November 1971), UNGA Res 31/6A (26 October 1976), UNGA Res 402 (22 December 1976), UNGA Res 407 (25 May 1977), UNGA Res 32/105N (14 December 1977), UNGA Res 34/93 G (12 December 1979), UNGA Res 37/43 (3 December 1982) and UNGA Res 37/69A (9 December 1982).

[21] Hersch Lauterpacht, *Recognition in International Law* (CUP 1947) 8. On this construction, see Vidmar, 'The Concept of State' (n 3).

[22] Crawford, *The Creation of States* (n 7) 93; Borgen, 'The Language of Law' (n 15) 12–13; Dugard and Raič, 'The Role of Recognition' (n 15) 110.

[23] Crawford, *The Creation of States* (n 7) 23, 25; *Deutsche Continental Gas-Gesellschaft v Polish State* (1929) 5 Annual Digest of Public International Law Cases 11, 13; 'Opinion No 1 of the Badinter Commission of 29 November 1991' reprinted in Pellet, 'The Opinions of the Badinter Arbitration Committee' (n 7) 182; 'Opinion No 10 of the Badinter Commission of 4 July 1992' reprinted in Pellet, 'The Opinions of the Badinter Arbitration Committee' (n 7) 90.

[24] Vidmar, 'Legal Effects of Recognition' (n 15); Vidmar, 'The Concept of State' (n 3); Brad Roth, 'Secessions, Coups and the International Rule of Law: Assessing the Decline of the Effective Control Doctrine' (2010) 11 Melbourne Journal of International Law 1 (hereafter Roth, 'Secessions, Coups and the International Rule of Law'); Peters, 'Statehood after 1989' (n 8); Dugard and Raič, 'The Role of Recognition' (n 15) 99.

[25] Vidmar, 'The Annexation of Crimea' (n 3) 373; Jure Vidmar, 'Territorial Integrity and the Doctrine of Statehood' (2013) 44 George Washington International Law Review 101, 109; Vidmar, 'Legal Effects of Recognition' (n 15).

[26] For an overview, see Daniel Thürer and Thomas Burri, 'Self-Determination' in Rüdiger Wolfrum (ed), *Max Planck Encyclopedia of Public International Law* (online edn, OUP 2008).

this concept being caught between international law and domestic law[27] or between international and domestic arrangements.[28]

The same degree of deferral of meaning is observed in the way in which authors approach the idea of *effectiveness* in the discourse on the law of statehood. Indeed, the very deference to facts and practice that is expressed by the idea of effectiveness is often construed as a legal principle called the 'principle' or 'doctrine' of effective control.[29] In that sense, effectiveness is supposedly disciplined by international law.[30] As a legal principle, it is even meant to have two dimensions, namely an internal and an external one.[31]

The work of self-difference can also be appreciated in the common claims that *uti possidetis* and self-determination,[32] as well as recognition and secession,[33] work in tandem. The same holds for the recurrent resort by authors to the idea of *mutual compensation* or *mutual calibration* between the paradigms of the discourse on the law of statehood. Such mutual compensation and calibration between meaning-deferring forms translates itself into claims accord-

---

[27]   Walter and von Ungern-Sternberg, 'Self-Determination and Secession' (n 3) 4–5.

[28]   See gen. Malcolm N Shaw, 'The Heritage of States: The Principle of Uti Possidetis Juris Today' (1996) 67 British Yearbook of International Law 75; Marcelo G Kohen, *Possession contestée et souveraineté territoriale* (Presses Universitaires de France 1997); Babara Delcourt and others (eds), *Démembrements d'Etat et délimitation territoriale: l'uti possidetis en question(s)* (Bruylant 1999); Anouche Beaudouin, *Uti possidetis et sécession* (Dalloz 2011); Anne Peters, 'The Principle of Uti Possidetis Juris: How Relevant is it for Issues of Secession?' in Christian Walter, Antje van Ungern-Sternberg, and Kavus Abuschov (eds), *Self-Determination and Secession in International Law* (OUP 2014) (hereafter Peters, 'The Principle of Uti Possidetis Juris'); Giuseppe Nesi, 'Uti Possidetis Doctrine' in Rüdiger Wolfrum (ed), *Max Planck Encyclopedia of Public International Law* (online edn, OUP 2018). See also Case Concerning the Frontier Dispute *(Burkina Faso v Republic of Mali)* (Judgment) [1986] ICJ Rep 554 [23] (hereafter *Burkina Faso v Mali*); 'Opinion No 3 of the Badinter Commission of 11 January 1992' reprinted in Pellet, 'The Opinions of the Badinter Arbitration Committee' (n 7) 184, para 3.

[29]   Roth, 'Secessions, Coups and the International Rule of Law' (n 24); Peters, 'Statehood after 1989' (n 8).

[30]   Christakis, 'The State as a "Primary Fact"' (n 4).

[31]   The internal dimension of *effectivité* pertains to the ability of the authority that claims a monopoly on the exercise of public authority on a piece of territory to actually impose its will—and enforce its decisions—on the people living in that territory. For its part, the external dimension of *effectivité* relates to the ability of that entity to enter into inter-state relations and claim state-like existence in the international arena of states. On this distinction, see Jean d'Aspremont, 'Regulating Statehood: the Kosovo Status Settlement' (2007) 20 Leiden Journal of International Law 654.

[32]   Peters, 'The Principle of Uti Possidetis Juris' (n 28) 126.

[33]   'Dugard and Raič, 'The Role of Recognition' (n 15) 94.

ing to which territorial integrity calibrates the principle of self-determination,[34] legality compensates for lack of effectiveness,[35] illegality neutralizes effectiveness,[36] democracy compensates for lack of effectiveness,[37] *uti possidetis* and self-determination work together,[38] *uti possidetis* calibrates secession,[39] human rights calibrate sovereignty,[40] human rights and self-determination constitute criteria of statehood,[41] and self-determination is adjusted though the saltwater theory as well as a possible doctrine of remedial secession.[42] Such compensations and calibrations constitute wonderful expressions of the work of the self-difference of the forms of the discourse on the law of statehood.

The self-difference of the forms populating the discourse on the law of statehood is sometimes touched on or acknowledged by authors, albeit in meaning-centric terms. It is said, for instance, that the law of statehood is informed by "a dialectics of might and right."[43] By the same token, reference is sometimes made to the "twilight" in the law of statehood,[44] or the idea that the law of statehood is caught in a constant oscillation.[45] Likewise, mention is made of the "inherent duality" of secession.[46] In the same vein, it is said

[34]   Vidmar, 'Remedial Secession' (n 3).
[35]   Peters, 'Statehood after 1989' (n 8).
[36]   For a discussion, see Vidmar, 'The Concept of State' (n 3).
[37]   See Jean d'Aspremont, 'Legitimacy of Governments in the Age of Democracy' (2006) 38 New York University Journal of International Law and Politics 877. See contra Vidmar, 'The Annexation of Crimea' (n 3). On this debate in general, see Vidmar, *Democratic Statehood* (n 10).
[38]   Peters, 'The Principle of Uti Possidetis Juris' (n 28) 126.
[39]   Malcolm N Shaw, 'Peoples, Territorialism and Boundaries' (1997) 3 European Journal of International Law 478; Peters, 'The Principle of Uti Possidetis Juris' (n 28) 110–12. On the idea that uti possidetis does not apply in cases of secession, however, see Marcelo Kohen, 'Introduction' in Marcelo Kohen (ed), *Secession: International Law Perspectives* (CUP 2006) 15.
[40]   Vidmar, 'Remedial Secession' (n 3) 38.
[41]   Dugard and Raič, 'The Role of Recognition' (n 15) 96.
[42]   See Antonello Tancredi, 'A Normative "Due Process" in the Creation of States through Secession' in Marcelo Kohen (ed), *Secession: International Law Perspectives* (CUP 2006) 176; Christian Tomuschat, 'Secession and Self-Determination' in Marcelo Kohen (ed), *Secession: International Law Perspectives* (CUP 2006) 42; Dugard and Raič, 'The Role of Recognition' (n 15) 106; Walter and von Ungern-Sternberg, 'Self-Determination and Secession' (n 3) 1. For more skeptical views on the idea of remedial secession, see Christakis, 'The Case of Crimea' (n 3); Vidmar, 'Remedial Secession' (n 3).
[43]   Peters, 'Statehood after 1989' (n 8).
[44]   Roth, 'Secessions, Coups and the International Rule of Law' (n 24) 48.
[45]   Corten, 'Are There Gaps' (n 6) 234–35.
[46]   Susanna Mancini, 'Secession and Self-Determination' in Michel Rosenfeld and András Sajó (eds), *The Oxford Handbook of Comparative Constitutional Law* (OUP 2012) 481.

that the principle of effectiveness has a dual meaning,[47] or that this principle works as a "bridge-concept which brings together the factual and legal side of statehood."[48]

2.   SELF-DIFFERENCE AND ARTICLE 38 OF THE STATUTE OF THE INTERNATIONAL COURT OF JUSTICE

"The International Court of Justice shall apply the sources of international law." This is the command famously addressed to the International Court of Justice by Article 38 of its Statute. Article 38 provides nothing more, and nothing less, than a command that the Court must apply the sources of international law. This entails, in common understandings of Article 38, that, subject to decision *ex aequo et bono* if the parties agree thereto, this provision represses modes of decision-making that are not based on the sources. And yet, this section argues, Article 38 is a legal form that both represses and empowers the Court, which can be understood as the work of self-difference. Indeed, as is shown in the following paragraphs, the repressive command explicitly formulated by Article 38 is inhabited by the trace of a conferral of a dramatic mode of decision-making to the Court.

Before elucidating Article 38's repressive command to the Court on the one hand and its dramatic empowerment of the Court on the other, a preliminary remark is warranted on the particular manifestation of self-difference that is discussed in this section. That a repressive construction be simultaneously constitutive of an uncontested and unrivaled empowerment is nothing idiosyncratic. After all, it is no coincidence that the word "command" in English can refer to either order or mastery. In fact, the relationship between repression and mastery that is construed here as the work of self-difference corresponds to a structure of discourses that has often been acknowledged in the literature.[49]

---

[47] Peters, 'Statehood after 1989' (n 8).

[48] Ibid.

[49] See gen. Jacques Derrida, *L'écriture et la différence* (Editions du Seuil 1967) 12; Michel Foucault, *L'archéologie du savoir* (Gallimard 1969) 205 (hereafter Foucault, *L'archéologie du savoir*); Bruno Latour, *Nous n'avons jamais été modernes. Essai d'anthropologie symétrique* (La Découverte 1997) 77 (hereafter Latour, *Jamais été modernes*). On the idea that slavery and power work together, see Roland Barthes, *Leçon* (Seuil 1978) 15. On the idea that the paradox between universality and particularism cannot be solved because one cannot exist without one another, see Ernesto Laclau, *Emancipation(s)* (Verso 2007) 34. On the idea that life and death are distinct but work together, see Jacques Derrida, *La vie la mort (séminaire 1975–1976)* (Le Seuil 2019).

Unsurprisingly, this is an expression of the work of self-difference that can also be observed elsewhere in the international legal discourse.[50]

As far as the work of self-difference in Article 38 is concerned, attention must first turn to the repressive and constraining character of Article 38. Indeed, Article 38 of the Statute of International Court of Justice contains a single but strict command: the International Court of Justice shall apply the sources of international law. This command to apply the sources of international law is rather exclusive. Indeed, this is a command addressed to the Court and to the Court only. Article 38 compels no one else to apply the sources of international law.[51] This command is also exclusive because Article 38 contains no instruction for the Court other than this command to apply the sources of international law. Thus, Article 38 provides that the Court—and the Court only—shall apply—and shall do nothing else in addition to applying—the sources of international law. The command of Article 38 is particularly demanding as well.[52] Article 38, for instance, requires the application of specific legal materials and not others. Accordingly, the Court cannot decide by way of applying domestic law, roman law, canon law, FIFA

---

[50] I have found a similar pattern in international criminal law where the principle of legality introduced at Nuremberg, originally designed to curtail the expansion of international criminal law, came to justify the very expansion it was meant to curtail. See Jean d'Aspremont, 'The Two Cultures of International Criminal Law' in Kevin Heller and others (eds), *Oxford Handbook of International Criminal Law* (OUP 2020).

[51] On the idea that Article 38 creates an internal rule for the Court, see Prosper Weil, 'Le droit international en quête de son identité' (1992) 237 Collected Courses of the Hague Academy of International Law 139; René-Jean Dupuy, 'La pratique de l'article 38 du Statut de la Cour internationale de Justice dans le cadre des plaidoiries écrites et orales' in UN Office of Legal Affairs (ed), *Collection of Essays by Legal Advisers of States, Legal Advisers of International Organizations and Practitioners in the Field of International Law* (United Nations 1999) 379; Alain Pellet, 'Article 38' in Andreas Zimmermann and others (eds), *The Statute of the International Court of Justice. A Commentary* (2nd edn, OUP 2012) 759. The idea that Article 38 creates a rule binding the Court has been confirmed by the Court itself on several occasions. See Continental Shelf (*Tunisia v Libyan Arab Jamahiriya*) [1982] ICJ Rep 18 [23]; Delimitation of the Maritime Boundary in the Gulf of Maine Area *(Canada v United States of America)* (Judgement) [1984] ICJ Rep 290 [83] (hereafter *Canada v USA*); Military and Paramilitary Activities in and against Nicaragua *(Nicaragua v United States of America)* (Merits) [1986] ICJ Rep 14 [187] (hereafter *Nicaragua v USA*); *Burkina Faso v Mali* (n 28) [42]; Maritime Delimitation in the Area Between Greenland and Jan Mayen *(Denmark v Norway)* (Judgment) [1993] ICJ Rep 38 [52]; Jurisdictional Immunities of the State *(Germany v Italy)* (Judgment) [2012] ICJ Rep 99 [55].

[52] This has sometimes been challenged. See Joe Verhoeven who argues that article 38 only gives 'indications' to the Court. See Joe Verhoeven, 'Considérations sur ce qui est commun. Cours général de droit international public' (2002) 334 Collected Courses of the Hague Academy of International Law 109.

law, or the law of the international space station. It must apply the sources of international law. More importantly, Article 38 simultaneously compels the Court to a specific action, that is, an application. The Court must *apply* the sources of international law. Its decisions must thus be produced by the action of applying the sources.[53] In other words, by virtue of Article 38, there are only so many actions that the Court can perform: to decide, the Court must apply the sources. The foregoing should suffice to show that Article 38 is a fundamentally repressive construction. By providing that the International Court of Justice shall apply the sources of international law, Article 38 restricts the mode of decision-making available to the Court, as well as the legal materials the Court can rely on. The Court is thus subdued into some specific modes of decision, themselves articulated around certain legal materials.[54]

The repressive character of Article 38 is confirmed by the *travaux préparatoires* of the Statute of the Permanent Court of International Justice. In this respect, and notwithstanding the originist thinking which the following denotes,[55] it is relevant to recall the discussions within the Advisory Committee of Jurists on Thursday July 1, 1920 after the presentation by Baron Descamps about his proposition for a provision about the rules to be applied by the Court.[56] Indeed, as soon as Descamps finished introducing his proposition, of what was to become Article 38, members of the Advisory Committee of Jurists stressed how important it would be to define the rules to be applied by the Court in order to induce states to accept the—then envisaged, compulsory—

---

[53] This is also emphasized by Article 38's reference to the role of the Court ("whose function is to decide in accordance with international law such disputes as are submitted to it").

[54] It must be acknowledged that Article 38 does not have the monopoly on the repression of the power of the Court and thus the alienation of law-making. For instance, Article 59 of the Statute could also be read in this way. Yet, the repression—and thus the alienation of law-making—by Article 38 is most notable given the extent to which Article 38 is the referent for anything related to the sources of international law. See gen. Chris Brown, 'Article 59' in Andreas Zimmermann and others (eds), *The Statute of the International Court of Justice. A Commentary* (2nd edn, OUP 2012).

[55] See also Chapter 1, section 5 and the remark in the introduction of this chapter.

[56] The project of Baron Descamps is reproduced in Advisory Committee of Jurists, 'Procès-Verbaux of the Proceedings of the Committee' (15th June–24th July 1920) with Annexes (Van Langenhuysen Brothers 1920), Annex no 3 to the meeting of 1st July 1920, 306 (hereafter Advisory Committee of Jurists, 'Procès-Verbaux'). When the project of Statute was adopted by the Assembly of the League of Nations in December 1920, the command which Baron Descamps introduced on 1st of July 1920 had made its way to the Statute of the Permanent Court of International Justice without any substantive alteration. See League Nations Assembly, 'Records of the First Assembly of the League of Nations, Plenary Meetings' (1923) 500.

jurisdiction of the Court.[57] For the Advisory Committee of Jurists, Article 38 was primarily a marketing measure to enhance the acceptability of the new Court in the eyes of the major powers represented in the League of Nations by presenting the Court as a very benign body whose modes of decision-making would be very constrained. In this context, it is no surprise that the sources of international law mentioned in Article 38 were themselves never discussed by the Advisory Committee of Jurists.[58] The attention of the members of the Committee was, rather, almost exclusively drawn to issues pertaining to a (dreaded) hypothetical situation involving the Court declaring itself incompetent because of a lack of applicable rules (*non liquet*).[59] Interestingly, the passionate debates on general principles of law confirmed that Article 38 was all about repressing the modes of decision-making available to the Court where there was lack of applicable legal material.[60] The *travaux* thus show that Article 38 was conceived by its authors as a repressive construction, the function of which was to legitimize and justify the very object of what it represses, that is, the Court's power to decide. It is in the repression of the Court's power to decide and the restriction placed on the Court's modes of decision-making with a view to making the Court look more benign to states that the *raison d'être* of Article 38 lies. It could even be said that, if not to repress the Court's power to decide, there would have been no Article 38.[61]

And yet, the uncontested repressive character of Article 38 simultaneously bears the trace of the elevation of the International Court of Justice into the master of the sources of international law.[62] Indeed, the international lawyer naturally turns to the International Court of Justice's judgments and advisory opinions to find authoritative guidance as to how international law ought to be ascertained.[63] To put it in another way, there seems to be no resistance

---

[57]   Advisory Committee of Jurists, 'Procès-Verbaux' (n 56) 293.

[58]   Loder made the point that the sources themselves did not call for any discussion right after Baron Descamps' presentation of its project about the rules to be applied by the Court. See Advisory Committee of Jurists, 'Procès-Verbaux' (n 56) 294.

[59]   Advisory Committee of Jurists, 'Procès-Verbaux' (n 56) 296.

[60]   Advisory Committee of Jurists, 'Procès-Verbaux' (n 56) 322–325.

[61]   Although the power that Article 38 was meant to justify was not made automatically opposable to all parties to the statute as the compulsory jurisdiction of the Court was scraped from the Statute, Article 38 notably survived the scaling down of the power it was meant to support.

[62]   I have further examined the various facets of the mastery of the Court over the sources of international law in Jean d'Aspremont, 'The International Court of Justice as the Master of the Sources' in Carlos Espósito and Kate Parlett (eds), *The Cambridge Companion to the International Court of Justice* (CUP 2021).

[63]   See Hugh Thirlway, *The Sources of International Law* (OUP 2014) 1–30. See the remarks of Jean d'Aspremont, 'Book review of H. Thirlway, *The Sources of International Law*' [2014] German Yearbook of International Law 57.

toward the Court being the principle *meta*-lawmaker; that is, the maker of the modes of lawmaking.[64] The Court's mastery of the sources of international law is actually unrivaled. Few would ever dare to claim that this role should be rather bestowed upon scholars.[65] Even the International Law Commission has explicitly relinquished its own authority to the Court when it comes to defining (or refining) the criteria to ascertain international law.[66] As a result, whenever the international lawyer is pressed to justify the functioning of the sources of international law or the foundations thereof, she looks to the Court.

Thus, Article 38, while restricting the modes of decision-making available to the Court as well as the legal materials the Court can rely on, also empowers the Court and elevates it to the unrivaled and uncontested master of the sources. In other words, the repression of the Court's modes of decision-making by Article 38's command that the Court applies the sources of international law is what enables the Court to be a master of the sources of international law. That repression and mastery go together is the work of self-difference as it is understood here. It is in defining what it is to decide by applying the sources of international law, and thus in defining the scope of repression of Article 38's command, that the Court asserts its mastery on the sources and, more generally, on the ascertainment of international law. Article 38 thus constitutes

---

[64]   It must be acknowledged that such assertion of power of the sources is sometimes contested. For instance, the Court is sometimes stigmatised for the liberty it has taken with the doctrine of sources and its adoption of "new rules of recognition" at convenience (Abraham Sofaer, 'Adjudication in the International Court of Justice: Progress through Realism' (1989) 44 Rec. A.B. City N.Y. 462, 477). For an overview of the criticisms of the International Court of Justice, see A Mark Weisburd, *Failings of the International Court of Justice* (OUP 2016).

[65]   Sometimes the international lawyer recognizes that the design of the structures of international legal argumentation and of their main doctrines is bound to be a scholarly enterprise. This is well illustrated by the candidness of Roberto Ago in his famous course on "the international delict" at the Hague Academy in 1938—which paved the way for the subsequent codification of the subject after the Second World War—and where he recognizes that the making of the main patterns of argumentative structure is a matter of scholarly choices. See eg Roberto Ago, 'Le délit international' (1938) 68 Collected Courses of the Hague Academy of International Law 420–421 (hereafter Ago, 'Le délit international'). See also Charles de Visscher, *Théories et Réalités en Droit International Public* (4th edn, Pedone 1970) 171.

[66]   See ILC, 'First report on formation and evidence of customary international law, by Sir Michael Wood, Special Rapporteur' (17 May 2013) UN Doc A/CN.4/663, para 54. See also ILC, 'Third report on identification of customary international law' (27 March 2015) UN Doc A/CN.4/682, para 4. It is also interesting to note that the International Court of Justice is mentioned 45 times in the International Law Commission's 2018 conclusions on identification of customary international law: see ILC, 'Draft Conclusions on Identification of Customary International Law, with Commentaries' (2018) UN Doc A/73/10, 117ff.

a form that denotes a very severe divided identity, one that is the expression of its self-difference and that allows its meaning to be deferred.

3.   SELF-DIFFERENCE AND THE LAW OF INTERNATIONAL RESPONSIBILITY

The discourse on the law of international responsibility provides a third illustration of how the forms of the international legal discourse point away to other forms by virtue of their self-difference and thereby differ in meaning. In fact, the discourse on the law of international responsibility is commonly construed as a set of legal forms through which the determination and allocation of the burden of compensation for a prior harm is debated. Said differently, allowing the determination and allocation of the burden of compensation for prior harm is what these forms are supposed to achieve. In the dominant discourse on the law of international responsibility, these forms are of two kinds, some of them pertaining to the establishment of responsibility and others relating to the determination of the contents of responsibility.[67] Altogether, these forms are deemed to perform a power-constraining and power-rationalizing role[68] while simultaneously inviting international actors to act with diligence and care.[69]

---

[67]   As is well known, responsibility in international law has not been confined to compensation *stricto sensu*: other—mostly restorative—consequences have been attached to the establishment of responsibility. In other words, the reparatory function of international responsibility has been supplemented with restorative functions. The restorative understanding of legality is usually traced back to Ago. See Ago, 'Le délit international' (n 65) 426–427, 429. See also ICL, 'Second report on State responsibility, by Roberto Ago, Special Rapporteur—the origin of international responsibility' (20 April 1970) UN Doc A/CN.4/233.

[68]   This is usually what informs the traditional and popular idea that "power breeds responsibility." See Clyde Eagleton, *The Responsibility of States in International Law* (New York University Press 1928) 206. See also Clyde Eagleton, 'International Organizations and the Law of Responsibility' (1950) 76 Collected Courses of the Hague Academy of International Law 385–386. For some critical remarks on these assertions and the various types of power which breed responsibility, see André Nollkaemper, 'Power and Responsibility in International Law' in Adriana Di Stefano (ed), *Un Diritto Senza Terra? Funzioni E Limiti de Principio Di Territorialità Nel Diritto Internazionale E Dell'Unione Europea/A Lackland Law? Territory, Effectiveness and Jurisdiction in International and European Law* (Giappichelli 2015). It should be noted that the constraining and rationalizing of power is certainly not specific to responsibility. Primary obligations can also be understood as seeking to rationalize and constrain power.

[69]   A common association also holds that responsibility serves the international rule of law. See Simon Chesterman, 'An International Rule of Law?' (2008) 56 American Journal of Comparative Law 331; Arthur Watts, 'The International Rule of Law' (1993) 36 German Yearbook of International Law 15.

And yet the forms that constitute the discourse on the law of international responsibility simultaneously bear the trace of forms enabling the very subject which they seek to constrain, which is yet another expression of self-difference as it is understood here.[70] Indeed, the forms of the discourse on the law of international responsibility, albeit aimed at constraining, blaming, and shaming some actor and subsequently subduing them to a range of obligations, simultaneously constitute those very actors. More specifically, the forms of the discourse on the law of international responsibility always bear the trace of the forms constitutive of the very power they subdue and thus of the legal forms that make that power possible. In that sense, the accountability mechanism of international responsibility is similarly an enabling mechanism. The forms of the discourse on the law of international responsibility thus have a divided identity as they constitute the subjects which they seek to subdue, and draw on all the other forms that make such a constitution of the subject possible.[71] Whether the forms constitutive of the discourse on the law of international responsibility are enabling more than they are constraining is not a relevant question here because one goes with the other, or to put it more clearly, one is the other, which manifests the very work of self-difference as it is understood here.

Such deferral of meaning is particularly noticeable in the forms pertaining to the responsibility of states for internationally wrongful acts.[72] It suffices here to give a few examples. For instance, all the powers exercised by the individuals in their capacity as organ or individual and which are, by virtue of Articles

---

[70]   This self-difference is sometimes captured through the claim that law structures and constitutes politics and powers: see Christian Reus-Smit, 'The Politics of International Law' in Christian Reus-Smit (ed), *The Politics of International Law* (CUP 2009) 14–44. See also Christian Reus-Smit, 'Politics and International Legal Obligation' (2003) 9 European Journal of International Law 591.

[71]   I have elaborated on this duality of the discourse on the law of international responsibility elsewhere. See Jean d'Aspremont, 'International Responsibility and the Constitution of Power: International Organizations Bolstered' in Ana Sofia Barros, Cedric Ryngaert and Jan Wouters (eds), *International Organizations and Member State Responsibility* (Brill 2016).

[72]   Philip Allott, 'State Responsibility and the Unmaking of International Law' (1988) 29 Harvard International Law Journal 1, 13 (hereafter Allott, 'Unmaking of International Law'). In the same vein, Koskenniemi has claimed that responsibility is as much a sword as a shield. See Martti Koskenniemi, 'Doctrines of State Responsibility' in James Crawford and others (eds), *The Law of International Responsibility* (OUP 2010) 51. Note that Allott has deemed such a constitution of power as being very detrimental to international law as a whole. See Allott, 'Unmaking of International Law' (above) 2. He argues that "the consumers—the people of the world—may have been less well served". He adds: "It is unlikely that anyone but a government official would regard the confirmation of government power as the purpose of law."

4–11 of the Articles on Responsibility of States for Internationally Wrongful Acts, nourishing the conduct of the states, are thus recognized as power at the international level in the first place. The same holds for the situations of attribution of responsibility dealt with in Articles 16–18, which give legal existence to the powers to aid and assist, to direct and control, or to coerce, without such powers having a prior existence to the Articles on Responsibility of States for Internationally Wrongful Acts.[73] Another example is provided by the circumstances precluding wrongfulness designed in Articles 20–26, which are very constitutive of a compelling form of power at the international level. For some scholars, circumstances precluding wrongfulness have even constituted the most dramatic constitution of power under the Articles on Responsibility of States for Internationally Wrongful Acts, such a recognition having been deemed socially harmful.[74]

It is submitted here that the self-difference of the forms on international responsibility, and thus the deferral of meaning, can prove even more tangible when it comes to the forms of the discourse on the responsibility of international organizations for internationally wrongful acts. Indeed, the latter bear even more visibly the trace of the forms constitutive of the power of the international organizations they subdue. To illustrate the extent to which the Articles on the Responsibility of International Organizations for Internationally Wrongful Acts[75] make international organizations powerful entities, it suffices here to take those provisions which construct the possibility of international organizations aiding, coercing, or directing (member) states (Articles 14–16). It does not seem controversial to claim that had the discourse on the law of international responsibility not provided for such categories, the possibility of international organizations exerting such power would not have belonged to the world of possibilities of the international legal discourse. Said differ-

---

[73] Note that Fry acknowledges that attributed responsibility "presumes control." See James D Fry, 'Attribution of Responsibility' in André Nollkaemper and Ilias Plakokefalos (eds), *Principles of Shared Responsibility in International Law* (CUP 2014) 128.

[74] Allott, 'Unmaking of International Law' (n 72) 16–24; Vaughan Lowe, 'Precluding Wrongfulness or Responsibility: A Plea for Excuses' (1999) 10 European Journal of International Law 405; Theodore Christakis, 'Les "circonstances excluant l'illicéité": une illusion d'optique?' in Olivier Corten and others, *Droit du Pouvoir— Pouvoir du Droit: Mélanges en l'honneur de Jean Salmon* (Bruylant 2007); Helmut Aust, 'Circumstances Precluding Wrongfulness' in André Nollkaemper and Ilias Plakokefalos (eds), *Principles of Shared Responsibility in International Law: An Appraisal of the State of the Art* (CUP 2014) 176–179.

[75] ILC, 'Articles on the Responsibility of International Organizations for Internationally Wrongful Acts' (26 April–3 June, 4 July–12 August 2011) UN Doc A/CN.4/L.778.

ently, those provisions make it a possibility that an international organization could aid, coerce or direct its (member) states.[76] This finding is, of course, not limited to those provisions pertaining to the attribution of responsibility to international organizations for aid, coercion, or direction. Yet, the above-mentioned examples should suffice to show the extent to which the Articles on the Responsibility of International Organizations for Internationally Wrongful Acts bear the trace of forms constitutive of international organizations as hugely powerful creatures, thereby illustrating the work of self-difference and the perpetual deferral of meaning.

4.   SELF-DIFFERENCE AND INTERNATIONAL LEGAL PRACTICE

It is submitted in this section that deferral of meaning is also at work in the references by forms of the international legal discourse to what is commonly called "practice," that is, a form that works as a shorthand for "reality" or "the actual world." In previous sections, it has already been shown that the common necessity of the contemporary international legal discourse to draw on practice manifests some very strong meaning-centrism, either through a type of reifying thinking[77] or through a type of deliverability thinking.[78] In this section, it is argued that references to practice by forms of the international legal discourse are themselves caught in the deferral of meaning and thus provide yet another example of the work of self-difference.

The work of self-difference that is discussed in this section is yet slightly different from that with which the previous sections grappled. In fact, the deferral of meaning discussed here is one that is partly self-referential, for it relates to a discursive situation where forms point away to other forms that then point away to yet other forms but also point back to the forms which had originally deferred meaning to them. This entails, as far as the forms of the international legal discourses that refer to practice are concerned, that meaning is deferred by the forms of the international legal discourse to practice which, as a form, refers back to the original meaning-deferring form that had referred to practice in the first place. In other words, attention is paid here to the fact that forms of the international legal discourse that refer to practice are already

---

[76]   It must be acknowledged that these provisions on aid, coercion, and direction come with a strong flavor of being of a textbook-case nature. This criticism is one of those given in Jean d'Aspremont, 'Abuse of the Legal Personality of International Organizations and the Responsibility of Member States' (2007) 4 International Organizations Law Review 91.

[77]   See Chapter 2, Section 3.1

[78]   See Chapter 2, Section 2.2.

inhabited by the traces of the practice which they refer to, while that practice is itself already bearing the trace of the forms of the international legal discourse that refer to it.[79]

The type of self-referential deferral of meaning that is discussed here corresponds to what I have called elsewhere a mode of "self-confirming thinking."[80] Self-confirming thinking is an expression that seeks to capture the dialectical relationship between the word and the world,[81] and more specifically the idea that the word is in the world and the world is in the word.[82] Here, the relationship between the forms of the international legal discourse and practice is not depicted as an expression of self-confirming thinking—which rather describes a discursive effect[83]—but as a deferral of meaning which epitomizes the sovereignty of forms about international legal thought and practice.[84]

---

[79] Jacques Derrida, *The Beast and the Sovereign*, vol 2 (University of Chicago Press 2011) 5, 9, 140.

[80] See Jean d'Aspremont, *The Discourse on Customary International Law* (OUP 2021) ch 6. See also Jean d'Aspremont, 'A Worldly Law in a Legal World' in Andrea Bianchi and Moshe Hirsch (eds), *International Law's Invisible Frames* (OUP 2021).

[81] See gen. Michel Foucault, *Les mots et les choses* (Gallimard 1966) 58. See also Latour, *Jamais été modernes* (n 49) 24; Emmanuel Levinas, *Altérité et transcendance* (Fata Morgana 1995) 17. This is not to say that dualism is unknown from pre-modern thought. Previously, the distinction between the body and the spirit brought about an important mode of dualistic thinking. See Jacques Le Goff, 'L'homme médiéval' in Jacques Le Goff (ed), *L'Homme médiéval* (Editions du Seuil 1989) 15.

[82] Timothy Mitchell, *Questions of Modernity* (University of Minnesota Press 2000) 17. See also Latour, *Jamais été modernes* (n 49) 57. See also Bruno Latour, *La fabrique du droit. Une ethnographie du Conseil d'Etat* (La Découverte 2004) 235 (hereafter Latour, *La fabrique du droit*). On the idea that modern science is based on the output of facts that it has created itself, see Henri Bergson, *La pensée et le mouvant* (Flammarion 2014) 251.

[83] This discursive effect is what Jacques Derrida has called the formidable "simulacrum effect" of language. See Jacques Derrida, *The Beast and the Sovereign*, vol 1 (University of Chicago Press 2011) 289 (hereafter Derrida, *The Beast and the Sovereign*). On the invincibility of such discursive effects, see Timothy Mitchell, *Colonising Egypt* (CUP 1991) xiii; George Steiner, *Errata: An Examined Life* (Weidenfeld and Nicholson 1997) 88; Steven L Winter, *A Clearing in the Forest: Law, Life and Mind* (The University of Chicago Press 2001) 67–68; John Law, *After Method: Mess in Social Science Research* (Routledge 2004) 32–37; Foucault, *L'archéologie du savoir* (n 49) 204; Latour, *La fabrique du droit* (n 82) 235; Latour, *Jamais été modernes* (n 49) 56. For an early theorization of self-confirming thinking, see Gaston Bachelard, *Le nouvel esprit scientifique* (Presses universitaires de France 1934).

[84] In Lacanian terms, this is captured through the idea that existence is a product of language. Language brings things into existence. This led Lacan to distinguish the real that precedes the language and is killed by it and the reality which is constituted by language, calling for an understanding of the real does not precede pre-language but exists alongside it. See gen. Jacques Lacan, *Ecrits* (Seuil 1966) 848. On this aspect of Lacan,

A good illustration of such self-referential deferral of meaning by the forms of the international legal discourse that refer to practice is provided by the mainstream understanding of the ascertainment of practice[85] and *opinio juris*[86] for the sake of the identification of customary international law. In fact, customary international law is one of these instances where such self-referential deferral of meaning is most tangible. Indeed, the identification of customary international law always necessitates that the "existence" as well as the content of a given rule of customary international law be tested, demonstrated, or contested through the finding of practice and *opinio juris* pertaining to that rule. In that sense, the "existence" and the content of a customary rule is always deferred to practice and the possible sense of obligation *vis-à-vis* that practice. At the same time, such practice and the possible sense of obligation *vis-à-vis* that practice are not out there ready to be observed, but are the reflection of the pre-existing representations of that behavior by the forms whose "existence" and content is being tested, demonstrated, or contested. In other words, the practice and the possible sense of obligation *vis-à-vis* such practice to which the forms of the discourse on customary international law point away in turn point back to the forms whose "existence" and content is being tested, demonstrated, or contested. As a result, the forms of customary international law—and thus all the words, idioms, aphorisms, and texts that compose it—defer meaning to practice while the latter, as form, defers meaning to the former.[87] Customary international law is a common site for such self-referential deferral of meaning.

---

see Bruce Fink, *The Lacanian Subject: Between Language and Jouissance* (Princeton University Press 1995) 24–25.

[85]   See ILC Conclusion 8, para 1 in ILC, 'Draft Conclusions on Identification of Customary International Law, with Commentaries' (2018) UN Doc A/73/10, 64 (hereafter UN Doc A/73/10) which reads as follows: "The relevant practice must be general, meaning that it must be sufficiently widespread and representative, as well as consistent." See the ILC Commentary in UN Doc A/73/10 (n 85) 137, paras 5–7; *Nicaragua v USA* (n 51) [186]; Fisheries case (*United Kingdom v Norway*) (Judgment) [1951] ICJ Rep 131; *Canada v USA* (n 51) [81].

[86]   See ILC Conclusion 9 in UN Doc A/73/10 (n 85) 138. See also North Sea Continental Shelf *(Federal Republic of Germany v Denmark; Federal Republic of Germany v Netherlands)* (Judgment) [1969] ICJ Rep 3 [76]–[77]; *Nicaragua v USA* (n 51) [206].

[87]   For a further elaboration on this aspect of customary international law, see Jean d'Aspremont, *The Discourse on Customary International Law* (OUP 2021) ch 6.

4.   After meaning

The forms of the international legal discourse are sovereign. They reign over the international legal discourse and need no meaning to do what they do. In fact, as was shown in the previous chapters, the forms of the international legal discourse perpetually point away to other forms by virtue of their self-difference and condemn meaning to be perpetually absent. As a result of its absence, meaning can no longer be the cause and origin of the forms of the international legal discourse. The main take-away from the previous chapters is that the main modes of engagement with international law must be rethought, as much as possible, short of all meaning-centric moves, and especially short of the common modes of originist thinking, of deliverability thinking, and of reifying thinking that dominate international legal thought and practice.

This chapter elaborates on the implications of engaging with international law short of meaning-centrism. It was mentioned in the introduction that de-necessitating meaning-centrism brings about a de-necessitating of the quest for an origin, of the quest for content, and of the quest for reality.[1] It is time now to shed light on what such de-necessitating moves more concretely entail for the international lawyer's day-to-day engagements with the words, idioms, aphorisms, and texts of international law. In elucidating some of the day-to-day consequences of a move away from the dominant meaning-centrism of international legal thought and practice, this chapter sketches the contour of a new scholarly attitude toward textuality in international law.[2]

---

[1]   See Chapter 1, Section 4.

[2]   It is argued here that the discussion of the implications of the sovereignty of forms for the critical attitude ought not to be conducted under the banner of "deconstruction." There are several reasons for keeping the idea of deconstruction at bay. First, deconstruction has come to mean so many different things to so many different people that it would be very cacophonic, if not unintelligible, to try to capture the possible consequences of the sovereignty of forms through the deconstruction. Second, and more fundamentally, approaching the implications of the sovereignty of forms through the notion of deconstruction would permit yet another slippage into meaning-centrism, for it presumes that deconstruction constitutes some sort of meaningful attitude, method, practice which can then be transposed and translated to legal studies. For a criticism of the way in which the work of Derrida has been used in the US critical scholarship, see Terry Eagleton, *The Function of Criticism* (Verso 2005) 98–101 (hereafter Eagleton, *The Function of Criticism*).

This chapter zeroes in on seven implications of the de-necessitating of the meaning-centric modes of engagement with international law, namely those pertaining to interpretation (1), the international lawyer herself (2), the critical attitude (3), the study of the history of international law (4), the exercise of comparison (5), the translation of international legal texts (6), and the practice of referencing (7).

Because the following account of the possible implications of the sovereignty of forms is not an account of something 'out there', 'fixed', or 'meaningful', but amounts to—nothing more and nothing less than—words, idioms, aphorisms and texts themselves caught in the deferral of meaning, the trace of other forms that can possibly inhabit the following sections is always mentioned in the title. This is a way to acknowledge that the following sections are nothing more than forms having a divided identity and being inhabited by the trace of other forms.

It will be noted by the reader that, in the following sections, the implications of the sovereignty of forms for the international lawyer's main modes of engagement with international law are discussed at a high level of abstraction and generality. The justification for such a choice is two-fold. First, I have had the chance to elaborate on several of such implications elsewhere, and also intend to continue to do so in the future. Second, refraining from spelling out very precisely what the sovereignty of forms possibly entails for those engaging with the forms of the international legal discourse is yet another way to acknowledge that the sovereignty of forms never leads to one fixed or universal experience, for it is itself caught in the infinite deferral of meaning.

1.   INTERPRETATION (A FORM-ENABLING HAPPENING)

The international lawyer is trained to interpret the words, idioms, aphorisms, and texts of international law as well as the origin, the context, the authors, the agendas, and the effects of such words, idioms, aphorisms, and texts. The international lawyer has also acquired a number of aptitudes that allow her to respond to, evaluate, contest, and question the interpretations made of such words, idioms, aphorisms, and texts by others. It is similarly in interpretive terms that the international lawyer commonly depicts her daily activities: engaging with international law is commonly represented as an interpretive business. In fact, she sees courtrooms, classrooms, and law journals as being saturated with debates on how to interpret international law, what goals the interpretation of international law should serve, what interpretation hides, what drives interpretation, how interpretation discriminates, what kind of world interpretation shapes, and so on. In sum, international law is thought, represented, practiced, and taught as an omnipresent and permanent interpretive activity. Interpretation is not only omnipresent and permanent in the (self-) representation of the international lawyer's activity. It is, above all, commonly represented as being centered on a quest for meaning.[3] For the international lawyer, interpretation is always reduced to meaning-determination interpretation. Indeed, in international legal thought and practice, interpretation is commonly construed in an hermeneutic fashion, that is, as being a meaningful activity about the determination of meaning carried and delivered by the forms of the international legal discourse as well as the determination of their meaningful contexts, meaningful origin, meaningful authors, meaningful addressees, meaningful effects, and so on.[4]

As can probably be anticipated, the claim made in this book about the sovereignty of forms and the need to de-necessitate deliverability thinking has major consequences for the abovementioned (self-) representations of what the international lawyer does, especially for her hermeneutic tradition. In fact, if the forms of the international legal discourse, as has been argued in the previous chapters, neither carry nor deliver meaning, there are simply no meanings to be determined or found, be it that of forms themselves or that of their origin, context, authors, agendas, effects, and so on. Basically, interpretation cannot be about determining any meaning whatsoever, for the latter is always absent.[5] The sovereignty of forms accordingly contradicts the dominant approach to interpretation based on *hermeneutics* and the search for meaning that is witnessed in the international legal discourse. Instead, the claim made in this book about the absence of meaning and the need to de-necessitate deliverability thinking dominating international legal thought and practice supports

---

[3]   On the idea that interpretation is traditionally deployed as "technology of analytical knowledge," see Pierre Legrand, 'Siting Foreign Law: How Derrida Can Help' (2011) 21 Duke Journal of Comparative and International Law 595, 598 (hereafter Legrand, 'Siting Foreign Law').

[4]   See Chapter 1, Section 2.2; Chapter 2, Section 2.1.

[5]   Pierre Legrand writes that if interpreters seek to determine meaning, they are condemned to impotence. See Pierre Legrand, 'Foreign Law: Understanding Understanding' (2011) 6 Journal of Comparative Law 67, 84 (hereafter Legrand, 'Understanding Understanding'). On the idea that literature seems to have long understood that the forms are not just a carrier and delivery as signified, see Maurice Merleau-Ponty, *Signes* (Gallimard 1960) 379–380.

an understanding of interpretation as *poetics*[6] and thus how international legal texts do what they do through the traces of other texts.[7]

It is acknowledged here that the move from hermeneutics to poetics that accompanies the sovereignty of forms can be perceived as rather tragic for the international lawyer who has been trained in the hermeneutic tradition to seek and determine meaning through interpretation. Indeed, how many failed arguments, failed articles, failed judgments, failed interviews, failed careers and, possibly, failed loves and failed lives for interpretative postures that have been deemed invalid despite meaning being perpetually absent from the words, idioms, aphorisms, and texts of international law? Yet, as it is argued in this section, the sovereignty of forms and the absence of meaning does not entail a repudiation or discontinuation of interpretation. In fact, the point made here is not that interpretation as meaning-determination ought to stop. Actually, one cannot call for a stop to interpretation as meaning-determination, for, as it is submitted here, such interpretation never started and never was there. More specifically, even if interpretation is commonly experienced and theorized as an activity geared toward the determination of meaning, interpretation has actually never been determining meaning, for meaning was always absent. This is why the argument made here cannot be that interpretation as meaning-determination should be halted. What ought to be contested is the common experience and theorization of interpretation as being about the deter-

---

[6]   On the distinction between a tradition based on hermeneutics and one based on poetics, see Jonathan Culler, *Structuralist Poetics: Structuralism, Linguistics, and the Study of Literature* (2nd edn, Routledge 2002) vii–viii (hereafter Culler, *Structuralist Poetics*). It is important to emphasize that the understanding of poetics advocated here is different from that of Culler. For the latter, poetics ought to remain structuralist and seek to account for the rules, the conventions, and the procedures whereby texts do what they do. As the following paragraphs should make clear, the poetics advocated here shares neither the "scientific" and explanatory ambitions of Culler's structuralist poetics nor its attempt to formulate general and universal laws out of the literary experience generated by the reading of international legal texts.

[7]   See Jacques Derrida's famous statement about the two ways in which one can interpret the structure in *L'Ecriture et la différence* (Seuil 1967) 427 ("There are, then, two interpretations of interpretation [...] One seeks to decipher, dreams of deciphering a truth [...] escaping the play and the order of the sign and lives like a banishment the necessity of interpretation. The other [...] asserts the play and attempts to go beyond man and humanism, the name of man being the name of this being which [...] has dreamt of full presence, reassuring foundation, [...] and the end of play. [...] [T]hese two interpretations of interpretation [...] are absolutely irreconcilable even though we live them simultaneously and reconcile them within an obscure economy").

mination of meaning carried and delivered by the forms of the international legal discourse.[8]

If meaning has always been absent from legal forms, what has the international lawyer been doing all these years when conducting what they call the interpretation of the words, idioms, aphorisms, and texts of international law? In other words, if interpretation has not been about determining meaning, what has it been about? It is submitted here that what the international lawyer calls interpretation has always been about *soliciting a meaning that is hoped for* but that is never to come. Importantly, such solicitation for meaning is never made in vain. Indeed, when soliciting a meaning that is condemned to remain absent, the interpreter awakens the deferral of meaning.[9] Said differently, when one purports to interpret a rule, one does not give meaning to that rule but puts into motion the deferral of meaning. In that sense, in soliciting a meaning that she hopes for, the international lawyer enables the form to defer meaning, and, in doing so, enables the form to be a form.[10] This is why interpretation is better experienced and theorized, not as a meaning-determining process, but as *form-enabling happening*, that is, an event consisting of igniting the words, idioms, aphorisms, and texts of international law to do what forms do, that is, defer meaning.

That interpretation, as it is argued here, has never been about determining meaning, but a happening that puts the deferral of meaning into motion begs the—theoretical, normative, and deontological—question of how the international lawyer should approach interpretation. In other words, if not an exercise of hermeneutics but a form-enabling happening, what is interpretation concretely about? The following paragraphs mention five major consequences

---

[8] I have myself been guilty over the past decade of repeatedly reducing interpretation to a content-determination process. See Jean d'Aspremont, 'The Multidimensional Process of Interpretation: Content-Determination and Law-Ascertainment Distinguished' in Andrea Bianchi, Daniel Peat and Matthew Windsor (eds), *Interpretation in International Law* (OUP 2015). See also Jean d'Aspremont, 'Sources in Legal-Formalist Theories: The Poor Vehicle of Legal Forms' in Samantha Besson and Jean d'Aspremont (eds), *The Oxford Handbook of the Sources of International Law* (OUP 2017). This terminology has been espoused by Panos Merkouris and others, 'Final Report of the ILA Study Group on Content and Evolution of the Rules of Interpretation' in International Law Association Report of the Seventy-Ninth Biennial Conference (Kyoto 2020) (International Law Association, Kyoto 2020).

[9] On the idea of awakening the trace, see Legrand, 'Siting Foreign Law' (n 3) 610. See also the remarks of Vincent Forray and Sébastien Pimont, *Décrire le droit ... et le transformer. Essai sur la décriture du droit* (Dalloz 2017) 222 (hereafter Forray and Pimont, *Décrire le droit*).

[10] On the idea that the form, if allocated a definite and fixed meaning, ceases to be a form, see Roland Barthes, *Le Bruissement de la langue. Essais critiques IV* (Seuil 1984) 109 (hereafter Barthes, *Essais critiques IV*).

of the de-necessitating of meaning-centrism for interpretation and of the corresponding understanding of interpretation as a form-enabling happening.

The first consequence pertains to the very words, idioms, aphorisms, and
texts of international law. Such forms cannot be approached as potentially
carrying or being able to deliver a unitary meaning, for they are spaces[11] where
something is happening.[12] In such spaces, meaning is always passing but never
stopping. Actually, failing to deliver meaning is part of the performativity of
the words, idioms, aphorisms, and texts of international law.[13] In that sense, the
words, idioms, aphorisms, and texts of international law can be construed as
a *site of infinite passage*[14]—or wandering spaces[15]—with thousands of entries
and exits.[16] The fact that the reader experiences the text as having a unitary
meaning is irrelevant.[17] Indeed, the reader's experience of a semantic unity,
and the verbalization of that experience, are themselves caught in the deferral
of meaning. Actually, engaging with the words, idioms, aphorisms, and texts
of international law in terms of determinacy, indeterminacy, subjectivity, or
objectivity becomes preposterous,[18] the notions of determinacy, indetermi-

---

[11]   See Roland Barthes, *L'aventure sémiologique* (Seuil 1985) 13 (hereafter Barthes,
L'aventure sémiologique). See also Roland Barthes, *S/Z* (Seuil 1970) 10–11 (hereafter
Barthes, *S/Z*); Barthes, *Essais critiques IV* (n 10) 56.

[12]   On the idea of text as an event, see Pierre Legrand, 'The Same and the Different'
in Pierre Legrand and Roderick Munday (eds), *Comparative Legal Studies: Traditions
and Transitions* (CUP 2003) 244 (hereafter Legrand, 'The Same and the Different').
See also Pierre Legrand, '"Il n'y a pas de hors-texte": Intimations of Jacques Derrida as
Comparatist-at-Law' in Peter Goodrich and others (eds), *Derrida and Legal Philosophy*
(Palgrave Macmillan 2008) 143 (hereafter Legrand, 'Il n'y a pas de hors-texte').

[13]   Anne Orford, 'Critical Intimacy: Jacques Derrida and the Friendship of Politics'
(2005) 6 German Law Journal 31, 40 (hereafter Orford, 'Critical Intimacy').

[14]   On the idea of passage in the text, see Barthes, *Essais critiques IV* (n 10) 75. On
the idea that the text is a volume of traces and deferrals, see Barthes, *L'aventure sémiologique* (n 11) 13.

[15]   On the idea of wandering, see Peter Goodrich, 'Europe in America:
Grammatology, Legal Studies, and the Politics of Transmission' (2001) 101 Columbia
Law Review 2063 (hereafter Goodrich, 'Europe in America'). Pierre Legrand speaks of
tracing as meandering. See Legrand, 'Understanding Understanding' (n 5) 154.

[16]   Barthes, *S/Z* (n 11) 17.

[17]   Jonathan Culler, *On Deconstruction: Theory and Criticism after Structuralism*
(Routledge 2008) 132 (hereafter Culler, *On Deconstruction*). See also the remarks of
Paul de Man, *The Resistance to Theory* (University of Minnesota Press 1986) 9–10
(hereafter de Man, *The Resistance to Theory*).

[18]   On the idea that the etymological root of determinacy is terminus, which con-
notes with both boundary and conclusion, see Peter Goodrich, 'Sleeping with the
Enemy: An Essay on the Politics of Critical Legal Studies in America' (1993) 68
New York University Law Review 389, 407 (hereafter Goodrich, 'Sleeping with the
Enemy'). See also the remarks of Fuad Zarbiyev, *Le discours interprétatif en droit
international* (Bruylant 2015) 109–118.

nacy, subjectivity, objectivity being condemned to belong to the order of the imaginary, given the infinite possibilities offered by the forms of the international legal discourse.[19]

The second consequence follows the first one and pertains to how interpretation should be theorized and conducted. This is where the poetics advocated here become more tangible. If the words, idioms, aphorisms, and texts of international law are sites of infinite passage, interpretation should be about appreciating words, idioms, aphorisms, and texts' plenitude[20] as well as their infinite possibilities in terms of deferral of meaning.[21] This attitude particularly entails letting oneself be *surprised* by the text[22] without predetermining the outcome of one's reading.[23] In that sense, interpretation is a type of slow and meticulous reading[24] that refuses linearity[25] as well as any pre-assigned sender and pre-assigned recipient.[26] It is a reading geared toward the intimacy, the excessive, and the singular of the form.[27] It is a reading that metonymizes the

---

[19]   On this idea, see Barthes, *S/Z* (n 11) 15. For an overview of different approaches to indeterminacy, see Cameron A Miles, 'Indeterminacy' in Jean d'Aspremont and Sahib Singh (eds), *Concepts for International Law: Contributions to Disciplinary Thought* (Edward Elgar Publishing 2019) 447.

[20]   Goodrich, 'Europe in America' (n 15) 2048.

[21]   Barthes, *S/Z* (n 11) 11, 20. In the same vein, see Legrand, 'Il n'y a pas de hors-texte' (n 12) 131.

[22]   On the idea of being "surprised," see Anne Orford, 'Critical Intimacies: Reading International Law' in Peter Goodrich and others (eds), *Derrida and Legal Philosophy* (Palgrave MacMillan 2008) 115 (hereafter Orford, 'Reading International Law').

[23]   Jacques Derrida, *La Carte Postale* (Flammarion 1980) 10 ("il est mauvais de prédestiner sa lecture") (hereafer Derrida, *La Carte Postale*).

[24]   For a similar understanding of Derrida's work, see Culler, *On Deconstruction* (n 17) ii. See also Peter Goodrich and others, 'Introduction: A Philosophy of Legal Enigmas' in Peter Goodrich and others (eds), *Derrida and Legal Philosophy* (Palgrave Macmillan 2008) 12 (hereafter Goodrich and others, 'Introduction') ("Derrida demanded that we read legal texts more closely, read more attentively and justly, that we give time and listen to the pathologies, traumas, and conflicts that are expressed through them"). See also Simon Critchley, 'Derrida's Influence on Philosophy … And on My Work' (2005) 6 German Law Journal 25, 27 (hereafter Critchley, 'Derrida's Influence'); Orford, 'Reading International Law' (n 22) 115; Orford, 'Critical Intimacy' (n 13) 31.

[25]   Legrand, 'Il n'y a pas de hors-texte' (n 12) 131.

[26]   Derrida, *La Carte Postale* (n 23) 11.

[27]   This is an attitude that Anne Orford associates with the work of Jacques Derrida. See Orford, 'Reading International Law' (n 22) 115; Orford, 'Critical Intimacy' (n 13) 31. See also Anne Orford, *Reading Humanitarian Intervention* (CUP 2003) 38 (hereafter Orford, *Reading Humanitarian Intervention*). In the same vein, see also Pierre Legrand, 'On the Singularity of Law' (2006) 47 Harvard International Law Journal 517 (hereafter Legrand, 'Singularity of Law').

words, idioms, aphorisms, and texts of international law in all directions.[28] It is about searching for all the possible frauds of the forms.[29] It is about nurturing the texts' enigmas.[30] In short, interpretation is a type of infinite and always unfinished[31] overinterpretation.[32]

The type of slow, meticulous, metonymizing, and surprise-inducing reading that stops short of anticipating any outcome that is envisaged here warrants an important observation. Such a reading cannot be reduced to *oppositional reading*. This observation is important because oppositional reading—and thus the understanding of the divided identity of forms as a binary identity—is a move often observed in critical literature,[33] a move that is probably inherited from traditional structuralism.[34] In fact, if reading, as is often witnessed in the critical literature, seeks to generate the opposite outcome of the words, idioms, aphorisms, and texts concerned, such reading becomes meaning-centric as it presupposes an original meaning which it will seek to frustrate or contradict. As was said earlier, the trace of the other in the form cannot be reduced to the trace of the opposite other.[35] The slow, meticulous, metonymizing, and surprise-inducing reading that stops short of anticipating any outcome which is envisaged here cannot be reduced to this common oppositional reading because it is a reading that metonymizes in all directions and that stops short

---

[28]   Avita Ronell, 'Saying Goodbye: An Amateur Video' in Peter Goodrich and others (eds), *Derrida and Legal Philosophy* (Palgrave MacMillan 2008) 245 (hereafter Ronell, 'Saying Goodbye').

[29]   Roland Barthes, *Leçon* (Seuil 1978) 16 (speaking of salutary deception, "tricherie salutaire") (hereafter Barthes, *Leçon*). Cf the notion of symptomatic reading of Ntina Tzouvala, *Capitalism as Civilisation. A History of International Law* (CUP 2020) 7–19 (hereafter Tzouvala, *Capitalism*).

[30]   Goodrich and others, 'Introduction' (n 24) 14 (for Peter Goodrich, the enigmas are the signs of a passage of something).

[31]   On the idea of the science of reading as a science of in-exhaustion, see Barthes, *Essais critiques IV* (n 10) 47. On the idea that interpretation of the legal text can never be completed, see Legrand, 'Understanding Understanding' (n 5) 84. In the same vein, see Tzouvala, *Capitalism* (n 29) 14.

[32]   On the idea of over-interpretation, see Jacques Derrida, *Papier Machine* (Galilée 2001) 27 (hereafter Derrida, *Papier Machine*). In relation to international legal studies, see Tzouvala, *Capitalism* (n 29) 13 ("Importantly, these silences and dark spots of our texts do not simply exist somewhere, ready to be discovered. Rather, the silences are the product of the questions we choose to ask the text, the problematic that informs our own reading").

[33]   See gen. Jack M Balkin, 'Deconstructive Practice and Legal Theory' (1987) 96 Yale Law Journal 743, 765 (hereafter Balkin, 'Deconstructive Practice'); Jack M Balkin, 'Deconstruction's Legal Career' (2005) 27 Cardozo Law Review 722–729 (hereafter Balkin, 'Deconstruction's Legal Career').

[34]   See the remarks of Culler, *Structuralist Poetics* (n 6) 16–17.

[35]   See Chapter 1, Section 3.2.

of postulating a hierarchy prior to the reading. The reading promoted here thus departs from the oppositional reading occasionally witnessed in the literature.[36] This is also why the reading promoted here is better presented as a type of overinterpretation rather than a misreading.[37]

The third consequence of the de-necessitating of meaning-centrism for interpretation is presented here as a non-consequence. Interpretation as an attitude of being surprised by the words, idioms, aphorisms, and texts of international law and appreciating the latter as sites of infinite passage do not entail that everything goes.[38] Meaning cannot be deferred at whim and according to the preferences of the interpreter, precisely because interpretation and all that is vested in it—preferences, agendas, imagination, and so on—are themselves caught in the deferral of meaning. The deferral of meaning always hinges on the other forms to which meaning is deferred at the moment the interpreter solicits meaning from the form. In other words, the deferral of meaning, albeit nomadic and always ever-changing,[39] is thus dependent on the other forms which are available to the interpreter and that she sees traced in the text.[40] This latter point is important, for it indicates that the approach to interpretation that follows the de-necessitating of deliverability thinking advocated here cannot

---

[36]   For some similar reservations towards the methodological unpicking of binary oppositions, see Critchley, 'Derrida's Influence' (n 24) 26. See contra for a promotion of oppositional reading in international legal studies, see Tzouvala, *Capitalism* (n 29) 9–10 (drawing on Bennett Capers, 'Reading Back, Reading Black' (2006) 35 Hofstra Law Review 9–22). See also contra Juan M Amaya-Castro and Hassan El Menyawi, 'Moving Away from Moving Away: A Conversation about Jacques Derrida and Legal Scholarship' (2005) 6 German Law Journal 101, 109–110.

[37]   Cf Roland Barthes, who speaks of "manhandling" (malmener) the text. See Barthes, *S/Z* (n 11) 15. See also Edward Said, *The World, the Text, and the Critic* (Harvard University Press 1983) 39 (hereafter Said, *The World, the Text, and the Critic*). On misreading in relation to international legal studies, see also Orford, *Reading Humanitarian Intervention* (n 27) 38-40. On the idea that the deferral of meaning by forms pointing away to other forms is unstoppable, see Richard Harland, *Superstructuralism. The Philosophy of Structuralism and Post-Structuralism* (Routledge 1987) 135 (hereafter Harland, *Superstructuralism*). See also Tzouvala, *Capitalism* (n 29) 8–10.

[38]   Jacques Derrida, *L'Ecriture et la différence* (Seuil 1967) 427 (hereafter Derrida, *Ecriture*); Culler, *On Deconstruction* (n 17) 132. See also the remarks of Balkin, 'Deconstructive Practice' (n 33) 776–777, 785; Balkin, 'Deconstruction's Legal Career' (n 33) 719.

[39]   Legrand, 'Understanding Understanding' (n 5) 145, 154.

[40]   This is different from claims that vests the determination of meaning in the community of interpreters which continues to be meaning-centric and rests on a type of deliverability thinking. Cf Stanley Fish, *Is There a Text in This Class? The Authority of Interpretive Communities* (Harvard University Press 1980) 147 (hereafter Fish, *Is There a Text in This Class?*). See also Chapter 1, Section 3.2.

be reduced to a replacement of the problems of hermeneutics by the pleasure of infinite creation[41] as well as a glorification of the aleatory.[42] The deferral of meaning is never aleatory, anarchical, and accidental.

This dependency of the deferral of meaning enabled by interpretation on the forms available to the interpreter entails a fourth consequence. Because deferral of meaning hinges on the forms available to the interpreter and to which the forms being interpreted will point away, the latter cannot just hide behind the words, idioms, aphorisms, and texts of international law. Such forms do what they do—and they often do terrible things—by virtue of the deferral of meaning enabled by the interpreter and, more specifically, the forms that the latter vest into the forms being interpreted. Being responsible for the deferral of meaning by the forms of the international legal discourse and for vesting forms into forms, the interpreter is inevitably instrumental in what the words, idioms, aphorisms, and texts of international law do.[43] De-necessitating meaning-centrism, far from entailing a withdrawal of the interpreter from the text and her abdication from any responsibility *vis-à-vis* the world,[44] maximizes her ethical responsibility.[45]

A fifth and last consequence pertains to the existing state of the scholarship on interpretation. Such literature is replete with sophisticated meta-language that is meant to provide the 'analyst' with a critical distance from the interpretations being carried out. For instance, it is now common to capture or evaluate the constraints on the determination of meaning by the interpreter through wide and sophisticated notions like epistemic community,[46] commu-

---

[41]   This is a charge made by Culler, *Structuralist Poetics* (n 6) 289.

[42]   Ibid, 295.

[43]   See contra on the idea that the removal of the signified entails a removal of human control Harland, *Superstructuralism* (n 37) 135.

[44]   Legrand, 'Singularity of Law' (n 27) 526.

[45]   See Jacques Derrida, 'The Force of Law: The "Mystical Foundation of Authority"' (1989) 11 Cardozo Law Review 920, 956, 961. See also Derrida, *Papier Machine* (n 32) 341–342. See also Goodrich, 'Europe in America' (n 15) 2068; Legrand, 'Siting Foreign Law' (n 3) 624; Forray and Pimont, *Décrire le droit* (n 9) 343–366; Petra Gehring, 'Force and "Mystical Foundation" of Law: How Jacques Derrida Addresses Legal Discourse' (2005) 6 German Law Journal 151; Adam Thurschwell, 'Specters and Scholars: Derrida and the Tragedy of Political Thought' (2005) 6 German Law Journal 87; Florian Hoffmann, 'Epilogue: In Lieu of Conclusion' (2005) 6 German Law Journal 197, 199; Costas Douzinas, 'Violence, Justice, Deconstruction' (2005) 6 German Law Journal 171.

[46]   Peter Haas, 'Introduction: Epistemic Communities and International Policy Coordination' (1992) 46 International Organization 1, 2–3; Peter Haas, 'International Environmental Law: Epistemic Communities' in Daniel Bodansky, Jutta Brunnée, and Ellen Hey (eds), *The Oxford Handbook of International Environmental Law* (OUP 2007).

nity of practice,[47] interpretive community,[48] juridical field,[49] invisible college,[50] communified professional group,[51] law-appliers,[52] *auctoritatis interpositio*,[53]

---

[47] Emanuel Adler, *Communitarian International Relations: The Epistemic Foundations of International Relations* (Routledge 2005) 15.

[48] Stanley Fish, 'Fish v. Fiss' (1984) 36 Stanford Law Review 1325, 1331–1332; Fish, *Is There a Text in This Class?* (n 40) 13–14. The notion of interpretive community has enjoyed considerable success in international legal scholarship. See eg Ian Johnstone, 'Treaty Interpretation: The Authority of Interpretive Communities' (1990) 12 Michigan Journal of International Law 371; Detlev F Vagts, 'Treaty Interpretation and the New American Ways of Law Reading' (1993) 4 European Journal of International Law 472ff, 480ff; Ian Johnstone, 'Security Council Deliberations: The Power of the Better Argument' (2003) 14 European Journal of International Law 437, 439; Efthymios Papastavridis, 'Interpretation of Security Council Resolutions under Chapter VII in the Aftermath of the Iraqi Crisis' (2007) 56 International and Comparative Law Quarterly 83; Andrea Bianchi, 'The International Regulation of the Use of Force: The Politics of Interpretive Method' (2009) 22 Leiden Journal of International Law 665; Veronika Fikfak and Benedict Burnett, 'Domestic Court's Reading of International Norms: A Semiotic Analysis' (2009) 22 International Journal for the Semiotics of Law 437ff; Fuad Zarbiyev, *Le discours interprétatif en droit international: une approche critique et généalogique* (PhD thesis, Geneva Graduate Institute of International and Development Studies 2009) 98ff; Andrea Bianchi, 'Textual Interpretation and (International) Law Reading: The Myth of (In)determinacy and the Genealogy of Meaning' in Pieter HF Bekker, Rudolf Dolzer and Michael Weibel (eds), *Making Transnational Law Work in the Global Economy: Essays in Honour of Detlev Vagts* (CUP 2010) 34ff and 51ff; Jean d'Aspremont, 'Wording in International Law' (2012) 25 Leiden Journal of International Law 575 (hereafter d'Aspremont, 'Wording').

[49] Pierre Bourdieu, 'The Force of Law: Toward a Sociology of the Juridical Field' (1987) 38 Hastings Law Journal 805.

[50] Oscar Schachter, 'The Invisible College of International Lawyers' (1977) 72 Northwestern University Law Review 217.

[51] See the notion of "speaking-listening" developed by Harold Berman, *Law and Language: Effective Symbols of Community* (CUP 2013) 38.

[52] The notion of law-applier emerged in the context of the rule-based approach to international law. It finds roots in British analytical jurisprudence as well as German legal positivism. It quickly proved insufficient as it often remained equated with the idea of judicial authority. In recent years, the concept of law-applying authority has been subject to some dilution and pluralization in general theory of law and jurisprudence. See Keith Culver and Michael Giudice, *Legality's Borders: An Essay in General Jurisprudence* (OUP 2010).

[53] The idea of *auctoritatis interpositio* is borrowed from Carl Schmitt, although it is used to refer to the Kantian idea—systematized by Kelsen—that by virtue of the indeterminacy of rules law is ultimately dependent upon human judgement. See Carl Schmitt, *Politische Theologie: Vier Kapitel zur Lehre von der Souveränität* (Duncker und Humblot 1979) 41. See the discussion of that question by Nikolas Rajkovic, 'Rules, Lawyering, and the Politics of Legality: Critical Sociology and International Law's Rule' (2014) 27 Leiden Journal of International Law 331.

topois,[54] "social practice,"[55] argumentative practice,[56] nomos,[57] belief system,[58] and so on.[59] What matters to highlight here is that these analytical vocabularies are not only premised on the idea that interpretation is meaning-determining. They also presuppose the possibility of a meta-language through which interpretation can be examined, discussed, and evaluated. If anything, the foregoing should have shown that any experience and theorization of interpretation through a meta-language is an impossibility, for such meta-vocabulary is itself caught in the very deferral of meaning enabled by the exercises of interpretations it seeks to examine, discuss, or evaluate.[60] In that sense, the abovementioned theorizations often constitute distractions that prevent the international lawyer from appreciating that the forms of the international legal discourse as well as all the forms which she vests in interpretation are sites of infinite passage and that interpretation is best construed as a form-enabling happening.

---

[54]   See Friedrich V Kratochwil, *Rules, Norms, and Decisions: On the Conditions of Practical and Legal Reasoning in International Relations and Domestic Affairs* (CUP 1989) 38. It must be acknowledged that gospels, as they are understood here, do not strictly mirror the four main lists of topoi given by Kratochwil (see at 232). Yet, gospels share the same structuring effects. It must also be highlighted that gospels are not exclusive of other constraints of reasoning being deployed in international legal argumentation.

[55]   See Martti Koskenniemi, 'Between Commitment and Cynicism: Outline for a Theory of International Law as Practice' in Martti Koskenniemi, *The Politics of International Law* (Hart Publishing 2011) 271. See also Sahib Singh, 'International Law as a Technical Discipline: Critical Perspectives on the Narrative Structure of a Theory' in Jean d'Aspremont, *Formalism and the Sources of International Law* (OUP 2013) 236.

[56]   Ingo Venzke, 'International Law as an Argumentative Practice: On Wohlrapp's The Concept of Argument' (2016) 7 Transnational Legal Theory 9. See also Jean d'Aspremont, *Epistemic Forces in International Law: Foundational Doctrines and Techniques of International Legal Argumentation* (Edward Elgar Publishing 2015) (hereafter d'Aspremont, *Epistemic Forces*).

[57]   See Robert Cover, 'The Supreme Court, 1982 Term—Foreword: Nomos and Narrative' (1983) 97 Harvard Law Review 4.

[58]   John Hart Ely, 'Constitutional Interpretivism: Its Allure and Impossibility' (1978) 53 Indiana Law Journal 399; Arthur Allen Leff, 'Unspeakable Ethics, Unnatural Law' [1979] Duke Law Journal 1229, 1231, 1245–1247; Pierre Schlag, 'Law as the Continuation of God by Other Means' (1997) 85 California Law Review 427; Jean d'Aspremont, *International Law as a Belief System* (CUP 2017) (hereafter d'Aspremont, *Belief System*).

[59]   See also the discussion of these concepts in Jean d'Aspremont, *Epistemic Forces in International Law* (Edward Elgar 2016) 1–30; Jean d'Aspremont, 'The Professionalisation of International Law' in Jean d'Aspremont and others (eds), *International Law as a Profession* (CUP 2017) 19.

[60]   Barthes, *Essais critiques IV* (n 10) 17.

2. THE INTERNATIONAL LAWYER (THE MEANING-SOLICITER)

The previous chapters have scarcely mentioned the international lawyer, be it as an agent of the international legal discourse or a user of its forms.[61] The absence of the international lawyer so far is not a coincidence.[62] The sovereign forms do not share their sovereignty over the international legal discourse.[63] Yet, it is submitted here that acknowledging the sovereignty of forms and de-necessitating meaning-centrism ought not to entail a complete obliteration of the international lawyer from the study of international legal thought and practice. It is true that, when approached as the *author* of the forms of the international legal discourse, and notwithstanding the possible biographical value thereof, the international lawyer is an irrelevant figure. As was said, the author of the form, just like the context, is part of the form.[64] That is not exclusive, however, of paying heed to the international lawyer's role as a *user* of forms. After all, the work of the form as form, and thus the deferral of meaning, is always put into motion by the international lawyer soliciting a meaning from the form, a meaning that she hopes for. By soliciting a meaning from the form,

---

[61]   On the role of the subject in critical legal scholarship, see David Kennedy, 'Critical Theory, Structuralism and Contemporary Legal Scholarship' (1986) 21 New England Law Review 209, 249 (hereafter Kennedy, 'Critical Theory'); Mikhail Xifaras, 'Théorie des personnages juridiques' (2017) 2 Revue française de droit administratif 275. For various accounts of the international legal discourse centered on the international lawyer, see David Kennedy, 'The Mystery of Global Governance' (2008) 34 Ohio Northern University Law Review 827; David Kennedy, *A World of Struggle: How Power, Law and Expertise Shape Global Political Economy* (Princeton University Press 2016). Some of my previous works similarly put the emphasis on the international lawyer and her projects. See d'Aspremont, 'Wording' (n 48); d'Aspremont, *Epistemic Forces* (n 56).

[62]   Roland Barthes famously speaks of the death of the author. See Barthes, *Essais critiques IV* (n 10) 61. See also Stanley Fish, 'With the Compliments of the Author: Reflections on Austin and Derrida' (1982) 8 Critical Inquiry 693–721. For a different take on the possibility to study discourse without paying attention to the users of the discourse and the question of agency, see the comments of Quentin Skinner, *The Foundations of Modern Political Thought*, vol 1 (CUP 1998) xii. See also Michael Polanyi, *Personal Knowledge: Towards a Post-Critical Philosophy* (The University of Chicago Press 1958) 309. For an attempt to reconcile structure and agency in social sciences, see however Maurice Mandelbaum, *Purpose and Necessity in Social Theory* (Johns Hopkins University Press 2019).

[63]   On the idea that divisible sovereignty is no longer sovereignty and that the sovereign ought not to respond to anything or anyone as it would otherwise not be sovereign, see Jacques Derrida, *The Beast and the Sovereign*, vol 2 (University of Chicago Press 2011) 57, 76–77.

[64]   See Chapter 1, Section 3.

the international lawyer comes to bring the self-identity of the form to existence,[65] thereby rolling out the deferral of meaning.[66] By soliciting a meaning from the form, the international lawyer simultaneously induces, prods, supports, constructs the traces of other forms in the form,[67] and thus pours more forms into the very forms from which she solicits meaning. And this is no different whether one speaks of the judge, the scholar, the counsel, the legal adviser, the activist, and so on.[68]

It is important to stress once more that although she puts in motion the deferral of meaning, the international lawyer is by no means the author thereof.[69] Indeed, the deferral of meaning has always been awaiting its unfolding by the international lawyer.[70] Yet, the international lawyer is heavily implicated in the deferral of meaning. And her implication is not trivial. In fact, as the foregoing has shown, she is implicated not only in the prompting of the deferral of meaning but also in the configuration thereof.[71] This is why, even after meaning-centrism has been de-necessitated, the international lawyer ought to be studied and scrutinized, neither as the cause or origin of an absent meaning nor as the author of the deferral of meaning, but as the one who initiates and configures the deferral of meaning through her solicitation of meaning from the form.[72]

What is there to learn from the international lawyer's prompting and configuration of the deferral of meaning, that is, from the international lawyer as a user of the form? It is argued here that the international lawyer's hope for meaning—and all the affects, desires, ambitions, and passions that drive

---

[65]   Pierre Legrand speaks of "awakening the trace." See Legrand, 'Siting Foreign Law' (n 3) 610.
[66]   Cf Jonathan Culler, who speaks of "meaning moving through the reader." See Culler, *Structuralist Poetics* (n 6) 35.
[67]   Legrand, 'Understanding Understanding' (n 5) 82.
[68]   On the various professions of the international lawyer, see Jean d'Aspremont and others (eds), *International Law as a Profession* (CUP 2017).
[69]   Although the subject activates the deferral of meaning, she is not the author of the deferral of meaning, for she is caught, as a subject, in the deferral of meaning. See Jacques Derrida, *Positions* (Editions de Minuit 1972) 40–41 (hereafter Derrida, *Positions*). Cf the idea that performativity always comes with a certain enactment, see Judith Butler, *Notes Toward a Performative Theory of Assembly* (Harvard University Press 2018) 31–32.
[70]   Legrand, 'Siting Foreign Law' (n 3) 609.
[71]   Legrand, 'Il n'y a pas de hors-texte' (n 12) 133. See also Legrand, 'Understanding Understanding' (n 5) 79; Legrand, 'Siting Foreign Law' (n 3) 609–610 and 614–615; Forray and Pimont, *Décrire le droit* (n 9) 222–223.
[72]   On the idea that reading is writing, see Derrida, *Papier Machine* (n 32) 27.

that hope[73]—may be a formidable source of scholarly insights. Likewise, and without them being necessarily distinguishable from the hope that triggers them, the study of international lawyers' moves, techniques, and strategies of solicitation of meaning from the form can prove equally enriching.

And yet, one should not lose sight of the fact that, as the international lawyer draws attention, she herself becomes a form caught in the deferral of meaning. Said differently, the international lawyer cannot evade being an absent self. In fact, the international lawyer, as a user of the discourse cannot be approached as a contextual element external to the deferral of meaning she is prodding and configuring.[74] We can neither know nor pin down the international lawyer whom we refer to when we study international legal thought and practice from the vantage point of the user of the form. In our engagement with the user of the form, we should remember that the international lawyer is yet another form indefinitely pointing away to other forms.

3.   THE CRITICAL ATTITUDE (OVER-LOYALTY TO THE FORM)

This section elaborates on the consequences of the sovereignty of forms and of the de-necessitating of meaning-centrism for the critical attitude in international legal scholarship. Before doing so, a few preliminary observations must be formulated on what the critical attitude in international legal scholarship refers to here. In the international legal literature, being 'critical' is a routine self-portrayal. And it has been so for a long time. Actually, being critical could even be deemed the condition of scholarship since the advent of modern thought. In fact, modern thought is commonly associated with a critical questioning of the necessities that govern action, perception, experience, and discourses[75] and a contestation of those necessities that are unacknowledged and unconsented.[76] The modern mind even invented a word for such 'critical' consciousness: *Enlightenment*. Being enlightened has often meant nothing more than the awareness and evaluation of the necessities governing actions,

---

[73]   See eg David Kennedy, 'The Disciplines of International Law and Policy' (1999) 12 Leiden Journal of International Law 9, 84–87 (hereafter Kennedy, 'The Disciplines'); See also Martti Koskenniemi, 'Between Commitment and Cynicism: Outline for a Theory of International Law as Practice' in Jean d'Aspremont and others (eds), *International Law as a Profession* (CUP 2017). In that respect, see also the forthcoming work of Sahib Singh.

[74]   See Chapter 1, Section 3.

[75]   Eagleton, *The Function of Criticism* (n 2) 9–10; Hayden White, *Tropics of Discourse: Essays in Cultural Criticism* (Johns Hopkins University Press 1978) 1 (hereafter White, *Tropics of Discourse*).

[76]   See the famous 'What is Enlightenment?' by Immanuel Kant.

perceptions, experiences, and discourses[77] and the corresponding confidence in one's ability to de-fatalize[78] such necessities. With the Enlightenment, everyone, including the international lawyer, is invited to be critical.[79] Whilst such modern 'critical' consciousness about unacknowledged and unconsented necessities has continued to inform international legal scholarship until today,[80] a new form of 'critical' evaluation of international law is said to have emerged in the last 20 years of the 20th century.[81] Allegedly drawing on the "linguistic turn" in humanities,[82] this new critical take on international law—commonly called *critique*—has been aiming to show the modern consciousness that informs international legal thought and practice is a form of false consciousness.[83] Whilst critique has, to some extent, been a continuation of the modern project,[84] it has distanced itself from the latter's liberal reformism[85]

---

[77]   Michel Foucault, *Le gouvernement de soi et des autres: Cours au Collège de France (1982–1983)* (Gallimard Le Seuil 2008) 15–16.

[78]   I borrow this term from Nikolas Rose, *Governing the Soul: The Shaping of the Private Self* (Free Association Books 1999) xii.

[79]   Eagleton, *The Function of Criticism* (n 2) 21.

[80]   David Kennedy has claimed that in the late 19th century and early 20th century, international lawyers were far more aware of the traditional system's contradictions and ambiguities than is commonly assumed. See Kennedy, 'The Disciplines' (n 73) 92.

[81]   For an exposition and criticism of the standard narrative about the rise of critical international legal scholarship, see Akbar Rasulov, 'What is Critique? Notes Towards a Sociology of Disciplinary Heterodoxy in Contemporary International Law' in Jean d'Aspremont and others (eds), *International Law as a Profession* (CUP 2017) 207–219.

[82]   See gen. Richard Rorty (ed), *The Linguistic Turn: Essays in Philosophical Method* (The University of Chicago Press 1992).

[83]   Kennedy, 'Critical Theory' (n 61) 245.

[84]   It has sometimes been claimed that the critique that emerged in the last part of the 20th century did not surface all of a sudden but drew on modernity itself, for it is an expression of modernity being defeated by its own criteria of validity and universality. Said differently, this critique is a repudiation that modernity has inflicted upon itself. See gen. Peter Sloterdijk, *Critique of Cynical Reason* (University of Minnesota 1987). See also Jean-François Lyotard, *La Condition Postmoderne* (Editions de Minuit 1979) 51 (hereafter Lyotard, *Condition Postmoderne*); Theodor Adorno and Max Horkheimer, *Dialectic of Enlightenment* (Verso 1997) 7–9. Cf the notion of autoimmunity of Jacques Derrida, *The Beast and the Sovereign*, vol 2 (University of Chicago Press 2011) 84 (For Derrida, autoimmunity consists "for a living body in itself destroying, in enigmatic fashion, its own immunitary defenses, in auto-affecting itself, then, in an irrepressibly mechanical and apparently spontaneous automatic, fashion, with an ill which comes to destroy what is supposed to protect against ill and safeguard immunity").

[85]   Kennedy, 'Critical Theory' (n 61) 216.

and has generally promoted an attitude of suspicion toward all modern claims of universality together with a sensibility for contingency.[86]

There is no doubt that the impact of late 20th-century critique on international legal thought has been wide-ranging,[87] including on the thoughts of the author of these lines.[88] This chapter is certainly not the place to take stock of the various ways in which critique upended international legal thought over the last decades. What matters, instead, is to reflect on the implications of the sovereignty of forms and the de-necessitating of meaning-centrism for the critical attitude that seems to have informed international legal thought for so long, either as a traditional modern contestation of unacknowledged and unconsented necessities or as a suspicion toward claims of universality.

As was indicated earlier, the critical attitude that emerged in international legal scholarship at the end of the 20th century drawing on the "linguistic turn" in the humanities did not bring about a discontinuation of meaning-centrism, the meaning delivered by the forms of the international legal discourse remaining at the heart of its scrutiny of the international legal discourse.[89] This is why the claim made in this book that meaning is always absent from forms and that the latter reign sovereignly over the international legal discourse is not without consequences about how the critical attitude ought to be understood and continued.

At this stage, it is important to emphasize once more that claiming that meaning is absent from forms because it is always deferred does not entail that the forms of the international legal discourse do not warrant scrutiny. It is recalled here that the forms of the international legal discourse do all what they do not by virtue of any content they carry and deliver but by virtue of the meaning they defer. That meaning is perpetually deferred by forms can thus never be a reason for passivity or complacency toward the forms of the international legal discourse. It is quite the opposite. The sovereignty of forms calls for the greatest scrutiny of the latter. The following paragraphs accord-

---

[86] It is about reviving the estrangement that comes with the child's "why" question and re-experiencing the arbitrariness of the necessities around which discourses are organized. Eagleton, *The Function of Criticism* (n 2) 88–89. For an example in international legal studies, see Ingo Venzke and Keven Jon Heller, *Contingency in International Law: On the Possibilities of Different Legal Histories* (OUP 2021).

[87] See eg the short stocktaking provided by Martti Koskenniemi, 'The Politics of International Law—20 Years Later' (2009) 20 European Journal of International Law 7. See the remarks of Jean d'Aspremont, 'Martti Koskenniemi, the Mainstream and Self-Reflectivity' (2016) 29 Leiden Journal of International Law 625.

[88] See Jean d'Aspremont, 'Critique, and the True Believer's Experience (Hommage à Pierre Schlag)' [2019] SSRN 1 <https://ssrn.com/abstract=3497764> accessed 24 May 2021.

[89] See Chapter 1, Section 1; Chapter 2, Sections 2.2, 2.3; Chapter 4, Section 1.

ingly shed light on the type of scrutiny of forms which the de-necessitating of meaning-centrism calls for.

The main consequence of the sovereignty of forms, as is understood here, is that being critical in international legal scholarship cannot be about unearthing hidden meaning, shedding light on preferred or privileged meanings, or showing the absence of meaning. In fact, as meaning is always absent, it is futile to seek to discover some hidden meaning, to search for privileges in the attribution of meaning, and to claim that there is no meaning.[90] Instead, the critical attitude, like any other engagement with the forms, must appreciate the forms of the international legal discourse as forms, that is, as sites of infinite passage where forms perpetually point away to other forms.[91] Said differently, the critical attitude has better focus on forms, their self-difference, the deferrals of meaning they possibly enable, and what such possible deferrals of meaning do to the world.

It is important to emphasize that, if the critical attitude is a critique of forms, the critical attitude cannot be outside the forms which it scrutinizes.[92] Indeed, and this is another consequence of the sovereignty of forms for the critical attitude, any critical engagement with international law is, at the moment it turns to the forms of the international legal discourse to scrutinize them, caught in the chain of supplements and the process of deferral of meaning by the very forms it scrutinizes.[93] Even if it seeks a transgression of such forms, the critical attitude always falls within the sovereignty of the forms it engages with.[94] The critical attitude can thus presume neither an external location nor an external evaluative tool. The location from which the critical inquiry is conducted and the evaluative tools which such critical inquiry deploys are always part of the

---

[90]   On the idea that there is no hidden meaning for everything is deferred and that one should not seek a hidden meaning, see Derrida, *Papier Machine* (n 32) 398.

[91]   See Chapter 4, Section 1.

[92]   Barthes, *Leçon* (n 29) 34; Derrida, *Ecriture* (n 38) 412–413; Barthes, *Essais critiques IV* (n 10) 17, 80; Barthes, *L'aventure sémiologique* (n 11) 14; Roland Barthes, *Le degré zéro de l'écriture* (Editions du Seuil 1972) 66; Gilles Deleuze, *Critique et Clinique* (Editions de Minuit 1993) 9, 16 (hereafter Deleuze, *Critique et Clinique*); White, *Tropics of Discourse* (n 75) 126–127; Derrida, *Positions* (n 69) 21, 35; Jacques Derrida, *De la Grammatologie* (Editions de Minuit 1967) 21, 25 (hereafter Derrida, *Grammatologie*); Derrida, *Ecriture* (n 38) 46.

[93]   See gen. Pierre Schlag, '"Le Hors de Texte, C'est Moi": The Politics of Form and the Domestication of Deconstruction' (1990) 11 Cardozo Law Review 1631. See also Jean d'Aspremont, 'Critical Histories of International Law and the Repression of Disciplinary Imagination' (2019) 7 London Review of International Law 89 (hereafter d'Aspremont, 'Critical Histories'); Kennedy, 'Critical Theory' (n 61) 273; Balkin, 'Deconstructive Practice' (n 33) 765.

[94]   On the idea that transgression always presupposes that the limit is at work, see Derrida, *Positions* (n 69) 35.

forms under its scrutiny.[95] In short, there is never any meta-critique of forms possible.[96]

The abovementioned impossibility for the critical attitude to be external to the forms it scrutinizes and thus the impossibility to rely on any type of meta-language or meta-evaluative tool leave the critical attitude in international legal scholarship with no other choice than being loyal to the forms it scrutinizes. In that sense, the critical attitude cannot do without a certain commitment to forms.[97] Yet, and this is the main argument developed in this section, the critical attitude's loyalty to forms must not be rehabilitative or complacent[98] but, on the contrary, should be pushed so far as it turns itself into

[95]   For an attempt to uphold the possibility of internal critique that is not conventionalist and that criticizes the very norm it relies on, see however Rahel Jaeggi, *Critique of Forms of Life* (Ciaran Cronin tr, Belknap Press 2018) 187–203 (such a critique is what she calls immanent critique).

[96]   Such posture is sometimes met with the objection that it rests on a performative contradiction. See Jürgen Habermas, *The Philosophical Discourse of Modernity: Twelve Lectures* (Frederik Lawrence tr, Polity Press 1987) 185–186, 279 (hereafter Habermas, *The Philosophical Discourse of Modernity*). See also Alasdair MacIntyre, *Three Rival Versions of Moral Inquiry: Encyclopaedia, Genealogy, and Tradition* (University of Notre Dame Press 1990) 55–56. This is also a charge that has surprisingly been raised against Michel Foucault's archeological work. See Hubert L Dreyfus and Paul Rabinow, *Michel Foucault: Beyond Structuralism and Hermeneutics* (2nd edn, University of Chicago Press 1983) 88, 99. Such objection could not be more at loggerheads with the de-necessitating of meaning-centrism attempted here, for it is based on the belief in the possibility of a meta-scientific vantage point, and thus the possibility of a meta-language. On the rebuttal of that objection and the idea that being part of what it scrutinizes is the very condition of critique, see Michel Foucault, *Les mots et les choses* (Gallimard 1966) 12; White, *Tropics of Discourse* (n 75) 142–43, 252–53; Paul Ricoeur, *La mémoire, l'histoire, l'oubli* (Seuil 2000) 399; Lyotard, *Condition Postmoderne* (n 84) 107 ; Derrida, *Ecriture* (n 38) 46; Said, *The World, the Text, and the Critic* (n 37) 26; Michel Foucault, *Naissance de la biopolitique: Cours au Collège de France (1978–1979)* (Gallimard Seuil 2004) 37.

[97]   On the idea of commitment to formalism as well as the idea that research is primarily a matter of writing and form, see Barthes, *Essais critiques IV* (n 10) 87, 374. Cf Martti Koskenniemi's plea for a culture of formalism in Martti Koskenniemi, *The Gentle Civilizer of Nations: The Rise and Fall of International Law 1870–1960* (CUP 2001) 502–509; Martti Koskenniemi, 'What is International Law For?' in Malcolm Evans (ed), *International Law* (2nd edn, OUP 2006) 69–70. See also Martti Koskenniemi, 'Carl Schmitt, Hans Morgenthau and the Image of Law in International Relations' in Michael Byers (ed), *The Role of Law in International Politics: Essays in International Relations and International Law* (OUP 2000) 32–33. On the various manifestations of the attachement to formalism in international legal thought, see the remarks of Umut Özsu, 'Legal Form' in Jean d'Aspremont and Sahib Singh (eds), *Concepts for International Law: Contributions to Disciplinary Thought* (Edward Elgar Publishing 2019) 629–35.

[98]   Goodrich, 'Europe in America' (n 15) 2050.

treason and betrayal.[99] In other words, the critical attitude's loyalty to the form should be a type of *over-loyalty*.[100]

A few illustrations of such over-loyalty to forms ought to be provided. Being over-loyal to the form can, for instance, involve pushing originist thinking[101] to a breaking point in order to show that the proclaimed origin of a form lies with other forms and is simply an empty self-referential move.[102] Likewise, one can also push deliverability thinking[103] to the edge of the abyss by overloading the forms with all the forms that the interpreter can possibly have access to and to which meaning can be possibly deferred[104] with a view to saturating the form concerned or exposing its margins.[105] In the same vein, one can push reifying thinking[106] to a point where the form and the world are no longer distinguishable.[107]

Over-loyalty to the form, as is understood here, may also impinge on the format of writing. For instance, because it owes less to the meaning-centric conventions of the traditional law article model—including the meaning-centric necessities to observe and derive—the essay, whether published as

---

[99] Derrida, *Positions* (n 69) 15. See also Derrida, *Papier Machine* (n 32) 383. In the same vein, see Culler, *On Deconstruction* (n 17) 86.

[100] Cf the ideas of confidence turned against itself and of love for systems' point of collapse discussed by Brian Dillon, *Essayism* (Fizcarraldo Editions 2017) 41–42. Cf with the idea of over-commitment (*sur-adhésion*) ascribed to critique by Laurent De Sutter, *Hors La Loi. Théorie de l'anarchie juridique* (Les Liens qui Libèrent 2021) 56–57. Cf Legrand, 'Siting Foreign Law' (n 3) 613 ("Tracing thus appears as a radicalization of legal positivism indebted to the very legal positivism which it radicalizes").

[101] On originist thinking, see Chapter 1, Section 2.1.

[102] This is what I have tried to do in d'Aspremont, *Belief System* (n 58). See also Jean d'Aspremont, 'Three International Lawyers in a Hall of Mirrors' (2019) 32 Leiden Journal of International Law 367.

[103] On deliverability thinking, see Chapter 1, Section 2.2.

[104] Scourging the margins is the lesson which Avita Ronell feels Jacques Derrida taught her. See Ronell, 'Saying Goodbye' (n 28) 246. On the immense critical capacity that comes with tracing the traces, see Legrand, 'Understanding Understanding' (n 5) 82.

[105] This is what I have tried to do in Jean d'Aspremont, 'The Literary Performances of the Tipping Point' in John Haskell and Jean d'Aspremont (eds), *Tipping Points in International Law* (CUP 2021).

[106] On reifying thinking, see Chapter 1, Section 2.3.

[107] This is what I have tried to do in Jean d'Aspremont, 'A Worldly Law in a Legal World' in Andrea Bianchi and Moshe Hirsch (eds), *International Law's Invisible Frames* (OUP 2021). Cf Derrida, *Grammatologie* (n 92) 53.

a self-standing essay or as a book chapter,[108] takes the forms more seriously.[109] In that sense, the essay probably facilitates an over-loyalty to the forms of the discourse as it is envisaged here.[110]

The novelty of the abovementioned critical moves ought not to be exaggerated, of course. In fact, many of them will probably look like *déjà vu*. The difference, however, lies in that the abovementioned critical moves are achieved without the strong positing of any meaning, any origin, or any cause to the forms of the international legal discourse under scrutiny.[111] In particular, the critical moves mentioned above avoid oppositional reading. Likewise, they do not seek to reverse pre-established hierarchies.[112] The over-loyal critical attitude envisaged here is a critical attitude that is spared by a logocentric detour. Said differently, it is a critical attitude that directly appeals to forms' resistance to themselves[113] in a way that allows a reinvention of the form by the form but without presuming or anticipating a specific meaning.[114]

It is expected that the over-loyalty to the form promoted here will be deemed textualist because it can be perceived as reducing the international

---

[108] For some critical remarks on the extent to which peer-review induces self-censorship and the greater instrumentality of book chapters in original and polemical thinking, see Jean d'Aspremont, 'Destination: the Wasteland of Academic Overproduction (Part 1)' (*EJIL:Talk!*, 3 February 2020) <https://www.ejiltalk.org/destination-the-wasteland-of-academic-overproduction-part-1/> accessed 24 May 2021; Jean d'Apremont, 'Destination: the Wasteland of Academic Overproduction (Part 2)' (*EJIL:Talk!*, 3 February 2020) <https://www.ejiltalk.org/destination-the-wasteland-of-academic-overproduction-part-2/> accessed 25 May 2021.

[109] Theodor W Adorno, 'The Essay as Form' (1984) 32 New German Critique 151, 160 (hereafter Adorno, 'The Essay as Form'). For Adorno, the essay is the critical form par excellence.

[110] Adorno, 'The Essay as Form' (n 109) 164.

[111] On the impossibility of being completely outside the structure and meaning-centrism, see Chapter 1, Introduction and Section 5.

[112] It should be recalled here that, according to the understanding of self-difference espoused here, the divided identity of forms is not a binary identity and the trace of the other in the form is not the trace of an opposite. As long as the other that inhabits the form constitutes its opposite, there is a presupposition of a fixed referent by virtue of which the opposition is constructed and apprehended. Construing self-difference as a binary identity and thus understanding the trace of the other as a trace of the opposite amounts to a meaning-centric move that empties the sovereignty of forms. The other within the selfsame is not the opposite other but only *an* other. See Chapter 1, Section 3.2.

[113] On the idea that the language of literary theory is the language of resistance to theory, see de Man, *The Resistance to Theory* (n 17).

[114] Deleuze, *Critique et Clinique* (n 92) 9, 16. This also corresponds to the idea of counter-interpellation by Jean-Jacques Lercercle, *De l'interpellation. Sujet, langue, idéologie* (Editions Amsterdam 2019) 97, 157. Cf Judith Butler, *Gender Trouble: Feminism and the Subversion of Identify* (2nd edn, Routledge 1990) 42.

legal discourse to texts and legal research to a mere literary genre. These charges are well known. They have long been raised against post-structuralist literary theory.[115] It is submitted here that these features of the critical attitude promoted here ought not to constitute deficiencies, let alone anything to be apprehensive of. For sure, the critical attitude advocated here is textualist and reduces legal scholarship to a literary genre.[116] But this is precisely where its merits lie. The foregoing should suffice to show that, for the critical attitude, loyalty to the form is neither an exile nor a prison, but is the very move that liberates the international lawyer from meaning-centrism while empowering her from within the forms of the international legal discourse.[117]

4.   HISTORY (SCRIPT)

As was discussed above,[118] even after the "historical turn" in international legal thought, most engagements with the history of international law have remained meaning-centric in the sense that they have continued to seek to unearth meaningful stories, meaningful causalities, meaningful continuities and discontinuities, meaningful injustices, meaningful inequalities, and meaningful tragedies from the past. The sovereignty of forms, and especially the de-necessitating of originist thinking, calls for revisiting the international lawyer's engagement with the past.

---

[115] These are charges made by Richard Rorty against Foucault, Derrida, Hayden White, and Paul de Man. See Richard Rorty, *Consequences of Pragmatism* (University of Minneapolis 2011) 139–141, 150–151. See the remarks of Jürgen Habermas in Giovanna Borradori, *Philosophy in a Time of Terror: Dialogues with Jürgen Habermas and Jacques Derrida* (University of Chicago Press 2003) 13–15. See also Habermas, *The Philosophical Discourse of Modernity* (n 96) 161–210. See also the critical remarks on textualism by Said, *The World, the Text, and the Critic* (n 37) 4–5.

[116] This is an approach to law that is reminiscent of the literary theory of authors like de Man, *The Resistance to Theory* (n 17) 11; White, *Tropics of Discourse* (n 75) 121; Hayden White, *The Content of the Form: Narrative Discourse and Historical Representation* (Johns Hopkins University Press 1987) 35–37 (hereafter White, *The Content of the Form*); Ludwig Wittgenstein, *Culture and Value* (Peter Winch tr, University of Chicago Press 1980) 36 (hereafter Wittgenstein, *Culture and Value*); Barthes, *Essais critiques IV* (n 10) 17–18, 63–69; Roland Barthes, 'Le discours de l'histoire' (1967) 6 Social Science Information 63; Paul Ricoeur, *Temps et récit*, vol 1 (Seuil 1983) (hereafter Ricoeur, *Temps et récit*, vol 1); Paul Veyne, *Les Grecs ont-ils cru à leurs mythes? Essai sur l'imagination constituante* (Seuil 1983) (hereafter Veyne, *Imagination constituante*); Paul Ricoeur, *Temps et récit*, vol 2 (Seuil 1984) (hereafter Ricoeur, *Temps et récit*, vol 2). Cf Goodrich, 'Sleeping with the Enemy' (n 18) 407.

[117] Barthes, *Leçon* (n 29) 15–16, 34.

[118] On the historical turn, see Chapter 2, Section 1.3.

Before elaborating on the consequences of the sovereignty of forms and the de-necessitating of originist thinking for the international lawyer's engagement with history, it is important to emphasize that the claim made here, and according to which the forms of the international legal discourse have no origin, source, author, and context external to the forms themselves, does not entail that it is irrelevant to study and explore past words, idioms, aphorisms, and texts, including the material conditions of their inscription, and the ideologies they carry. In fact, the international lawyer simply cannot do without past words, idioms, aphorisms, and texts.[119] Retrieving and reconstructing past words, idioms, aphorisms, and texts for the sake of the present constitutes a central component of the international legal discourse, certainly since the "modernization" of international law.[120] What is more, past words, idioms, aphorisms, and texts are among the best materials at hand to scrutinize past injustices, past inequalities, past tragedies, and so on which the international legal discourse is responsible for.[121] The question raised by the sovereignty of forms is thus not whether one should turn a blind eye to past words, idioms, aphorisms, and texts but rather which kind of engagement with past words,

---

[119] Tzouvala, *Capitalism* (n 29) 7; Anne Orford, 'On International Legal Method' (2013) 1 London Review of International Law 166, 172, 175 (hereafter Orford, 'International Legal Method'); Anne Orford, 'International Law and the Limits of History' in Wouter Werner, Marieke de Hoon and Alexis Galán (eds), *The Law of International Lawyers: Reading Martti Koskenniemi* (CUP 2015) (hereafter Orford, 'Limits of History'); Thomas Kleinlein, 'International Legal Thought: Creation of a Tradition and the Potential of Disciplinary Self-Reflection' in Giuliana Ziccardi Capaldo, *The Global Community: Yearbook of International Law and Jurisprudence 2016* (OUP 2016) 812. See also Matthew Craven, 'The Invention of a Tradition: Westlake, The Berlin Conference and the Historicisation of International Law' in Luigi Nuzzo and Miloš Vec, *Constructing International Law: The Birth of a Discipline* (Klostermann 2012); Kate Purcell, 'Faltering at the Critical Turn to History: "Juridical Thinking" in International Law and Genealogy as History, Critique, and Therapy' (2015) 15 Jean Monnet Working Paper 1, 13–15.

[120] In fact, it is probably the formalization of a 'doctrine of sources' at the beginning of the 20th century that most decisively entrenched such necessity to organize the past in the making of international legal discourses. In the same vein, see Rose Parfitt, 'The Spectre of Sources' (2014) 25 European Journal of International Law 297, 298.

[121] See gen. Roland Barthes, *Mythologies* (Editions du Seuil 1957) 215 ("plus un système est spécifiquement défini dans ses formes, et plus il est docile à la critique historique"). See also the remarks of Antony Anghie, 'Domination' in Jean d'Aspremont and Sahib Singh (eds), *Concepts for International Law: Contributions to Disciplinary Thought* (Edward Elgar Publishing 2019) 223–224. For some recent illustrations of a critical use of past words, idioms, aphorisms, and texts for the sake of shedding light on past injustices, past inequalities, past tragedies, see Rose Parfitt, *The Process of International Legal Reproduction: Inequality, Historiography, Resistance* (CUP 2019); Tzouvala, *Capitalism* (n 29).

idioms, aphorisms, and texts ought to be promoted in international legal thought.

Whilst upholding the necessity of international lawyers' engagement with past words, idioms, aphorisms, and texts, the claim made here is that such engagement ought not to be governed by meaning-centrism, and especially its originist variant. It is submitted here that revealing or attributing a meaning to past words, idioms, aphorisms, and texts is not the only way in which one can engage with past words, idioms, aphorisms, and texts. It is the aim of the following paragraphs to sketch out a type of engagement with the past that is not meaning-centric and which does not beg for meaningful stories, meaningful causalities, meaningful continuities and discontinuities, meaningful injustices, meaningful inequalities, meaningful tragedies from the past and, more generally, a meaningful past. It is more specifically argued here that the international lawyer's engagement with past words, idioms, aphorisms, and texts should better be a-historical, a-contextual, un-real, a-methodological, and, above all, scriptorial.[122]

First, and however paradoxical this may sound at first glance, the international lawyer's engagement with past words, idioms, aphorisms, and texts should be *a-historical*. Concretely, such past words, idioms, aphorisms, and texts ought not to be approached as if they belong to a past. Indeed, the deferral of meaning in which past words, idioms, aphorisms, and texts are caught is always out of time.[123] Such past words, idioms, aphorisms, and texts are part of the words, idioms, aphorisms, and texts that compose the present as much as the latter are part of the past words, idioms, aphorisms, and texts found in the past. In that sense, the international lawyer's engagement with past words, idioms, aphorisms, and texts ought not to formally and explicitly distinguish

---

[122] Albeit from a slightly different angle and through a different vocabulary, I have already promoted such type of engagement with the past elsewhere. See d'Aspremont, 'Critical Histories' (n 93). See also Jean d'Aspremont, *The Critical Attitude and the History of International Law* (Brill 2019).

[123] In that sense, it could be contended that the engagement with past words, idioms, aphorisms, and texts that is envisaged here is very structuralist, as it promotes a synchronic rather than diachronic approach to words, idioms, aphorisms, and texts. Yet, it is not clear whether the distinction between synchronism and diachronism is relevant to describe the type of engagement under discussion here. In fact, the synchronism that the approach promoted here denotes is not one that is geared towards determinacy of the present. On the idea that self-identity does not belong to the order of synchronism and diachronism, see Derrida, *Positions* (n 69) 39, 41; Jacques Derrida, *Marges de la Philosophie* (Editions de Minuit 1972) 17 (hereafter Derrida, *Marges*).

between a past and a present. The engagement with the past is always an engagement with the present, and vice-versa.[124]

Second, the international lawyer's engagement with past words, idioms, aphorisms, and texts should be *a-contextual*.[125] As long as words, idioms, aphorisms, and texts are thought as having been caused by the pre-existing meaning that they are meant to carry and deliver, engagement with the past cannot turn a blind eye to the origin, source, location, authors, effects, and, more generally, to the context at work in the loading of that meaning onto the forms. Yet, once originist thinking has been de-necessitated and the sovereignty of forms acknowledged, it is no longer possible to consider a contextual approach to the past, that is, an approach that presupposes a context external to the past words, idioms, aphorisms, and texts of international law under scrutiny and which is the cause of the meaning the latter allegedly carry and deliver.[126] The context of the past form, and thus its source, its cause, or its author, are already in the form. For the sake of the international lawyer's engagement with the past, what is commonly called the context is at best *a moment* of the international legal discourse.

Third, the international lawyer's engagement with past words, idioms, aphorisms, and texts should be *un-real*. This entails breaking away from the common understanding of history as a type of discourse that provides a form-

---

[124] Cf the idea of genealogy of Michel Foucault, *Surveiller et Punir* (Gallimard 1975) 30–32. See the remarks of David Garland, 'What Is a "History of the Present"? On Foucault's Genealogies and Their Critical Preconditions' (2014) 16 Punishment and Society 365, 369–371. See also Nathaniel Berman, 'In the Wake of Empire' (1999) 14 American University International Law Review 1515, 1521; Ellen K Feder, 'Power/ Knowledge' in Dianna Taylor (ed), *Michel Foucault: Key Concepts* (Routledge 2014). For a recent use of the notion of genealogy in international legal studies, see Ingo Venzke, 'Cracking the Frame? On the Prospects of Change in a World of Struggle' (2016) 27 European Journal of International Law 831.

[125] See the remarks of Anne Orford about the loss in critical attitude that may be brought about by the turn to history and its embrace of contextualism. See Orford, 'Limits of History' (n 119) 301–306. Anne Orford sees pleas in favor of a more rigorous contextualism as well as the necessity to use historical protocols as being conducive to conservatism. See also Orford, 'International Legal Method' (n 119) 170–177. See also the remarks of Matthew Craven, 'Introduction: International Law and Its Histories' in Matthew Craven, Malgosia Fitzmaurice, and Maria Vogiatzi (eds), *Time, History and International Law* (Brill 2007) 12–13.

[126] See Derrida, *Grammatologie* (n 92) 87. Cf the criticism of causality in the discourse on the past by Paul Ricoeur, *Histoire et vérité* (Seuil 1955) 33–34; Michel Foucault, *L'archéologie du savoir* (Gallimard 1969) 34 (hereafter Foucault, *L'archéologie du savoir*). See also Wittgenstein, *Culture and Value* (n 116) 62 ("there is nothing more stupid than the chatter about cause and effect in history books").

less past with meaning-giving form and creates an *effet du réel*[127] (reality effect[128]) in the present.[129] In other words, the international lawyer's engagement with past words, idioms, aphorisms, and texts should be an engagement with the past that resolutely rejects scientificity, truth-searching, and universality.[130] Anything else would bring about a resurgence of the meaning-centric modes of thought which this book is trying to de-necessitate.

Fourth, the international lawyer's engagement with past words, idioms, aphorisms, and texts should be *a-methodological*. In particular, it should not espouse any pre-defined mode of investigation that is recognized as properly "historical,"[131] for doing so would both presuppose meaningful forms external to the engagement with the past as well as anticipate a content for such past. It is true—and this is what distinguishes such an engagement with the past from dangerous and disgusting revisionist enterprises—that such a-methodological engagement with past words, idioms, aphorisms, and texts would still need to abide by some elementary empiricism and modes of factual evidence, even though the latter is itself always caught in the deferral of meaning. Likewise, such an a-methodological engagement with the past would need to meet some of the common social constraints that apply to the production of any discourse.

---

[127]   This description comes from Roland Barthes, 'Le discours de l'histoire' (1967) 6 Social Science Information 63, 74 (hereafter Barthes, 'Le discours de l'histoire').

[128]   This is how Alun Munslow translated Barthes's "effet réel." See Alun Munslow, 'Preface' in Keith Jenkins (ed), *On 'What is History': From Carr and Elton to Rorty and White* (Roultledge 1995) xiv.

[129]   Beverley Southgate, 'Postmodernism' in Aviezer Tucker (ed), *A Companion to the Philosophy of History and Historiography* (Wiley-Blackwell 2011) 541. See also Edward Hallett Carr, *What is History?* (2nd edn, CUP 1987) 25.

[130]   On the idea of history as a non-scientific discourse, see gen. White, *Tropics of Discourse* (n 75) 121–125; White, *The Content of the Form* (n 116) 35–37; Keith Jenkins (ed), *On 'What is History': From Carr and Elton to Rorty and White* (Roultledge 1995) 65, 82; Keith Jenkins, *Re-thinking History* (Routledge 2003) 65; Hayden White, *Metahistory. The Historical Imagination in the 19th-Century Europe* (Johns Hopkins University Press 2014) 428; Barthes, *Essais critiques IV* (n 10) 17–18 and 63–69; Barthes, 'Le discours de l'histoire' (n 127) 63; Ricoeur, *Temps et récit*, vol 1 (n 116); Ricoeur, *Temps et récit*, vol 2 (n 116); Veyne, *Imagination constituante* (n 116). For some critical remarks on how engagement with the past has traditionally been deployed by the international lawyer to uphold a feeling of scientificity of the field, see Anne Orford, 'Scientific Reason and the Discipline of International Law' (2014) 25 European Journal of International Law 369, 370 (hereafter Orford, 'Scientific Reason'); Orford, 'Limits of History' (n 119) 308; Luigi Nuzzo, 'The Birth of an Imperial Location: Comparative Perspectives on Western Colonialism in China' (2018) 31 Leiden Journal of International Law 569, 596.

[131]   In the same sense, see Anne Orford's plea against the idea that the international lawyer should embrace "historical methods": Orford, 'International Legal Method" (n 119); Orford, "Limits of History" (n 119) 302–303, 312.

And yet, such an accommodation of some minimal discursive constraints would still stop short of molding the engagement with past words, idioms, aphorisms, and texts into any kind of pre-established methodology.

Last but not least, the international lawyer's engagement with past words, idioms, aphorisms, and texts should be scriptorial. This entails an appreciation that past words, idioms, aphorisms, and texts can only be confronted by producing new words, idioms, aphorisms, and texts.[132] Engaging with past words, idioms, aphorisms, and texts is about pouring forms into forms and maximizing the deferral of meaning. It is about confronting the deferral of meaning in which past words, idioms, aphorisms, and texts are caught (and confronted with) more forms and thus more deferral of meaning.

5. COMPARISON (DE-COLONIZING THINKING)

The international lawyer has always had a strong affinity with comparison.[133] Comparison seems to be one of those intellectual operations which the international lawyer must be capable of undertaking when she invokes and applies international law. In fact, international law is built around, and draws upon, constructions requiring an exercise of comparison.[134] It suffices to mention here the well-known use of comparison in, for instance, the ascertainment of general principles of law,[135] the evaluation of the *practice and opinio juris* of states and international organizations for the sake of identifying custom,[136]

---

[132] Cf Foucault, *L'archéologie du savoir* (n 126) 41 (who argues that once we are freed from immediate forms of continuity, we can start constructing new statements and narratives).

[133] In the same vein, see William E Butler, 'Comparative Approaches to International Law' (1985) 190 Collected Courses of the Hague Academy of International Law 9, 30 (hereafter Butler, 'Comparative Approaches').

[134] For an overview, see Butler, 'Comparative Approaches' (n 133) 33–45. See also the literature cited by Anthea Roberts and others, 'Conceptualizing Comparative International Law' in Anthea Roberts and others (eds), *Comparative International Law* (OUP 2018) 4, note 7.

[135] See Article 38.1.c of the Statute of the International Court of Justice. On the idea that general principles of law do not constitute a source but a mode of interpretation by analogy, see Jean d'Aspremont, 'What Was Not Meant to Be: General Principles of Law as a Source of International Law' in Riccardo Pisillo Mazzeschi and Pasquale De Sena (eds), *Global Justice, Human Rights, and the Modernization of International Law* (Springer 2018) (hereafter d'Aspremont, 'What Was Not Meant to Be').

[136] See the ILC, 'Draft Conclusions on Identification of Customary International Law, with Commentaries' (2018) UN Doc A/73/10, 137: "In examining whether the practice is consistent it is of course important to consider instances of conduct that are in fact comparable, that is, where the same or similar issues have arisen so that such

the application of the standard of due diligence,[137] the enforcement of the obligation to make full reparation in the discourse on the law of international responsibility,[138] or the interpretation of international law.[139] The use of analogies with domestic law, which was praised early on as a tool for the development of international law,[140] similarly involves a comparison between domestic legal systems.[141] The margin of appreciation, which international courts rely on to calibrate the normative requirements of international human rights law, also entails an exercise of comparison.[142] Likewise, the law of international organizations is commonly studied through a comparison between the various practices of international organizations with a view to extracting some

---

instances could indeed constitute reliable guides." See also The Case of the S.S. 'Lotus' *(France v Turkey)* [1927] PCIJ Rep Series A No 10, 21.

[137] Corfu Channel Case *(United Kingdom of Great Britain and Northern Ireland v Albania)* [1949] ICJ Rep 4. See gen. Sarah Heathcote, 'State Omissions and Due Diligence: Aspects of Fault, Damage and Contribution to Injury in the Law of State Responsibility' in Karine Bannelier, Theodore Christakis, and Sarah Heathcote (eds), *The ICJ and the Evolution of International Law: The Enduring Impact of the 'Corfu Channel' Case* (Routledge 2012); Patrick Jacob, 'Le contenu de La responsabilité de l'Etat négligent' in Société française de droit international, *Le standard du due diligence et la responsabilité internationale: Journée SDFI d'études du Mans* (Pedone 2018).

[138] See Article 31 of the Articles on the Responsibility of States for Internationally Wrongful Acts. See Case Concerning the Factory at Chorzów *(Germany v Poland)* (Judgement) [1928] PCIJ Rep Series A No 9, 47 ("reparation must, so far as possible, wipe out all the consequences of the illegal act and reestablish the situation which would, in all probability, have existed if that act had not been committed"). For some remarks, see Brigitte Stern, 'The Obligation to Make Reparation' in James Crawford and others (eds), *The Law of International Responsibility* (OUP 2010).

[139] Daniel Peat, *Comparative Reasoning in International Courts and Tribunals* (CUP 2019) (hereafter Peat, *Comparative Reasoning*).

[140] Hersch Lauterpacht, *Private Law Sources and Analogies of International Law (with Special Reference to International Arbitration)* (Lawbook Exchange 2002, originally published by Longmans 1927).

[141] For an overview as well as some critical remarks, see Fernando Lusa Bordin, 'Analogy' in Jean d'Aspremont and Sahib Singh, *Concepts for International Law* (Edward Elgar Publishing 2018). See also Peat, *Comparative Reasoning* (n 139).

[142] For some criticisms of the use of comparative law method to determine the normative standard applied by the European Court of Human Rights, see Paolo Carozza, 'Uses and Misuses of Comparative Law in International Human Rights: Some Reflections on the Jurisprudence of the European Court of Human Rights' (1997) 73 Notre Dame Law Review 1217. For some critical remarks on the exercise of comparison in international human rights law, see Samantha Besson, 'Comparative Law and Human Rights' in Mathias Reimann and Reinhard Zimmermann (eds), *The Oxford Handbook of Comparative Law* (2nd edn, OUP 2019).

common principles or institutional patterns.[143] Scholarly reform projects like global constitutionalism,[144] or scholarly projects concerned with the reconceptualization of global governance, like global administrative law,[145] similarly require the use of comparison as well. In recent years, calls have even been made to turn the familiar tool of comparison into a central way to engage with international law and to embrace a new comparative "approach"[146] to international law called *Comparative International Law*.[147] Comparison has thus long informed international legal thought and practice and it does not seem that its centrality and popularity will abate any time soon.

It is submitted here that the sovereignty of forms and the corresponding de-necessitating of meaning-centrism outlined in the previous chapters suggest

---

[143] Henry Schermers and Niels Blokker, *International Institutional Law* (6th edn, Martinus Nijhoff Publishers 2018), at 4 ("we aim to offer a general framework for a better understanding of the [similarities and differences] between institutional rules of international organizations"). See the remarks of Jean d'Aspremont, 'The Law of International Organizations and the Art of Reconciliation' (2014) 11 International Organizations Law Review 428.

[144] See Erika de Wet, 'The International Constitutional Order' (2006) 55 International and Comparative Law Quarterly 51; Anne Peters, 'Compensatory Constitutionalism: The Function and Potential of Fundamental International Norms and Structures' (2006) 19 Leiden Journal of International Law 579; Anne Peters, 'The Merits of Global Constitutionalism' (2009) 16 Indiana Journal of Global Legal Studies 397; Anne Peters, 'Are We Moving towards Constitutionalisation of the World Community' in Antonio Cassese, *Realising Utopia: The Future of International Law* (OUP 2012); Erika de Wet, 'The Constitutionalisation of Public International Law' in Michel Rosenfeld and Andras Sajo (eds), *The Oxford Handbook of Comparative Constitutional Law* (OUP 2012) 1209.

[145] See eg the studies on Global Administrative Law by Benedict Kingsbury, Nico Krisch, and Richard B Stewart, 'The Emergence of Global Administrative Law' (2005) 68 Law and Contemporary Problems 3, 29; Carol Harlow, 'Global Administrative Law: The Quest for Principles and Values' (2006) 17 European Journal of International Law 1, 187.

[146] On the portrayals of comparative international law as an "approach" see Anthea Roberts, 'Is International Law International? Continuing the Conversation' (*EJIL: Talk!*, 9 February 2018) <https://www.ejiltalk.org/is-international-law-international-continuing-the-conversation/> accessed 24 May 2021.

[147] See eg Martti Koskenniemi, 'The Case for Comparative International Law' (2009) 20 Finnish Yearbook of International Law 1; Anthea Roberts, *Is International Law International?* (OUP 2017) 17. See also Lauri Malksoo, *Russian Approaches to International Law* (OUP 2015) 1; Anthea Roberts and others (eds), *Comparative International Law* (OUP 2018). For some critical remarks about the colonizing thinking at the heart of the international comparative law project, see Jean d'Aspremont, 'Comparativism and Colonizing Thinking in International Law' (2020) 57 Canadian Yearbook of International Law 89 (hereafter d'Aspremont, 'Comparativism and Colonizing Thinking').

that the international lawyer ought to revamp her use of comparison. In fact, comparison, whether to ascertain general principles, to establish principles of international institutional law, to evaluate compliance, or to calibrate the margin of appreciation, and so on is commonly carried out by the international law in a way that presupposes fixed and meaningful comparable objects as well as a fixed and meaningful referent of commonality—the so-called pre-comparative tertium—that is posited or asserted prior to the comparison. Yet, once one acknowledges the sovereignty of forms and the absence of meaning, one comes to appreciate that it is no longer possible to hold both the forms being compared and the forms constituting the pre-comparative tertium as having any kind of fixed meaning. Indeed, the exercise of comparison is inexorably absorbed in the chain of supplements constituting the deferral of meaning by the forms being compared as well as by the forms constituting the pre-comparative tertium.[148] As a result, and as has already been highlighted in critical comparative law,[149] the meaning of what is compared and the meaning of the pre-comparative tertium are always deferred and condemned to be absent from the exercise of comparison.[150]

The consequences of there being no meaning in the exercise of comparison, be it regarding its object or the comparative tertium, are tremendous for the exercise of comparison in international legal thought and practice. Three of these specific consequences must be mentioned here. First, comparison ought not to be pursued if it is conducted to capture a resemblance or a difference because comparison indefinitely multiplies avenues for meaning, be it in terms of resemblance or difference. In fact, comparison always has a multiplying effect on the deferral of meaning, be it about the object of the comparison or the comparative tertium.[151] For instance, if one carries out comparison for the sake of the ascertainment of general principles of law, both the postulation of a norm to be found in domestic legal system or the identification of the practices or rules of domestic legal systems that ought to be compared are bound to be the source of an indefinite semantic universe where no meaning can never be pinned or fixed.[152] The same holds for the ascertainment of principles

---

[148]   Legrand, 'The Same and the Different' (n 12) 309.

[149]   The claim has long been made with respect to comparative law. Legrand, 'Understanding Understanding' (n 5) 70. See also Pierre Legrand, *Negative Comparative Law: A Manifesto* (CUP 2021) (forthcoming) (hereafter Legrand, *Negative Comparative Law*).

[150]   On the idea that difference is "inexhaustible," see Legrand, 'The Same and the Different' (n 12) 285, 298.

[151]   Legrand, 'The Same and the Different' (n 12) 299.

[152]   For the reason, it seems that the great reluctance of international courts to resort to general principles of law—notwithstanding their having been designed as a lacunae-filling mechanism—cannot be contested. On the reluctance of the

of international institutional law where the exercise of comparison comes to multiply indefinitely the possibilities of divergent or convergent meaningful practices. In sum, if comparison is pursued to establish resemblances or differences, comparison always fails.[153]

A second consequence of the sovereignty of forms for the exercise of comparison in international legal thought and practice pertains to the impossibility of immersing oneself in the object of comparison and in the context thereof before conducting any exercise of comparison.[154] It is submitted here that strategies of immersion—that is, strategies of knowing the other like those promoted by those spearheading the abovementioned Comparative International Law—are accelerating the deferral of meaning and thus reinforcing the absence of the latter. This is why it is argued here that the international lawyer conducting a comparison must come to terms with the impossibility of contextualizing the exercise of comparison.[155] The same goes for strategies of self-immersion, that is strategies aimed at raising one's self-awareness about one's internalized intelligibility frameworks and pre-comparative tertium.[156] Whatever effort the international lawyer vests in contextualizing both the object of comparison and her act of comparison, she maximizes the deferral of meaning and further postpones meaning, be it of its object, of the comparative tertium, of herself, or of her intelligibility frameworks.

The third and possibly greatest consequence of the sovereignty of forms and the de-necessitating of meaning-centrism for the exercise of comparison may be found in its renewed relation with otherness.[157] In fact, meaning-centric

---

International Court of Justice to resort to general principles and the reasons thereof, see d'Aspremont, 'What Was Not Meant to Be' (n 135). See also Alain Pellet, 'Article 38' in Andreas Zimmermann and others (eds), *The Statute of the International Court of Justice: A Commentary* (2nd edn, OUP 2012) 767; Gleider Hernandez, *The International Court of Justice and the Judicial Function* (OUP 2014) 261.

[153] It is true that, for the international lawyer who has been trained in producing unitary knowledge about difference and resemblance by virtue of some predefined doctrines held as universal, such an anti-totalizing attitude will seem counter-intuitive, if not preposterous. On the idea that the correspondence of the self's apprehension of the "other" with the "other" also constitutes a very modern characteristic of knowledge, see Pierre Legrand, 'Comparative Legal Studies and the Matter of Authenticity' (2006) 1 Journal of Comparative Law 365, 396.

[154] In the same vein, Legrand, 'The Same and the Different' (n 12) 251–252.

[155] See Günter Frankenberg, 'Constitutional Transfer: The IKEA Theory Revisited' (2010) 8 International Journal of Constitutional Law 563, 571–75.

[156] On the idea that the foreign inevitably partakes in the constitution of the self, see Legrand, 'Understanding Understanding' (n 5) 70, 138.

[157] Whether an otherness that transcends the defining subject is ever possible and whether there can be alterity outside the defining subject constitutes a central philosophical question that ought not to be taken on here. On this question, see gen.

comparison, as is commonly conducted in international legal thought and practice, has always been a venture into colonizing thinking,[158] whereby an other is unilaterally defined, silenced, and spoken on behalf of.[159] Interestingly, the colonizing move that accompanies meaning-centric comparisons is something which has long been acknowledged in critical comparative law.[160] Such sensibility has been conspicuously lacking in the international legal literature interested in the exercise of comparison. Such colonizing thinking has even come to a head in the abovementioned Comparative International Law project.[161] It is argued here that, if meaning is absent from the exercise of comparison, the international lawyer is given the chance to avoid the pitfall—and the scandal!—of colonizing thinking. In fact, the sovereignty of forms and the corresponding de-necessitating of meaning-centrism allow the international lawyer to avoid systematically absorbing and appropriating the other and embracing a totalizing approach to alterity.[162] Said differently, the sovereignty of forms, as is understood here, enables the constant renewal of the experiences of alterity, the latter being sought, not for their contribution to any kind of knowledge about the world, but for unanticipated deferrals of

---

Emmanuel Levinas, *Totalité et Infini* (Martinus Nijhoff Publishers 1971). On this question in the context of modern thought, see also Bruno Latour, *Nous n'avons jamais été modernes. Essai d'anthropologie symétrique* (La Découverte 1997) 51–52.

[158] On the idea of colonizing gesture, see Judith Butler, *Gender Trouble* (2nd edn, Routledge 2007) 18 (hereafter Butler, *Gender Trouble*).

[159] On the discourses silencing the "others" they have created, see Michel de Certeau, *L'écriture de l'histoire* (Gallimard 1975) 15–20. See also Butler, *Gender Trouble* (n 158) 2–4.

[160] Gunter Frankenberg, 'Critical Comparisons: Re-thinking Comparative Law' (1985) 26 Harvard International Law Journal 411, 412, 422–423; David Nelken, 'Towards a Sociology of Legal Adaptation' in David Nelken and Johannes Feest (eds), *Adapting Legal Cultures* (Hart Publishing 2001) 16; H Patrick Glenn, 'Are Legal Traditions Incommensurable?' (2001) 49 American Journal of Comparative Law 133, 145; Legrand, 'The Same and the Different' (n 12) 246, 255, 261; Mitchel Lasser, 'The Question of Understanding' in Pierre Legrand and Roderick Munday (eds), *Comparative Legal Studies: Traditions and Transitions* (CUP 2003) 204, 219; Michael Werner and Bénédicte Zimmermann, 'Beyond Comparison: Histoire Croisée and the Challenge of Reflexivity' (2006) 45 History and Theory 30, 34; Legrand, 'Understanding Understanding' (n 5) 70.

[161] See d'Aspremont, 'Comparativism and Colonizing Thinking' (n 147).

[162] For a similar plea with respect to private international law, see Horatia Muir Watt, 'Discours sur les méthodes du droit international privé (des formes juridiques de l'inter-altérité). Cours général de droit international privé' (2018) 389 Collected Courses of the Hague Academy of International Law 363 (hereafter Muir Watt, 'Discours sur les méthodes de droit international privé'). For a similar plea with respect to comparative law, see Legrand, 'The Same and the Different' (n 12) 250, 307, 369, 373.

meaning.[163] The sovereignty of forms simultaneously helps the international lawyer reinforce her suspicion toward any perception of symmetry between the self and the other as well as any move geared toward an appropriation of the other by the self.[164] The sovereignty of forms and the de-necessitating of meaning-centrism can even be conducive to an attitude of pockmarked resistance toward any anticipation of meaning in the conduct of comparison in international legal thought and practice,[165] and thus be a formidable tool to contain colonizing thinking.[166]

6. TRANSLATION (IMPOSSIBILITY)

With a view to illustrating the implications of the sovereignty of forms for the question of interlingual translation in international law,[167] it is useful to start with a well-known story. It is a story that takes place in Beijing in the summer of 1863. The Zongli Yamen, that is, the governmental body in charge of foreign policy in imperial China during the late Qing dynasty, is in the midst of arduous negotiations with foreign powers and seeks to reinforce its negotiating position *vis-à-vis* those powers by resorting to the very authoritative international legal principles which foreign powers mobilize in their relations with one another. Having been convinced that Henry Wheaton's *Elements of International Law* (1836) is one of the most accepted authoritative treatises about international law among foreign powers, the Zongli Yamen hired William AP Martin

---

[163] Cf the idea of making the "other" an "interlocutor": see Legrand, 'The Same and the Different' (n 12) 250. Cf the notion of "hospitality" developed by Jacques Derrida, *De l'hospitalité* (Calmann-Levy Editions 1997). For some reflections on the idea of "hospitality" in private international law and for some reflections on the idea of "hosting," see Muir Watt, 'Discours sur les méthodes de droit international privé' (n 162).

[164] Legrand, 'The Same and the Different' (n 12) 304, 307.

[165] Derrida, *Ecriture* (n 38) 46.

[166] This attitude is what I have called elsewhere "counter-comparability." Counter-comparability refers to an attitude that refuses to define the "other" according to the categories of the "self," let alone silence it and speak on its behalf. See d'Aspremont, 'Comparativism and Colonizing Thinking' (n 147). Cf Legrand, *Negative Comparative Law* (n 149). See also Theodor W Adorno, *Negative Dialectics* (EB Ashton tr, Routledge 1973) 5; Theodor W Adorno, *Lectures on Negative Dialectics: Fragments of a Lecture Course 1965/1966* (Rolf Tiedmann ed, Rodney Livingstone tr, Polity Press 2008) 6. On this dimension of Adorno's negative dialectics, see Ross Wilson, *Theodor Adorno* (Routledge 2007) 59.

[167] On the distinction between interlingual, intralingual, and intersemiotic translations, see Roman Jakobson, 'On Linguistic Aspects of Translation' in Achilles Fang and Reuben Brower (eds), *On Translation* (Harvard University Press 1959) (hereafter Jakobson, 'On Linguistic Aspects').

to produce the translation of an international legal instrument that China crucially needed in its negotiations with foreign powers. William AP Martin was an American Presbyterian missionary who had been an interpreter during the negotiations for the 1858 Sino-American Treaty of Tianjin and who had already started the translation in Mandarin of one of Wheaton's *Elements of International Law*. A few months later, after intense scrutiny of Martin's translation and a comparison thereof with the other available translations of Wheaton's text, the Zongli Yamen initially approved Martin's translation and ordered four secretaries to assist Martin in revising and editing his first draft. The final and carefully inspected version of the translation was published by the Beijing Chongshiguan in 1864; 300 copies were sent to central and local offices. The same year, following an incident between Prussia and Denmark in Chinese territorial waters, the Zongli Yamen invoked the carefully and strategically edited Chinese translation of Wheaton's *Elements of International Law* to successfully argue for the illegality of the Prussian action. As a reward for his collaboration in the production of a Chinese version of Henry Wheaton's *Elements of International Law*, William AP Martin was made professor of international law at the Tongwen Guan Library, that is, the Academy of Foreign Languages, and later the first chancellor of the Imperial University of Peking.[168]

It is common to refer to this story of the Chinese efforts to produce a Chinese version of one of the most authoritative Western treatises of international law of the 19th century as an illustration of the extent to which the translation of international legal texts is never innocent and is always subject to sophisticated modes of control by certain actors with a view to enabling certain knowledge,

---

[168] See Chi-Hua Tang, 'China-Europe' in Anne Peters and Bardo Fassbender (eds), *The Oxford Handbook of the History of International Law* (OUP 2012) 705; Shin Kawashima, 'China' in Anne Peters and Bardo Fassbender (eds), *The Oxford Handbook of the History of International Law* (OUP 2012) 462–464; Stephen C Neff, *Justice Among Nations* (Harvard University Press 2014) 313; Maria Adele Carrai, 'The Politics of History in the Late Qing Era: William A.P. Martin and a History of International Law for China' (2020) 22 Journal of the History of International Law 269. In translation studies literature, see eg Lydia H Liu, 'Legislating the Universal: The Circulation of International Law in the Nineteenth Century' in Lydia H Liu (ed), *Tokens of Exchange: The Problem of Translation in Global Circulations* (Duke University Press 1999); Rune Svarverud, *International Law as World Order in Late Imperial China: Translation, Reception and Discourse. 1847–1911* (Brill 2007) 69–132; Emily Cheung and Maranatha Fung, 'The Hazards of Translating Wheaton's Elements of International Law into Chinese: Cultures of World Order Lost in Translation' in Anthony Carty and Janne Nijman (eds), *Morality and Responsibility of Rulers: European and Chinese Origins of a Rule of Law as Justice for World Order* (OUP 2018).

certain legal arguments, and certain types of globalization.[169] Yet, the sovereignty of forms and the corresponding de-necessitating of meaning-centrism promoted in this book help show that the processes of control and manipulation at work in the translation of international legal texts are not mere interventions in the meaning of such texts but ought to be understood as processes of maximizing of deferral of meanings by the superposition of new forms to the forms composing the international legal text being translated. In fact, from the perspective of the sovereignty of forms, control over and manipulation of the translation of international legal texts cannot be reduced to meaning-determining actions, for there is no meaning to be translated in the first place. As meaning is absent from the international legal texts being translated, translation cannot be a secondary and derived event in relation to an original text.[170] Actually, translation of international legal texts as translation of their meaning always constitutes an impossibility.[171]

If, by virtue of the sovereignty of forms, the translation of international legal texts as translation of their meaning is an impossibility, what does translation do? It is submitted here that, as meaning is always absent from the international

---

[169] Translation studies literature constantly refers to instances of controlled translation. As noted by Theo Hermans, "the history of translation suggests that, as a rule, translations have not been perceived as equal to their source texts at all and that, in addition, they are deployed in situations involving highly unequal power relations" (see Theo Hermans, *Translation in Systems: Descriptive and Systemic Approaches Explained* (Routledge 2020) 54). There is even a group of authors in translation studies that have come to be labeled the "manipulation group" or the "manipulative school" of translation studies. These scholars have defended the idea that all translation implies a degree of manipulation of the source text for a certain purpose. See eg André Lefevere, 'Mother Courage's Cucumbers: Text: System and Refraction in a Theory of Literature' (1982) 12 Modern Language Studies 3, 4; Theo Hermans (ed), *The Manipulation of Literature: Studies in Literary Translations* (Croom Helm 1985); Gideon Toury, *Descriptive Translation Studies and Beyond* (Benjamins 1995); Antoine Berman, 'Translation and the Trials of the Foreign' in Lawrence Venuti (ed), *The Translation Studies Reader* (Routledge 2004); Theo Hermans, *Translation in Systems: Descriptive and System-Oriented Approaches Explained* (Routledge 2014); Wenjie Li, 'A Systemic Approach to Manipulation in Translation—A Case Study of Ye Junjian's 1958 Translation of H.C. Andersen's Tales' in Lieven D'hulst, Carol O'Sullivan, and Michael Schreiber (eds), *Politics, Policy and Power in Translation History* (Frank & Timme 2016).
[170] See Jacques Derrida, 'Letter to a Japanese Friend' in David Wood and Robert Bernasconi (eds), *Derrida and Différance* (Northwestern University Press 1988) 5.
[171] On the idea that translation is another name for the impossible, see Jacques Derrida, *Le Monolinguisme de l'autre* (Galilée 1996) 103 ("la traduction est un autre nom de l'impossible"). See also Jacques Derrida, *Spectres de Marx* (Galilée 1993) 43. On this aspect of Derrida's work and for its application to comparative legal studies, see Legrand, 'Siting Foreign Law' (n 3) 616.

legal texts being the object of the translation, the translation of international legal texts like that of the abovementioned Henry Wheaton's *Elements of International Law* is always an act of production of forms that fuel the deferral of meaning in which the text being translated was already caught.[172] Said differently, the act of which translation is the shorthand is an act of production of new forms that further inflates the deferral of meaning already at work in the text being translated.[173] And the same goes for any attempt to immerse oneself in the translated text or the context of the act of translation.[174] In that sense, translation of international legal texts is better approached as another mode of maximization of the deferral of meaning. [175]

Translation being a mode of maximization of the deferral of meaning in which it is caught, the translated text and the text produced by the translation can no longer be distinguished from one another as they are both caught in the deferral of meaning, which also absorbs the translators' mind, constraints, agendas, strategies, and so on.[176] And this is what brings us back to the abovementioned story of the translation of Henry Wheaton's *Elements of International Law* by Zongli Yamen. If there cannot be any translation as translation of meaning, there cannot be any control over and manipulation of translation as translation of meaning. Any intervention on the text being translated is always caught in the deferral of meaning which it comes to fuel with new forms and from which it cannot be distinguished.

The abovementioned understanding of the translation of international legal texts should certainly not be construed as a curse, let alone as an obstacle to translation.[177] Actually, the translation of international legal texts is not different from the translation that is constantly at work in any engagement with the forms of the international legal discourse. Indeed, the moment the international lawyer puts into motion the deferral of meaning, she makes an act of translation, for the forms she engages point away to other forms. In that sense, translation should not be reduced to its inter-lingual impossibility but should be construed as the very act of engagement with forms. In that sense, one could

---

[172] On the idea that for who seeks meaning-equivalence and approaches translation, translation only multiplies confusion, see Jacques Derrida, 'Des Tours de Babel' in Joseph F Graham (ed), *Difference in Translation* (Cornell University Press 1985) 172.

[173] Cf Jacques Derrida, *Positions* (n 69) 41. On the idea that translation always entails the superposition of a sign to another sign, see Jakobson, 'On Linguistic Aspects' (n 167) 232–233.

[174] In the same vein, Legrand, 'The Same and the Different' (n 12) 251–252.

[175] Cf Legrand, 'Siting Foreign Law' (n 3) 616.

[176] In relation to comparative law, see Legrand, 'Understanding Understanding' (n 5) 138.

[177] See the remarks of George Steiner, *Errata: An Examined Life* (Weidenfeld and Nicholson 1997) 89.

say that the international lawyer is a permanent translator adrift in the deferral of meaning and never done with her task.

7. REFERENCES (HIGHWAY CONNECTORS)

The practice of referencing is well intrenched in international legal literature.[178] It is possibly one of the few remnants[179] of the earlier project of elevating international law to the status of social science[180] that produces knowledges about naturalistic and social realities.[181] The practice of referencing warrants attention here because footnotes and bibliographies are an important part of international law's inscriptions.[182] In fact, footnotes and bibliographies speak. They speak about origins, causes, influences, inspirations, implications,

---

[178] Vincent Genin recounts how Lieber (who had fought in the Prussian army against Napoleon's troops at Waterloo in 1815) contributed to the import of the German system of referencing to US law schools. See Vincent Genin, *Le laboratoire belge du droit international: Une communauté épistémique et internationale de juristes (1869–1914)* (Académie Royale des Sciences, des Lettres et de Beaux-Arts de Belgique 2018) 55–56. For a famous charge against referencing practices in the US legal academia, see Fred Rodell, 'Goodbye to Law Reviews' (1936) 23 Virginia Law Review 38.

[179] For a few exceptions, see Gregory Shaffer and Tom Ginsburg, 'The Empirical Turn in International Legal Scholarship' (2012) 106 American Journal of International Law 1. For an illustration, see Pierre-Hugues Verdier and Erik Voeten, 'How Does Customary International Law Change? The Case of State Immunity' (2015) 59 International Studies Quarterly (2015) 209. See also Jakob VH Holtermann and Mikael Rask Madsen, 'Toleration, Synthesis or Replacement? The "Empirical Turn" and Its Consequences for the Science of International Law' (2016) 29 Leiden Journal of International Law 1001. It must also be noted that such a turn to empirical studies of international law is not completely unprecedented. See eg the work of the New Haven School and in particular that of Myres S McDougal, 'Law and Power' (1952) 46 American Journal of International Law 102. See also the work of the legal process school, as illustrated by Abram Chayes and Antonia Handler Chayes, *The New Sovereignty: Compliance with International Regulatory Agreements* (Harvard University Press 1995). For a claim about the virtuosity of empirical sensitivity, see Jorge E Vinuales, 'On Legal Inquiry' in Denis Alland and others (eds), *Unity and Diversity of International Law: Essays in Honour of Professor Pierre-Marie Dupuy* (Martinus Nijhoff Publishers 2014) 72–75.

[180] See eg Lassa Oppenheim, 'The Science of International Law: Its Task and Method' (1908) 2 The American Journal of International Law 313.

[181] On this project, see gen. Orford, 'Scientific Reason' (n 130). See also Martti Koskenniemi, 'Letter to the Editors of the Symposium' (1999) 93 American Journal of International Law 351. See also Simon Chesterman, 'Herding Schrödinger's Cats: The Limits of the Social Science Approach to International Law' (2021) 22 Chicago Journal of International Law 1.

[182] On the idea that the legal academic's greatest achievement is to become a footnote, see Pierre Schlag, 'My Dinner at Langdell's' (2004) 52 Buffalo Law Review 851.

authority, contrasts, disagreements, and so on. Footnotes and bibliographies are never benign. The way in which they are designed, organized, sequenced, and filled is informed by specific universalizing strategies, certain desires in terms of self-image, a certain distribution of power in the profession and in the world, prior education and background, certain geographies, white mythologies, gender imbalances, and so on.[183]

Yet, like other inscriptions, footnotes and bibliographies do not carry or deliver any pre-existing meaning but contribute to the deferral of meaning. They are like any other forms and their sovereignty should be better acknowledged. Whilst footnotes are caught in the deferral of meaning like any other forms of the international legal discourse, they warrant specific scrutiny for they play a very pivotal role in the deferral of meaning. Actually, footnotes are like immense *highway connectors*: arriving at a footnote or a bibliographical inscription, the reader is able to go into a multitude of directions at high speed and yet has no choice but to continue to defer meaning. In that sense, it could be said that footnotes and bibliographies inflate and accelerate the deferral of meaning in which the words, idioms, aphorisms, and texts of international law are caught. For instance, whether the word "critical" in a piece of legal literature adjoins a reference to the work of Hersch Lauterpacht or that of Martti Koskenniemi will bring about a very different type of deferral of meaning. To take another example, the mention of "territory" or "investment" will induce a very different deferral of meaning depending on whether it is accompanied by a reference to the case-law of the International Court of Justice or by a reference to works in post-colonial studies.

Given how much they inflate and accelerate the deferral of meaning, one cannot overlook footnotes and bibliographies when reflecting upon the implications of the sovereignty of forms in international law. Being such important crossroads in the deferral of meaning, they warrant as much scrutiny as the rest of international law's words, idioms, aphorisms, and texts. And it is not only a matter of scrutiny. Given their role in the deferral of meaning in international legal thought and practice, footnotes and bibliographies should constitute a priority area for the international lawyer's correcting and re-balancing interventions.[184] They should particularly be turned into a mode of disruption of the universalizing strategies, distribution of power, geographies, white

---

[183] On the idea of white mythologies permeating forms, see Derrida, *Marges* (n 123) 247–324.

[184] As I told students at the Hague Academy of International Law in summer 2019, I am surprised that there have not been more calls for better gender balance and geographical diversity in referencing.

mythologies, gender imbalances, and so on that inform international law's inscriptions.[185]

---

[185] For an example of a use of a new typography to generate disorders and foil the work of the forms, see Derrida, *Papier Machine* (n 32) 159, 244. See also more generally, Jacques Derrida, *Glas* (Galilée 1974); Jacques Derrida, *La carte postale: De Socrate à Freud et au-delà* (Flammarion 1980).

Epilogue

Grand Central Terminal, New York, 16 June 2021, 14.03. I came late. Too late. The 14.02 service to New Haven had already departed. The next one was not for an hour. There was no point running any more. I was there, standing in the main concourse of the Terminal under its famous gigantic zodiac ceiling and having to kill an hour. I consciously turned my gaze away from the main split-flap departures board as I feared that the sight thereof would painfully remind me that I was now condemned to stand idle until the next service. As I was trying not to mull over what led me to arrive too late and what I should have done differently, I came to think how one always rushes through the Terminal's concourse and rarely takes pains to glance at the magnificence of the 12 constellations painted in gold leaf on its ceiling. Maybe missing my train today was my one opportunity to finally examine the splendors of Grand Central Terminal. After looking up at the ceiling for a few seconds, I came to feel that I was not in the mood for such an exercise of contemplation. I was still too angry at myself for missing my train to appreciate the marvels created by 20th-century human craftwork.

As I was struggling with remorse, my attention was drawn to the main concourse itself. It was noisy and bustling as it always is at this time of the day. So many travelers rushing in and out through its many entries and exits, all on a journey that began long before they reached this place. I looked closer. The place was teeming with travelers in haste, travelers who hurriedly cross the concourse, never stop and then vanish. Where were they coming from? Where were they going? Nobody could ever know, I thought. Even if one were to track these travelers' phones, no answer to those questions could ever be provided. The place they were coming from before reaching Grand Central Terminal was only a place that had succeeded another place. There was always a journey before their journey to Grand Central Terminal. And there was always another destination after their next destination. In a way, the journey that had led all these travelers to this main concourse today had begun before it began and would continue after it ended.

As I thought about the traveling without origin and end on which all these travelers had embarked, I found myself struck by the feeling that this place was surprisingly empty. In fact, the sight of this congested hallway was inextricably accompanied by a feeling it was deserted. That feeling bothered me. How could I experience a feeling of emptiness vis-a-vis this huge hallway thronged with so many travelers? Grand Central Terminal's main concourse is never empty, I told myself! I came to worry about the irrationality of my thoughts. Why on earth was I thinking that this gigantic and densely packed hallway was empty? Was I becoming insane?

I tried to suppress my thoughts about the emptiness of the place by thinking about the good time I expected to have in New Haven. Surely, once there, once with all those colleagues I cherish and whom I had not seen for so long, I would forget that I had missed my train and that I had had bizarre thoughts while standing in the middle of the main concourse of Grand Central Terminal. Irritatingly, as I was trying to repress the bizarre thought that the place was empty, this impression of emptiness was continuously being reinforced. The more I tried to repress it, the more I was caught by it. I could not just evade the thought that this place was empty. This place, I irremediably continued to feel, is empty. Yes, empty. As this impression of emptiness overwhelmed me, I even came to feel that I was hearing an echo, the echo one hears in an empty room. I tried to listen to the sounds coming from this huge concourse … No way! I could not believe what I was hearing. How is that possible? The echo I was actually hearing in this empty place was that of my own thoughts. In fact, I could hear the echo of my thoughts in the hallway. More precisely, the place was empty and I could hear the echo of my thinking of the place as being empty.

I felt terrified for a short moment. Maybe all these irrational thoughts about these travelers rushing in and out of the main concourse of Grand Central Terminal were the early symptoms of a mental disease. I was in my early forties. Isn't that an age where people suffering from chronic insanity start developing the first symptoms? Maybe in a couple of years I would have to be admitted to a mental health unit. What would my daughters think of me? What image would they keep of their dad? Or was I just a hypochondriac, as so many of my friends are? This thought of being in the early stage of a mental illness, however, proved short-lived as it was quickly displaced by the ever-returning thought that this place was empty and that I could hear the echo of my own thought about this place's very emptiness.

Still avoiding turning my gaze to the main departure board, I looked at my phone. It was now 14.08. Only five minutes had passed since I came into this hallway. In that short period of time, I thought, several hundred travelers must have transited here while I was caught in my idiotic, self-absorbed, and irrational thinking. Hundreds of these journeys without beginning and end had come to include a short passage in this hall in the five minutes that had just elapsed. Although the thought of the emptiness of the place still bothered me, I stopped trying to repress it.

In my attempt to move away from the irritation provoked by my feeling of this place being empty, I was helped by the arrival of another thought that came to equally bewilder me, namely, that not much had happened in this bustling and noisy hall in the last five minutes. Many travelers had crossed the hall without stopping and had vanished, none of them having ever completed the journey they were on. The journey of all these travelers is still going on at this very time, I thought. I reflected further on the idea that nothing had happened in the last five minutes in this bustling and noisy hall. Maybe it makes sense, I thought, that nothing happened here. How could anything possibly happen, as these travelers were unknown to me? Indeed, they had no identity. What is more, they were walking so fast, masking one another, that they did not even have a face I could possibly recognize had I known them. Actually, these travelers were just shapes moving in this gigantic hallway under a zodiac ceiling with 12 constellations painted in gold leaf. Had even one of them stumbled and spilled her coffee in front of me, nothing would have happened either, because I would not have been able to articulate a story with a proper subject. These travelers with no identity and no face were simply anonymous shapes on journeys without a beginning and an end. This hall was nothing more than a site of passage where shapes move in an erratic, meaningless, and anonymous manner. No proper happening could ever possibly be envisaged as far as these anonymous shapes in the hall on journeys without a beginning and an end were concerned.

I paused. After a few seconds, I suddenly rolled my eyes. Come on! The fact that these anonymous shapes in the hall on journeys without a beginning and an end could not constitute a happening could not mean that nothing had happened in the bustling and noisy hallway in the last minutes. No, no, no, no, I told myself. It can't be that nothing happened, because something irrefutably happened in the last minutes: my thinking was a happening. My disarticulated outpouring of thoughts since I came into this hall, whatever the individual merits of each of them, was an event taking place in this very hall. For that reason, it was not true that nothing had happened as these hundreds of travelers without any origin and destination transited through the main concourse. Thinking, and especially thinking about this hall's anonymous shapes, was a happening. Feeling a bit ashamed about my earlier thought about the lack of happening in the main concourse, I backtracked and changed my mind. A lot had happened in this hall since I arrived, I thought.

I had thus been wrong to think that nothing had happened since I stopped in the middle of the main concourse of the Terminal. But had I also been wrong to think that this hall was empty? I started to feel that I had to review that thought too. After all, all these travelers that had entered the main concourse before vanishing must have had a rich life made of successes, hopes, disappointments, treasons, generosity, missteps, affairs, and so on. These travelers couldn't be reduced to empty shapes entering the hall and vanishing a few dozen seconds later. As I was revisiting my earlier thought about the emptiness of the place,

I started to spot some of the travelers crossing the main concourse at that very moment. This one! Mmm, I am sure he must be an ambitious and greedy lawyer from one of these big law firms of Midtown. And this one! Maybe this one is going to visit her mum and let her know about her new boyfriend. And this one. He looks like the kindest person on earth, always caring for others. I felt like speaking to that shape to which I had just given an identity to my liking. That feeling, however, did not distract me from the major distribution of identities I had engaged in. What about this other traveler? She looks sad, as if she had been turned down for a job or failed an exam. I felt I wanted to go and speak to her to offer her some help or solace. And that other guy there … For a moment that probably lasted a minute or two, I found some amusement in projecting distinct identities on some of these moving shapes of the main concourse, inventing a life for each of them.

At some point, I gained a kind of consciousness of the ridiculous exercise I was actually conducting in the middle of the gigantic concourse of the Grand Central Terminal. I felt it was probably another bout of the irrational and idiotic thinking in which I had repeatedly lost myself today. As I was lamenting this other stupid thought exercise of mine, I came to think that this was maybe not that silly after all. I thought that, by inventing an identity for these travelers crossing the main concourse, I was confirming my earlier thought that this place was empty. I took a breath and reflected further on that. I suddenly felt relief. That was it! Yes! It all fell into place. I actually came to understand why I had been repeatedly struck by the emptiness of this noisy and bustling concourse: these travelers were just inscriptions and I had been filling these inscriptions with a content of my choice. Being on a journey with no origin and no destination and having no identity and recognizable face, they could only be inscriptions. This is how I had been treating them since I came into this main concourse.

At that moment, I came to experience some satisfaction at the thought that my own thinking could be as powerful as designing to my liking this hall and all the travelers that cross it. That little moment of satisfaction did, however, not last long, for two reasons. First, I felt myself ashamed of finding satisfaction in the discovery of the power of my thought and my ability to fill those shapes with a content of my choice. Second, I came to doubt that my invention of an identity for all these travelers crossing the main concourse was really at my entire discretion. It is true, I thought, I can decide to see in that person a greedy and ambitious lawyer of Midtown and in that other person a possible friend for whom I care and want to help. But those very identities, I thought, are not creations of mine. They are identities that are available to me by virtue of my own experience, my personal history, my language, my culture, my education, the world I can possibly imagine, my repertoire of possibilities, and so on. Also, I realized, the way in which I design a possible identity for such travelers hinges on the shape or image that these travelers project to me. In that sense, the way I invent an identity for all these travelers in this main concourse is not arbitrary, accidental, and fortuitous, let alone at my full discretion. Although I am the one making the final attribution of a certain identity to these anonymous travelers, I thought, my invention of an identity for these travelers is always caught in something much bigger, a flow of references, histories, affects, and meanings that I am mobilizing from somewhere—but I had no clue where from—and that I have not invented myself.

Suddenly the hall emptied. Travelers became scarce. This was the moment I realized that the fire alarm was ringing. I felt that it actually must have been ringing for possibly a minute or so. I had not realized it, for I had been too absorbed by my realization that I had no full discretion over the determination of identity of the vanishing shapes that were populating the main concourse. I experienced the sound of the fire alarm as rather painful. To protect myself from it, I put my fingers in my ears. This is when I was struck by what later proved the most extraordinary thoughts of all those I had had that day while standing in the middle of Grand Central Terminal's main concourse. I appreciate that the following is difficult to believe. I am however not lying when I say that I then felt that the shapes of these hundreds of travelers having hastily crossed the hallway since I arrived were … still in the hallway! Indeed, as I was standing in the middle of the main concourse with my fingers in my ears, I could remember them and see them entering and vanishing. I vividly felt that the place was replete with their trace and, paradoxically, could not be emptied by the fire alarm! Whilst these travelers had hastily crossed this place and vanished into one of the many exits of the concourse, they had left their trace, and their trace was still here with me in the main concourse. That made me think that, even as the place was forcefully emptied as a result of the fire alarm, the place was still full, full of the traces of all those travelers I had spotted earlier and who were on a journey without a beginning and an end.

This is when I felt someone touching my arm in a rather unpleasant manner. I turned. A security guard was standing next to me. He was urging me to leave the hall as I should have because of the fire alarm. I looked at him reverentially and apologized. That did not make him much friendlier. Without much thinking this time, I started to move in a direction which I had not chosen or considered. I just walked, knowing that this hall had so many entries and exits that it would have one for me wherever I walked. It was 14.20. As I left the hallway, I could still hear the echo of my thoughts and see the traces of these hundreds of fellow travelers. Surely, the 15.12 service to New Haven would be delayed or even canceled. Maybe I would not even make it to New Haven today. But it did not matter anymore. The journeys without beginning and end of these travelers I had spotted would be continued outside this hallway and without me. I felt at peace.

After meaning. The international lawyer always arrives after meaning has been deferred by the forms of the international legal discourse by virtue of their self-difference. This book has tried to make the reader sensitive to the idea that meaning is nowhere to be found in the international legal discourse. Having arrived after meaning, the international lawyer is left with forms and only forms, forms which perpetually point away to other forms, forms which sovereignly preside over international legal thought and practice.

Bibliography

CRITICAL, LITERARY, AND THEORETICAL WORKS

Adorno, TW, *Negative Dialectics* (E B Ashton tr, Routledge 1973)

Adorno, TW, 'The Essay as Form' (1984) 32 New German Critique 151

Adorno, TW, *Lectures on Negative Dialectics: Fragments of a Lecture Course 1965/1966* (Rolf Tiedmann ed, Rodney Livingstone tr, Polity Press 2008)

Adorno, TW and Horkheimer, M, *Dialectic of Enlightenment* (Verso 1997)

Althusser L, *For Marx* (Ben Brewster tr, Verso 2006)

Anderson, B, *Imagined Communities. Reflections on the Origin and Spread of Nationalism* (Verso 2016)

Bachelard, G, *Le nouvel esprit scientifique* (Presses universitaires de France 1934)

Barthes, R, *Mythologies* (Editions du Seuil 1957)

Barthes, R, 'Le discours de l'histoire' (1967) 6 Social Science Information 63

Barthes, R, *S/Z* (Seuil 1970)

Barthes, R, *Le degré zéro de l'écriture* (Editions du Seuil 1972)

Barthes, R, *Leçon* (Seuil 1978)

Barthes, R, *Le Bruissement de la langue. Essais critiques IV* (Seuil 1984)

Barthes, R, *L'aventure sémiologique* (Seuil 1985)

Bennington, G, *Jacques Derrida* (Seuil 1991)

Bergson H, *La pensée et le mouvant* (Flammarion 2014)

Borradori, G, *Philosophy in a Time of Terror: Dialogues with Jürgen Habermas and Jacques Derrida* (University of Chicago Press 2003)

Bourdieu, P, 'The Force of Law: Toward a Sociology of the Juridical Field' (1987) 38 Hastings Law Journal 805

Brogan, AA, 'The Original Difference' in David Wood and Robert Bernasconi (eds), *Derrida and Différance* (Northwestern University Press 1988)

Butler, J, *Gender Trouble: Feminism and the Subversion of Identity* (2nd edn, Routledge 1990)

Butler, J, *Gender Trouble* (2nd edn, Routledge 2007)

Butler, J, *Notes Toward a Performative Theory of Assembly* (Harvard University Press 2018)

Carr, EHH, *What is History?* (2nd edn, CUP 1987)

Culler, J, *Structuralist Poetics: Structuralism, Linguistics, and the Study of Literature* (Ithaca 1975)

Culler, J, *Literary Theory: A Very Short Introduction* (OUP 1997)

Culler, J, *Structuralist Poetics: Structuralism, Linguistics, and the Study of Literature* (Routledge, 2002)

Culler, J, *On Deconstruction: Theory and Criticism after Structuralism* (Routledge 2008)

de Certeau, M, *L'écriture de l'histoire* (Gallimard 1975)

de Man, P, *The Resistance to Theory* (University of Minnesota Press 1986)

de Saussure, F, *Course in General Linguistics* (Charles Bally and Albert Sechehaye eds, Open Court 1986)

Deleuze, G, *Critique et Clinique* (Editions de Minuit 1993)

Derrida, J, *De la Grammatologie* (Editions de Minuit 1967)

Derrida, J, *L'Ecriture et la différence* (Editions du Seuil 1967)

Derrida, J, *Marges de la Philosophie* (Editions de Minuit 1972)

Derrida, J, *Positions* (Editions de Minuit, 1972)

Derrida, J, *Glas* (Galilée 1974)

Derrida, J, *La carte postale: De Socrate à Freud et au-delà* (Flammarion 1980)

Derrida, J, 'Des Tours de Babel' in Joseph F Graham (ed), *Difference in Translation* (Cornell University Press 1985)

Derrida, J, 'Letter to a Japanese Friend' in David Wood and Robert Bernasconi (eds), *Derrida and Différance* (Northwestern University Press 1988)

Derrida, J, 'The Force of Law: The "Mystical Foundation of Authority"' (1989) 11 Cardozo Law Review 920

Derrida, J, *Spectres de Marx* (Galilée 1993)

Derrida, J, *Le Monolinguisme de l'autre* (Galilée 1996)

Derrida, J, *De l'hospitalité* (Calmann-Levy Editions 1997)

Derrida, J, *L'Université sans condition* (Galilée 2001)

Derrida, J, *Papier Machine* (Galilée, 2001)

Derrida, J, *Le problème de la genèse dans la philosophie de Husserl* (PUF 2010)

Derrida, J, *The Beast and the Sovereign*, vol 1 (University of Chicago Press 2011)

Derrida, J, *The Beast and the Sovereign*, vol 2 (University of Chicago Press 2011)

Derrida, J, *La voix et le phénomène: Introduction au problème du signe dans la phénoménologie de Husserl* (PUF 2016)

Derrida, J, *La vie la mort (séminaire 1975–1976)* (Le Seuil 2019)

Descombes, V, *Le Même et l'Autre. Quarante-cinq ans de philosophie française* (Editions de Minuit 1979)

Dillon, B, *Essayism* (Fizcarraldo Editions 2017)

Eagleton, T, *The Function of Criticism* (Verso 2005)

Feder, EK, 'Power/Knowledge' in Dianna Taylor (ed), *Michel Foucault: Key Concepts* (Routledge 2014)

Fink, B, *The Lacanian Subject: Between Language and Jouissance* (Princeton University Press 1995)

Fish, S, *Is There a Text in This Class? The Authority of Interpretive Communities* (Harvard University Press 1980)

Fish, S, 'With the Compliments of the Author: Reflections on Austin and Derrida' (1982) 8 Critical Inquiry 693

Fish, S, 'Fish v. Fiss' (1984) 36 Stanford Law Review 1325

Fish, S, *Doing What Comes Naturally* (Duke University Press 1989)

Foucault, M, *Les mots et les choses* (Gallimard 1966)

Foucault, M, *L'archéologie du savoir* (Gallimard 1969)

Foucault, M, *Surveiller et Punir* (Gallimard 1975)

Foucault, M, 'Politics and the Study of Discourse' in Graham Burchell, Colin Gordon and Peter Miller (eds), *The Foucault Effect: Studies in Governmentality* (University of Chicago Press 1991)

Foucault, M, The *Archaeology of Knowledge* (Routledge 2002)

Foucault, M, *Naissance de la biopolitique: Cours au Collège de France (1978–1979)* (Gallimard Seuil 2004)

Foucault, M, *Le gouvernement de soi et des autres: Cours au Collège de France (1982–1983)* (Gallimard Le Seuil 2008)

Glendinning, S, *Derrida: A Very Short Introduction* (OUP 2011)

Goodman, N, *Ways of Worldmaking* (Hackett Publishing 1978)

Harland, R, *Superstructuralism: The Philosophy of Structuralism and Post-Structuralism* (Routledge 1987)

Jaeggi, R, *Critique of Forms of Life* (Ciaran Cronin tr, Belknap Press 2018)

Jakobson, R, 'On Linguistic Aspects of Translation' in Achilles Fang and Reuben Brower (eds), *On Translation* (Harvard University Press 1959)

Jameson, F, *Late Marxism: Adorno or the Persistence of the Dialectic* (Verso 2007)

Jenkins, K (ed), *On 'What is History': From Carr and Elton to Rorty and White* (Routledge 1995)

Jenkins, K, *Re-thinking History* (Routledge 2003)

Lacan, J, *Ecrits* (Seuil 1966)

Laclau, E, *Emancipation(s)* (Verso 2007)

Latour, B, *Science in Action: How to Follow Scientists and Engineers Through Society* (Harvard University Press 1987)

Latour, B, *Nous n'avons jamais été modernes. Essai d'anthropologie symétrique* (La Découverte 1997)

Latour, B, *La fabrique du droit. Une ethnographie du Conseil d'Etat* (La Découverte 2004)

Latour, B, 'Why Has Critique Run out of Steam? From Matters of Fact to Matters of Concern' (2004) 30 Critical Inquiry 225

Latour, B, *An Inquiry into Modes of Existence: An Anthropology of the Moderns* (Harvard University Press 2013)

Law, J, *After Method: Mess in Social Science Research* (Routledge 2004)

Le Goff, J, 'L'homme médiéval' in Jacques Le Goff (ed), *L'Homme médiéval* (Editions du Seuil 1989)

Lercercle, J-J, *De l'interpellation. Sujet, langue, idéologie* (Editions Amsterdam 2019)

Levinas, E, *Altérité et transcendance* (Fata Morgana 1995)

Levinas, E, *Totalité et Infini* (Martinus Nijhoff Publishers 1971)

Li, W, 'A Systemic Approach to Manipulation in Translation—A Case Study of Ye Junjian's 1958 Translation of H.C. Andersen's Tales' in Lieven D'hulst, Carol O'Sullivan, and Michael Schreiber (eds), *Politics, Policy and Power in Translation History* (Frank & Timme 2016)

Lyotard, J-F, *La Condition Postmoderne* (Les Editions de Minuit 1979)

Lyotard, J-F, *Le Différend* (Editions de Minuit 1983)

MacIntyre, A, *Whose Justice? Which Rationality?* (Duckworth 1988)

MacIntyre, A, *Three Rival Versions of Moral Inquiry: Encyclopaedia, Genealogy, and Tradition* (University of Notre Dame Press 1990)

Malabou, C, and Derrida, J, *La Contre-Allée* (La Quinzaine Littéraire, 1999)

Merleau-Ponty, M, *Signes* (Gallimard 1960)

Mitchell, T, *Colonising Egypt* (CUP 1991)

Mitchell, T, *Questions of Modernity* (University of Minnesota Press 2000)

Munslow, A, 'Preface' in Keith Jenkins (ed), *On 'What is History': From Carr and Elton to Rorty and White* (Roultledge 1995)

Ricoeur, P, *Histoire et vérité* (Seuil 1955)

Ricoeur, P, *Temps et récit*, vol 1 (Seuil 1983)

Ricoeur, P, *Temps et récit*, vol 2 (Seuil 1984)

Ricoeur, P, *La mémoire, l'histoire, l'oubli* (Seuil 2000)

Ronell, A, 'Saying Goodbye: An Amateur Video' in Peter Goodrich and others (eds), *Derrida and Legal Philosophy* (Palgrave MacMillan 2008)
Rorty, R (ed), *The Linguistic Turn: Essays in Philosophical Method* (The University of Chicago Press 1992)
Rorty, R, *Consequences of Pragmatism* (University of Minneapolis 2011)
Rose, G, *The Dialectic of Nihilism: Post-Structuralism and Law* (Basil Blackwell 1984)
Rose, N, *Governing the Soul: The Shaping of the Private Self* (Free Association Books 1999)
Said, E, *Orientalism* (Routledge 1978)
Said, E, *The World, the Text, and the Critic* (Harvard University Press 1983)
Sapir, E, *Language. An Introduction to the Study of Speech* (Ishi Press 2014)
Skinner, Q, *The Foundations of Modern Political Thought*, vol 1 (CUP 1998)
White, H, *Tropics of Discourse: Essays in Cultural Criticism* (Johns Hopkins University Press 1978)
White, H, *The Content of the Form: Narrative Discourse and Historical Representation* (Johns Hopkins University Press 1987)
White, H, *Metahistory: The Historical Imagination in the 19th-Century Europe* (Johns Hopkins University Press 2014)
Wittgenstein, L, *Culture and Value* (Peter Winch tr, University of Chicago Press 1980)
Wood, D, 'Introduction' in David Wood and Robert Bernasconi (eds), *Derrida and Différance* (Northwestern University Press 1988)

INTERNATIONAL LAW, LEGAL THEORY, AND RELATED WORKS

Abi-Saab, G, 'Cours général de droit international public' (1987) 207 Collected Courses of the Hague Academy of International Law 9
Adler, E, *Communitarian International Relations: The Epistemic Foundations of International Relations* (Routledge 2005)
Ago, R, 'Le délit international' (1939) 69 Collected Courses of the Hague Academy of International Law 426
Ago, R, 'Positive Law and International Law' (1957) 51 American Journal of International Law 691
Allott, P, 'Language, Method and the Nature of International Law' (1971) 45 British Yearbook of International Law 79
Allott, P, 'State Responsibility and the Unmaking of International Law' (1988) 29 Harvard International Law Journal 1
Amaya-Castro, JM and El Menyawi, H, 'Moving Away from Moving Away: A Conversation about Jacques Derrida and Legal Scholarship' (2005) 6 German Law Journal 101
Anghie, A, 'Francisco De Vitoria and the Colonial Origins of International Law' (1996) 5 Social and Legal Studies 321
Anghie, A, *Imperialism, Sovereignty and the Making of International Law* (CUP 2004)
Anghie, A, 'The Evolution of International Law: colonial and postcolonial realities' (2006) 27 Third World Quarterly 740
Anghie, A, 'Domination' in Jean d'Aspremont and Sahib Singh (eds), *Concepts for International Law: Contributions to Disciplinary Thought* (Edward Elgar 2019)
Anzilotti, D, *Corso di Diritto Internazionale*, vol 1 (Athenaeum 1928)
Anzilotti, D, *Scritti di diritto internazionale pubblico* (Cedan Padova 1956)

Arangio-Ruiz, G, *L'Etat dans le sens du droit des gens et la notion de droit international* (Cooperativa Libraria Universitaria 1975)

Aust, A, *Modern Treaty Law and Practice* (2nd edn, CUP 2007)

Aust, H, 'Circumstances Precluding Wrongfulness' in André Nollkaemper and Ilias Plakokefalos (eds), *Principles of Shared Responsibility in International Law: An Appraisal of the State of the Art* (CUP 2014)

Balkin, JM, 'Deconstructive Practice and Legal Theory' (1987) 96 Yale Law Journal 743

Balkin, JM, 'Deconstruction's Legal Career' (2005) 27 Cardozo Law Review 719

Barberis, J, 'Le Concept de "traité international" et ses limites' (1984) 30 Annuaire français de droit international 239

Barreto, J-M, 'Cerberus: Rethinking Grotius and the Westphalian System' in Martti Koskenniemi, Walter Rech, and Manuel Jimenez Fonseca (eds), *International Law and Empire* (OUP 2017)

Basdevant, J, 'Règles générales du droit de la paix' (1936) 58 Collected Courses of the Hague Academy of International Law 471

Beaudouin, A, *Uti possidetis et sécession* (Dalloz 2011)

Bederman, D, *The Spirit of International Law* (Georgia University Press 2002)

Benvenisti, E, *The Law of Global Governance* (Brill 2014)

Benvenisti, E and Downs, GW, 'The Empire's New Clothes: Political Economy and the Fragmentation of International Law' (2007) 60 Stanford Law Review 595

Berman, A, 'Translation and the Trials of the Foreign' in Lawrence Venuti (ed), *The Translation Studies Reader* (Routledge 2004)

Berman, H, *Law and Language: Effective Symbols of Community* (CUP 2013)

Berman, N, 'In the Wake of Empire' (1999) 14 American University International Law Review 1515

Besson, S, 'Theorizing the Sources of International Law' in Samantha Besson and John Tasioulas (eds), *The Philosophy of International Law* (OUP 2010)

Besson, S, 'Comparative Law and Human Rights' in Mathias Reimann and Reinhard Zimmermann (eds), *The Oxford Handbook of Comparative Law* (2nd edn, OUP 2019)

Bianchi, A, 'The International Regulation of the Use of Force: The Politics of Interpretive Method' (2009) 22 Leiden Journal of International Law 665

Bianchi, A, 'Textual Interpretation and (International) Law Reading: The Myth of (In)determinacy and the Genealogy of Meaning' in Pieter HF Bekker, Rudolph Dolzer and Michael Weibel (eds), *Making Transnational Law Work in the Global Economy: Essays in Honour of Detlev Vagts* (CUP 2010)

Bianchi, A, 'Reflexive Butterfly Catching: Insights from a Situated Catcher' in Joost Pauwelyn and others (eds), *Informal International Lawmaking* (OUP 2012)

Bianchi, A, 'The Game of Interpretation in International Law: The Players, the Cards, and Why the Game is Worth the Candle' in Andrea Bianchi, Daniel Peat, and Matthew Windsor (eds), *Interpretation in International Law* (OUP 2015)

Bianchi A, *International Law Theories: An Inquiry into Different Ways of Thinking* (OUP 2016)

Bianchi, A, 'Epistemic Communities' in Jean d'Aspremont and Sahib Singh (eds), *Concepts for International Law: Contributions to Disciplinary Thought* (Edward Elgar Publishing 2019)

Bianchi, A, Peat, D, and Windsor, M (eds), *Interpretation in International Law* (OUP 2015)

Borgen, CJ, 'The Language of Law and the Practice of Politics: Great Powers and the Rhetoric of Self-Determination in the Cases of Kosovo and South Ossetia' (2009) 10 Chicago Journal of International Law 1

Bradley, C, 'Customary International Law Adjudication as Common Law Adjudication' in Curtis Bradley (ed), *Custom's Future: International Law in a Changing World* (CUP 2016)

Brierly, JL, 'The Basis of Obligation in International Law' in Hersch Lauterpacht (ed), *The Basis of Obligation in International Law and Other Papers* (Scientia Verlag Aalen 1977)

Brölmann, C, 'Law-Making Treaties: Form and Function in International Law' (2005) 74 Nordic Journal of International Law 383

Brown, C, 'Article 59' in Andreas Zimmermann and others, *The Statute of the International Court of Justice: A Commentary* (2nd edn, OUP 2012)

Brownlie, I, 'International Law at the Fiftieth Anniversary of the United Nations: General Course on Public International Law' (1995) 255 Collected Courses of the Hague Academy of International Law 9

Brunnée, J and Toope, S, 'International Law and Constructivism: Elements of an International Theory of International Law' (2000) 39 Columbia Journal of Transnational Law 19

Brunnée, J and Toope, S, 'Constructivism and International Law' in Jeffrey L Dunoff and Marck A Pollack (eds), *Interdisciplinary Perspectives on International Law and International Relations: The State of the Art* (CUP 2012)

Burazin, L, 'The Rule of Recognition and the Emergence of a Legal System' (2015) 27 Revus 115

Butler, WE, 'Comparative Approaches to International Law' (1985) 190 Collected Courses of the Hague Academy of International Law 9

Byers, M, *Custom, Power and the Power of Rules: International Relations and Customary International Law* (CUP 1999)

Carozza, P, 'Uses and Misuses of Comparative Law in International Human Rights: Some Reflections on the Jurisprudence of the European Court of Human Rights' (1997) 73 Notre Dame Law Review 1217

Carrai, MA, 'The Politics of History in the Late Qing Era: William A.P. Martin and a History of International Law for China' (2020) 22 Journal of the History of International Law 296

Carty, A, 'The Need to be Rid of the Idea of General Customary Law' (2018) 112 American Journal of International Law Unbound 319

Carty, A, *The Decay of International Law: A Reappraisal of the Limits of Legal Imagination in International Affairs* (Manchester University Press 2019)

Carty, A, 'International law and nervous states in the age of anger, the collapse of legal formalism and a return to natural law' in Rossana Deplano and Nicholas Tsagourias, *Research Methods in International Law* (Edward Elgar 2021)

Caspersen, N and Stansfield, G (eds), *Unrecognized States in the International System* (Routledge 2011)

Cass, DZ, 'Navigating the Newstream: Recent Critical Scholarship in International Law' (1996) 65 Nordic Journal of International Law 341

Cassese, A, 'States: Rise and Decline of the Primary Subjects of the International Community' in Bardo Fassbender and Anne Peters (eds), *Oxford Handbook on the History of International Law* (OUP 2012)

Charlesworth, H, 'The Sex of the State in International Law' in Ngaire Naffine and Rosmary Owens (eds), *Sexing the Subject of Law* (LBC Information Services 1997)

Charlesworth, H, 'Feminist Ambivalence about International Law' (2005) 11 International Legal Theory 1.

Charlesworth, H, 'Prefiguring Feminist Judgment in International Law' in Loveday Hodson and Troy Lavers (eds), *Feminist Judgments in International Law* (Hart Publishing 2019)

Charlesworth, H and Chinkin, C, *The Boundaries of International Law: A Feminist Analysis* (Manchester University Press 2000)

Charlesworth, H, Chinkin, C, and Wright, S, 'Feminist Approaches to International Law' (1991) 85 American Journal of International Law 613

Chaumont, C, 'Cours général de droit international public' (1970) 129 Collected Courses of the Hague Academy of International Law 333

Chayes, A and Chayes, AH, *The New Sovereignty: Compliance with International Regulatory Agreements* (Harvard University Press 1995)

Chesterman, S, 'An International Rule of Law?' (2008) 56 American Journal of Comparative Law 331

Chesterman, S, 'Herding Schrödinger's Cats: The Limits of the Social Science Approach to International Law' (2021) 22 Chicago Journal of International Law 1

Cheung, E and Fung, M, 'The Hazards of Translating Wheaton's Elements of International Law into Chinese: Cultures of World Order Lost in Translation' in Anthony Carty and Janne Nijman (eds), *Morality and Responsibility of Rulers: European and Chinese Origins of a Rule of Law as Justice for World Order* (OUP 2018)

Chimni, BS, 'Third World Approaches to International Law: A Manifesto' (2006) 8 International Community Law Review 18

Chinkin, C, 'A Mirage in the Sand? Distinguishing Binding and Non-Binding Relations Between States' (1997) 10 Leiden Journal of International Law 223

Christakis, T, *Le droit à l'autodétermination en dehors des situations de décolonisation* (La Documentation Francaise 1999)

Christakis, T, 'The State as a "Primary Fact": Some Thoughts on the Principle of Effectiveness' in Marcelo Kohen (ed), *Secession: International Law Perspectives* (CUP 2006)

Christakis, T, 'Les "circonstances excluant l'illicéité": une illusion d'optique?' in Olivier Corten and others, *Droit du Pouvoir—Pouvoir du Droit: Mélanges en l'honneur de Jean Salmon* (Bruylant 2007)

Christakis, T, 'Self-Determination, Territorial Integrity, and Fait Accompli in the Case of Crimea' (2015) 75 ZaöRV/Heidelberg Journal of International Law 75

Coates, BA, *Legalist Empire: International Law and American Foreign Relations in the Early Twentieth Century* (OUP 2016)

Collins, R, 'Taking Legal Positivism Beyond the State: Finding Secondary Rules?' in Luca Siliquini-Cinelli (ed), *Legal Positivism in a Global and Transnational Age* (Springer 2019)

Corten, O, 'Are There Gaps in the International Law of Secession?' in Marcelo Kohen (ed), *Secession: International Law Perspectives* (CUP 2006)

Cover, R, 'The Supreme Court, 1982 Term—Foreword: Nomos and Narrative' (1983) 97 Harvard Law Review 4

Craven, M, 'Introduction: International Law and Its Histories' in Matthew Craven, Malgosia Fitzmaurice, and Maria Vogiatzi (eds), *Time, History and International Law* (Brill 2007)

Craven, M, 'The Invention of a Tradition: Westlake, The Berlin Conference and the Historicisation of International Law' in Luigi Nuzzo and Miloš Vec, *Constructing International Law: The Birth of a Discipline* (Klostermann 2012)

Craven, M, 'Theorizing the Turn to History in International Law', in Anne Orford and Florian Hoffmann (eds), *The Oxford Handbook of the Theory of International Law* (OUP 2016)

Crawford, J, *The Creation of States in International Law* (2nd edn, OUP 2006)

Crawford, J, 'Overview of Part Three of the Articles on State Responsibility' in James Crawford and others (eds), *The Law of International Responsibility* (OUP 2010)

Crawford, J, *Chance, Order, Change: The Course of International Law, General Course of Public International Law* (Brill 2014)

Critchley, S, 'Derrida's Influence on Philosophy ... And on My Work' (2005) 6 German Law Journal 25

Culver, K and Giudice, M, *Legality's Borders: An Essay in General Jurisprudence* (OUP 2010)

D'Amato, A, 'Treaties as a Source of General Rules of International Law' (1962) 3 Harvard International Law Journal 1

D'Amato, A, 'The Neo-Positivist Concept of International Law' (1965) 59 American Journal of International Law 321

d'Aspremont, J, 'Legitimacy of Governments in the Age of Democracy' (2006) 38 New York University Journal of International Law and Politics 877

d'Aspremont, J, 'Abuse of the Legal Personality of International Organizations and the Responsibility of Member States' (2007) 4 International Organizations Law Review 91

d'Aspremont, J, 'Regulating Statehood: The Kosovo Status Settlement' (2007) 20 Leiden Journal of International Law 654

d'Aspremont, J, *Formalism and the Sources of International Law: A Theory of the Ascertainment of Legal Rules* (OUP 2011)

d'Aspremont, J, 'Wording in International Law' (2012) 25 Leiden Journal of International Law 575

d'Aspremont, J, 'Book Review of H. Thirlway, *The Sources of International Law*' [2014] German Yearbook of International Law 57

d'Aspremont, J, 'The Idea of "Rules" in the Sources of International Law' (2014) 84 British Yearbook of International Law 103

d'Aspremont, J, 'The Law of International Organizations and the Art of Reconciliation' (2014) 11 International Organizations Law Review 428

d'Aspremont, J, *Epistemic Forces in International Law. Foundational Doctrines and Techniques of International Legal Argumentation* (Edward Elgar Publishing 2015)

d'Aspremont, J, 'The Multidimensional Process of Interpretation: Content-Determination and Law-Ascertainment Distinguished' in Andrea Bianchi, Daniel Peat, and Matthew Windsor (eds), *Interpretation in International Law* (OUP 2015)

d'Aspremont, J, 'International Responsibility and the Constitution of Power: International Organizations Bolstered' in Ana Sofia Barros, Cedric Ryngaert, and Jan Wouters (eds), *International Organizations and Member State Responsibility* (Brill 2016)

d'Aspremont, J, 'Martti Koskenniemi, the Mainstream and Self-Reflectivity' (2016) 29 Leiden Journal of International Law 625

d'Aspremont, J, *International Law as a Belief System* (CUP 2017)

d'Aspremont, J and others (eds), *International Law as a Profession* (CUP 2017) d'Aspremont, J, 'The Professionalisation of International Law' in Jean d'Aspremont and others (eds), *International Law as a Profession* (CUP 2017)

d'Aspremont, J, 'Sources in Legal-Formalist Theories: The Poor Vehicle of Legal Forms' in Samantha Besson and Jean d'Aspremont (eds), *The Oxford Handbook of the Sources of International Law* (OUP 2017)

d'Aspremont, J, 'What Was Not Meant to Be: General Principles of Law as a Source of International Law' in Riccardo Pisillo Mazzeschi and Pasquale De Sena (eds), *Global Justice, Human Rights, and the Modernization of International Law* (Springer 2018)

d'Aspremont, J, 'Critical Histories of International Law and the Repression of Disciplinary Imagination' (2019) 7 London Review of International Law 89

d'Aspremont, J, 'Critique, and the True Believer's Experience (Hommage à Pierre Schlag)' [2019] SSRN 1, https://ssrn.com/abstract=3497764, accessed 24 May 2021

d'Aspremont, J, 'Three International Lawyers in a Hall of Mirrors' (2019) 32 Leiden Journal of International law 367

d'Aspremont, J, *The Critical Attitude and the History of International Law* (Brill 2019)

d'Aspremont, J, 'Comparativism and Colonizing Thinking in International Law' (2020) 57 Canadian Yearbook of International Law 89

d'Aspremont, J, 'Current Theorizations about the Treaty in International Law' in Duncan Hollis (ed), *The Oxford Guide to Treaties* (2nd edn, OUP 2020)

d'Aspremont, J, 'Destination: The Wasteland of Academic Overproduction (Part 1)' (EJIL:Talk!, 3 February 2020) accessed 24 May 2021

d'Apremont, J, 'Destination: the Wasteland of Academic Overproduction (Part 2)' (EJIL:Talk!, 3 February 2020) accessed 25 May 2021

d'Aspremont, J, 'International Law, Theory, and History: Ordering through Distinctions' in Jean d'Aspremont (ed), *The History and Theory of International Law*, vol 1 (Edward Elgar Publishing 2020)

d'Aspremont, J, *The Discourse on Customary International Law* (OUP 2020)

d'Aspremont, J, 'The Two Cultures of International Criminal Law' in Kevin Heller and others (eds), *Oxford Handbook of International Criminal Law* (OUP 2020)

d'Aspremont, J, 'Turntablism in the History of International Law' (2020) 22 Journal of the History of International Law 472

d'Aspremont, J, 'A Worldly Law in a Legal World' in Andrea Bianchi and Moshe Hirsch (eds), *International Law's Invisible Frames* (OUP 2021)

d'Aspremont, J, 'The International Court of Justice as the Master of the Sources' in Carlos Espósito and Kate Parlett (eds), *The Cambridge Companion to the International Court of Justice* (CUP 2021)

d'Aspremont, J, 'The Literary Performances of the Tipping Point' in John Haskell and Jean d'Aspremont (eds), *Tipping Points in International Law* (CUP 2021)

d'Aspremont, J, 'Legal Imagination and the Thinking of the Impossible', Leiden Journal of International Law (forthcoming)

d'Aspremont, J and Singh, S (eds), *Concepts for International Law. Contributions to Disciplinary Thought* (Edward Elgar Publishing 2019)

Danilenko, GM, *Law-Making in the International Community* (Martinus Nijhoff Publishers 1993)

De Sutter, L, *Hors La Loi. Théorie de l'anarchie juridique* (Les Liens qui Libèrent 2021)

de Vattel, E, *The Law of Nations* (Charles G Fenwick tr, Carnegie Institution of Washington 1916).

de Visscher, C, *Les effectivités du droit international public* (Pedone 1967) de Visscher, C, *Théories et Réalités en Droit International Public* (4th edn, Pedone 1970)

de Wet, E, 'The Constitutionalisation of Public International Law' in Michel Rosenfeld and Andras Sajo (eds), *The Oxford Handbook of Comparative Constitutional Law* (OUP 2012)

de Wet, E, 'The International Constitutional Order' (2006) 55 International and Comparative Law Quarterly 51

Delcourt, B and others (eds), *Démembrements d'Etat et délimitation territoriale: l'uti possidetis en question(s)* (Bruylant 1999)

Desautels-Stein, J, 'Structuralist Legal Histories' (2015) 78 Law and Contemporary Problems 37

Desautels-Stein, J, 'International Legal Structuralism: A Primer' (2016) 8 International Theory 201

Douzinas, C, 'Violence, Justice, Deconstruction' (2005) 6 German Law Journal 171

Dreyfus, HL and Rabinow, P, *Michel Foucault: Beyond Structuralism and Hermeneutics* (2nd edn, University of Chicago Press 1983)

Dugard, J and Raič, D, 'The Role of Recognition in the Law and Practice of Secession' in Marcelo Kohen (ed), *Secession: International Law Perspectives* (CUP 2006)

Dunoff, JL and Pollack, MA (eds), *Interdisciplinary Perspectives on International Law and International Relations: The State of the Art* (CUP 2013)

Dupont, C and Schultz, T, 'Towards a New Heuristic Model: Investment Arbitration as a Political System' (2016) 7 Journal of International Dispute Settlement 3

Dupuy, R-J, 'La pratique de l'article 38 du Statut de la Cour internationale de Justice dans le cadre des plaidoiries écrites et orales' in UN Office of Legal Affairs (ed), *Collection of Essays by Legal Advisers of States, Legal Advisers of International Organizations and Practitioners in the Field of International Law* (United Nations 1999)

Dworkin, R, *Law's Empire* (Harvard 1986)

Eagleton, C, *The Responsibility of States in International Law* (New York University Press 1928)

Eagleton, C, 'International Organizations and the Law of Responsibility' (1950) 76 Collected Courses of the Hague Academy of International Law 385

Ely, JH, 'Constitutional Interpretivism: Its Allure and Impossibility' (1978) 53 Indiana Law Journal 399

Erlanger, H and others, 'New Legal Realism Symposium: Is it Time for a New Legal Realism?' (2005) 2 Wisconsin Law Review 335

Eslava, L, Fakhri, M, and Nesiah, V, *Bandung, Global History and International Law: Critical Pasts and Pending Futures* (CUP 2017)

Fassbender, B, 'Westphalia, Peace of (1648)' in Rüdiger Wolfrum (ed), *The Max Planck Encyclopedia of Public International Law* (OUP 2012)

Fikfak, V and Burnett, B, 'Domestic Court's Reading of International Norms: A Semiotic Analysis' (2009) 22 International Journal for the Semiotics of Law 437

Fitzmaurice, G, 'Some Problems Regarding the Formal Sources of International Law' in Frederik Mari van Asbeck (ed), *Symbolae Verzijl, présentées au professeur J. H. W. Verzijl à l'occasion de son LXXX-ième anniversaire* (Martinus Nijhoff Publishers 1958)

Fitzmaurice, M, 'The Identification and Character of Treaties and Treaty Obligations Between States in International Law' (2003) 73 British Yearbook of International Law 141

Forray, V and Pimont, S, *Décrire le droit ... et le transformer. Essai sur la décriture du droit* (Dalloz 2017)

Forteau, M, 'L'Etat selon le droit international: une figure à géométrie variable' (2007) 111 Revue Générale de Droit International Public 737

Franck, T, *The Power of Legitimacy Among Nations* (OUP 1990)

Franck, T, *Fairness in International Law and Institutions* (Clarendon Press 1995)

Frankenberg, G, 'Critical Comparisons: Re-thinking Comparative Law' (1985) 26 Harvard International Law Journal 411

Frankenberg, G, 'Constitutional Transfer: The IKEA Theory Revisited' (2010) 8 International Journal of Constitutional Law 563

Frowein, JA, 'De Facto Regime' in Rüdiger Wolfrum (ed), *Max Planck Encyclopedia of Public International Law* (online edn, OUP 2013)

Fry, J, 'Attribution of Responsibility' in André Nollkaemper and Ilias Plakokefalos (eds), *Principles of Shared Responsibility in International Law* (CUP 2014)

Galindo, G, 'Martti Koskenniemi and the Historiographical Turn in International Law' (2005) 16 European Journal of International Law 539

García-Salmones Rovira, M, *The Project of Positivism in International Law* (OUP 2013)

Gardiner, R, *Treaty Interpretation* (2nd edn, OUP 2017)

Gardiner, R, 'The Vienna Convention Rules on Treaty Interpretation' in Duncan Hollis (ed), *The Oxford Guide to Treaties* (2nd edn, OUP 2020)

Garland, D, 'What Is a "History of the Present"? On Foucault's Genealogies and Their Critical Preconditions' (2014) 16 Punishment and Society 365

Gazzini, T, *Interpretation of International Investment Treaties* (Hart Publishing 2016).

Gehring, P, 'Force and "Mystical Foundation" of Law: How Jacques Derrida Addresses Legal Discourse' (2005) 6 German Law Journal 151

Genin, V, *Le laboratoire belge du droit international: Une communauté épistémique et internationale de juristes (1869–1914)* (Académie Royale des Sciences, des Lettres et de Beaux-Arts de Belgique 2018)

Glenn, HP, 'Are Legal Traditions Incommensurable?' (2001) 49 American Journal of Comparative Law 133

Goodrich, P, 'Law and Modernity' (1986) 49 The Modern Law Review 545

Goodrich, P, 'Sleeping with the Enemy: An Essay on the Politics of Critical Legal Studies in America' (1993) 68 New York University Law Review 389

Goodrich, P, 'Europe in America: Grammatology, Legal Studies, and the Politics of Transmission' 101 Columbia Law Review (2001) 2033–2084

Goodrich, P, 'J.D.' (2005) 6 German Law Journal 15

Goodrich, P and others (eds), *Derrida and Legal Philosophy* (Palgrave Macmillan 2008)

Goodrich, P and others, 'Introduction: A Philosophy of Legal Enigmas' in Peter Goodrich and others (eds), *Derrida and Legal Philosophy* (Palgrave Macmillan 2008)

Gross, L, 'The Peace of Westphalia, 1648–1948' (1948) 42 American Journal of International Law 29

Guzman, AT, *How International Law Works: A Rational Choice Theory* (OUP 2008)

Haas, P, 'Introduction: Epistemic Communities and International Policy Coordination' (1992) 46 International Organization 1

Haas, P, 'International Environmental Law: Epistemic Communities' in Daniel Bodansky, Jutta Brunnée, and Ellen Hey (eds), *The Oxford Handbook of International Environmental Law* (OUP 2007)

Habermas, J, *The Philosophical Discourse of Modernity: Twelve Lectures* (Frederik Lawrence tr, Polity Press 1987)

Hakimi, M, 'The Work of International Law' (2017) 58 Harvard International Law Journal 1

Hamamoto, S, 'A propos de deux clichés sur l'histoire du droit international en Asie de l'Est: une reconsidération de l'ordre mondial chinois et du discours de traités inégaux' in Pierre-Marie Dupuy and Vincent Chetail (eds), *The Roots of International Law: Liber Amicorum Peter Haggenmacher* (Martinus Nijhoff Publishers 2014)

Harlow, C, 'Global Administrative Law: The Quest for Principles and Values' (2006) 17 European Journal of International Law 1

Hart, HLA, *Essays in Jurisprudence and Philosophy* (Clarendon Press 1983)

Hart, HLA, *The Concept of Law* (2nd edn, OUP 1997)

Haskell, J, 'Hugo Grotius in the Contemporary Memory of International Law: Secularism, Liberalism, and the Politics of Restatement and Denial' in José María Beneyto and David Kennedy (eds), *New Approaches to International Law: The European and the American Experiences* (Asser Press 2012)

Haskell, J, 'The Traditions of Modernity within International Law and Governance: Christianity, Liberalism, and Marxism' (2014) 6 Human Rights and Globalization Law Review 29

Hathaway, OA and Shapiro, SJ, *The Internationalists: How a Radical Plan to Outlaw War Remade the World* (Simon & Schuster 2017)

Heathcote, S, 'State Omissions and Due Diligence: Aspects of Fault, Damage and Contribution to Injury in the Law of State Responsibility' in Karine Bannelier, Theodore Christakis, and Sarah Heathcote (eds), *The ICJ and the Evolution of International Law: The Enduring Impact of the 'Corfu Channel' Case* (Routledge 2012).

Hermans, T (ed), *The Manipulation of Literature: Studies in Literary Translations* (Croom Helm 1985)

Hermans, T, *Translation in Systems: Descriptive and System-Oriented Approaches Explained* (Routledge 2014)

Hermans, T, *Translation in Systems: Descriptive and Systemic Approaches Explained* (Routledge 2020)

Hernandez, G, *The International Court of Justice and the Judicial Function* (OUP 2014)

Higgins, R, *Problems and Process: International Law and How We Use It* (OUP 1994)

Higgins, R, 'Overview of Part Two of the Articles on State Responsibility' in James Crawford and others (eds), *The Law of International Responsibility* (OUP 2010)

Hillgenberg, H, 'A Fresh Look at Soft Law' (1999) 10 European Journal of International Law 499

Hirsch, M, *Invitation to the Sociology of International Law* (OUP 2015)

Hoffmann, F, 'Epilogue: In Lieu of Conclusion' (2005) 6 German Law Journal 197

Hollis, D, 'A Comparative Approach to Treaty Law and Practice' in Duncan Hollis et al (eds), *National Treaty Law and Practice* (Martinus Nijhoff Publishers 2005)

Hollis, D, 'Introduction to the Oxford Guide to Treaties' in Duncan Hollis (ed), *The Oxford Guide to Treaties* (OUP 2012)

Hollis, D, 'The Existential Function of Interpretation in International Law in Interpretation' in Andrea Bianchi, Daniel Peat, and Matthew Windsor (eds), *International Law in Interpretation in International Law* (OUP 2014)

Hollis, D, 'Interpretation' in Jean d'Aspremont and Sahib Singh (eds), *Concepts for International Law: Contributions to Disciplinary Thought* (Edward Elgar Publishing 2019)

Holtermann, JVH and Madsen, MR, 'Toleration, Synthesis or Replacement? The "Empirical Turn" and Its Consequences for the Science of International Law' (2016) 29 Leiden Journal of International Law 1001

Humphreys, S, *Theatre of the Rule of Law: Transnational Legal Intervention in Theory and Practice* (CUP 2010)

Jachtenfuchs, M and Krisch, N, 'Subsidiarity in Global Governance' (2016) 79 Law and Contemporary Problems 1

Jacob, P, 'Le contenu de La responsabilité de l'Etat négligent' in Société française de droit international, *Le standard du due diligence et la responsabilité internationale: Journée SDFI d'études du Mans* (Pedone 2018).

Jacqué, J-P, *Eléments pour une théorie de l'acte juridique en Droit international public* (Librairie générale de droit et de jurisprudence 1972)

Jeffery, R, *Hugo Grotius in International Thought* (Palgrave Macmillan 2006)

Jennings, R and Watts, KCMG QCO A (eds), *Oppenhein's International Law*, vol 1 (9th edn, Longman 1992)

Johnstone, I, 'Treaty Interpretation: The Authority of Interpretive Communities' (1990) 12 Michigan Journal of International Law 371

Johnstone, I, 'Security Council Deliberations: The Power of the Better Argument' (2003) 14 European Journal of International Law 437

Jouannet, E, 'A Critical Introduction' in Martti Koskenniemi (ed), *The Politics of International Law* (Hart Publishing 2011)

Jouannet, E, 'Universalism and Imperialism: The True–False Paradox of International Law?' (2007) 18 European Journal of International Law 379

Kammerhofer, J, 'Uncertainty in the Formal Sources of International Law: Customary International Law and Some of Its Problems' (2004) 15 European Journal of International Law 523

Kammerhofer, J, *Uncertainty in International Law: A Kelsenian Perspective* (Routledge 2010)

Kawashima, S, 'China' in Anne Peters and Bardo Fassbender (eds), *The Oxford Handbook of the History of International Law* (OUP 2012)

Kelsen, H, *General Theory of Law and State* (Harvard University Press 1945)

Kelsen, H, 'Law, State and Justice in the Pure Theory of Law' (1948) 57 Yale Law Journal 377

Kelsen, H, 'Théorie du droit international public' (1953) 84 Collected Courses of the Hague Academy of International Law 1

Kennedy, D, 'Critical Theory, Structuralism and Contemporary Legal Scholarship' (1986) 21 New England Law Review 209

Kennedy, D, *International Legal Structures* (Nomos 1987)

Kennedy, D, 'The Disciplines of International Law and Policy' (1999) 12 Leiden Journal of International Law 9

Kennedy, D, 'Tom Franck and the Manhattan School' (2003) 35 New York University Journal of International Law and Politics 397

Kennedy, D, 'A Left Phenomenological Critique of the Hart/Kelsen Theory of Legal Interpretation' in Duncan Kennedy, *Legal Reasoning, Collected Essays* (The Davies Book Publishers 2008)

Kennedy, D, 'The Mystery of Global Governance' (2008) 34 Ohio Northern University Law Review 827

Kennedy, D, 'The Hermeneutic of Suspicion in Contemporary American Legal Thought Law' (2014) 25 Critique 91

Kennedy, D, *A World of Struggle: How Power, Law and Expertise Shape Global Political Economy* (Princeton University Press 2016)

Kingsbury, B, 'The Concept of "Law" in Global Administrative Law' (2009) 20 European Journal of International Law 23

Kingsbury, B, Krisch, N, and Steward, R, 'The Emergence of Global Administrative Law' (2005) 68 Law and Contemporary Problems 3

Klabbers, J, *The Concept of Treaty in International Law* (Kluwer Publishing 1996)

Klabbers, J, 'The Commodification of International Law' in Hélène Ruiz Fabri, Emmanuelle Jouannet, and Vincent Tomkiewicz (eds), *Select Proceedings of the European Society of International Law*, vol 1 (Hart Publishing 2008)

Klabbers, J, 'Not Re-Visiting the Concept of Treaty' in Alexander Orakhelashvili and Sarah Williams (eds), *40 Years of the Vienna Convention on the Law of Treaties* (British Institute of International and Comparative Law 2010)

Klabbers, J, 'Virtuous Interpretation' in Malgosia Fitzmaurice, Olufemi Elias, and Panos Merkouris (eds), *Treaty Interpretation and the Vienna Convention on the Law of Treaties: 30 Years On*, vol 1 (Martinus Nijhoff Publishers 2010)

Kleinlein, T, 'International Legal Thought: Creation of a Tradition and the Potential of Disciplinary Self-Reflection' in Giuliana Ziccardi Capaldo, *The Global Community: Yearbook of International Law and Jurisprudence 2016* (OUP 2016)

Knop, K, 'Borders of the Imagination: The State in Feminist International Law' (1994) 88 Proceedings of the ASIL Annual Meeting 14

Kochi, T, *The Other's War: Recognition and the Violence of Ethics* (Birkbeck Law Press 2009)

Kohen, M, *Possession contestée et souveraineté territoriale* (Presses Universitaires de France 1997)

Kohen, M, 'Introduction' in Marcelo Kohen (ed), *Secession: International Law Perspectives* (CUP 2006)

Kooijmans, PH, 'Tolerance, Sovereignty and Self-Determination' (1996) 43 Netherlands International Law Review 211

Koskenniemi, M, 'Lauterpacht: The Victorian Tradition in International Law' (1997) 2 European Journal of International Law 215

Koskenniemi, M, 'Letter to the Editors of the Symposium' (1999) 93 American Journal of International Law 351

Koskenniemi, M, 'Carl Schmitt, Hans Morgenthau and the Image of Law in International Relations' in Michael Byers (ed), *The Role of Law in International Politics: Essays in International Relations and International Law* (OUP 2000)

Koskenniemi, M, *The Gentle Civilizer of Nations: The Rise and Fall of International Law 1870–1960* (CUP 2001)

Koskenniemi, M, 'What is International Law For?' in Malcolm Evans (ed), *International Law* (2nd edn, OUP 2006)

Koskenniemi, M, 'The Fate of International Law: Between Technique and Politics' (2007) 70 Modern Law Review 1

Koskenniemi, M, 'The Case for Comparative International Law' (2009) 20 Finnish Yearbook of International Law 1

Koskenniemi, M, 'The Politics of International Law—20 Years Later' (2009) 20 European Journal of International Law 7

Koskenniemi, M, 'Doctrines of State Responsibility' in James Crawford and others (eds), *The Law of International Responsibility* (OUP 2010)

Koskenniemi, M, 'Between Commitment and Cynicism: Outline for a Theory of International Law as Practice' in M Koskenniemi, *The Politics of International Law* (Hart Publishing 2011)

Koskenniemi, M, 'Empire and International Law: The Real Spanish Contribution' (2011) 61 University of Toronto Law Journal 1

Koskenniemi, M, 'A History of International Law Histories' in Bardo Fassbender and Anne Peters (eds), *Oxford Handbook on the History of International Law* (OUP 2012)

Koskenniemi, M, 'Histories of International Law: Significance and Problems for a Critical View' 27 Temple International and Comparative Law Journal (2013)

Koskenniemi, M, 'International Law and the Emergence of Mercantile Capitalism: Grotius To Smith' in Pierre-Marie Dupuy and Vincent Chetail (eds), *The Roots of International Law: Liber Amicorum Peter Haggenmacher* (Martinus Nijhoff Publishers 2014)

Koskenniemi, M, 'What is Critical Research in International Law? Celebrating Structuralism' (2016) 29 Leiden Journal of International Law 727

Koskenniemi, M, 'Between Commitment and Cynicism. Outline for a Theory of International Law as Practice' in Jean d'Aspremont and others (eds), *International Law as a Profession* (CUP 2017)

Koskenniemi, M, 'Introduction: International Law and Empire—Aspects and Approaches' in Martti Koskenniemi, Walter Rech, and Manuel Jimenez Fonseca (eds), *International Law and Empire* (OUP 2017)

Koskenniemi, M, *To the Uttermost Parts of the Earth: Legal Imagination and International Power 1300–1870* (CUP 2021)

Kratochwil Friedrich, V, *Rules, Norms, and Decisions. On the Conditions of Practical and Legal Reasoning in International Relations and Domestic Affairs* (CUP 1989)

Krisch, N, *Beyond Constitutionalism: The Pluralistic Structure of Postnational Law* (OUP 2010)

Kumar, V, 'Revolutionaries' in Jean d'Aspremont and Sahib Singh (eds), *Concepts for International Law: Contributions to Disciplinary Thought* (Edward Elgar Publishing 2019)

Lagerwall, A, 'The Duty Not to Recognise Unlawful Territorial Situations and the European Court of Human Rights' in Christina Binder and Konrad Lachmayer (eds), *European Court of Human Rights and Public International Law: Fragmentation or Unity?* (Nomos 2014)

Lasser, M, 'The Question of Understanding' in Pierre Legrand and Roderick Munday (eds), *Comparative Legal Studies: Traditions and Transitions* (CUP 2003)

Laurent, F, *Histoires du droit des gens et des relations internationales* (Hebbelynck 1850)

Lauterpacht, H, *Recognition in International Law* (CUP 1947)

Lauterpacht, H, *Private Law Sources and Analogies of International Law (with Special Reference to International Arbitration)* (Lawbook Exchange 2002, originally published by Longmans 1927)

Lauterpacht, H, *The Function of Law in the International Community* (2nd edn, OUP 2011)

Lawrence, T, *The Principles of International Law* (7th edn, Heath & Co 1915)

Lefeber, R and Raič, D, 'Frontiers of International Law Part One: The Chechen People' (1996) 9 Leiden Journal of International Law 1

Lefevere, A, 'Mother Courage's Cucumbers: Text: System and Refraction in a Theory of Literature' (1982) 12 Modern Language Studies 3

Leff, AA, 'Unspeakable Ethics, Unnatural Law' [1979] Duke Law Journal 1229

Legrand, P, 'The Same and the Different' in Pierre Legrand and Roderick Munday (eds), *Comparative Legal Studies: Traditions and Transitions* (CUP 2003)

Legrand, P, 'Comparative Legal Studies and the Matter of Authenticity' (2006) 1 Journal of Comparative Law 365

Legrand, P, 'On the Singularity of Law' (2006) 47 Harvard International Law Journal 517

Legrand, P, '"Il n'y a pas de hors-texte": Intimations of Jacques Derrida as Comparatist-at-Law' in Peter Goodrich and others (eds), *Derrida and Legal Philosophy* (Palgrave MacMillan 2008)

Legrand, P, 'Foreign Law: Understanding Understanding' (2011) 6 Journal of Comparative Law 67

Legrand, P, 'Siting Foreign Law: How Derrida Can Help' (2011) 21 Duke Journal of Comparative and International Law 595

Legrand, P, *Negative Comparative Law. A Manifesto* (CUP 2021) (forthcoming)

Lesaffer, R, 'International Law and Its History: The Story of an Unrequited Love' in Matthew Craven, Malgosia Fitzmaurice, and Maria Vogiatzi (eds), *Time, History and International Law* (Brill 2007) 40

Lesaffer, R, 'The Classical Law of Nations (1500–1800)' in Alexander Orakhelashvili (ed), *Research Handbook on the Theory and History of International Law* (Edward Elgar Publishing 2011).

Letsas, G, 'Strasbourg's Interpretive Ethic: Lessons for the International Lawyer' (2010) 21 European Journal of International Law 535

Lipson, C, 'Why Are Some International Agreements Informal' (1991) 45 International Organization 495

Liu, LH, 'Legislating the Universal: The Circulation of International Law in the Nineteenth Century' in Lydia H Liu (ed), *Tokens of Exchange: The Problem of Translation in Global Circulations* (Duke University Press 1999)

Lobban, M, 'English Approaches to International Law in the Nineteenth Century' in Matthew Craven, Malgosia Fitzmaurice, and Maria Vogiatzi (eds), *Time, History and International Law* (Brill 2007).

Lowe, V, 'Precluding Wrongfulness or Responsibility: A Plea for Excuses' (1999) 10 European Journal of International Law 405

Luhmann, N, *Social Systems* (John Bednarz and Dirk Baecker trs, Stanford University Press 1995)

Lusa Bordin, F, 'Analogy' in Jean d'Aspremont and Sahib Singh, *Concepts for International Law* (Edward Elgar Publishing 2018)

Macaulay, S, 'The New Versus the Old Legal Realism: Things Ain't What They Used to Be' (2005) 2 Wisconsin Law Review 365

Malksoo, L, *Russian Approaches to International Law* (OUP 2015)

Mancini, S, 'Secession and Self-Determination' in Michel Rosenfeld and András Sajó (eds), *The Oxford Handbook of Comparative Constitutional Law* (OUP 2012)

Mandelbaum, M, *Purpose and Necessity in Social Theory* (Johns Hopkins University Press 2019)

McCorquodale, R, 'Self-Determination: A Human Rights Approach' (1994) 43 International and Comparative Law Quarterly 24

McDougal, MS, 'Law and Power' (1952) 46 American Journal of International Law 102

Mejía-Lemos, D, 'On Self-Reflectivity, Performativity and Conditions for Existence of Sources of Law in International Law' (2014) 57 German Yearbook of International Law 289

Miéville, C, *Between Equal Rights: A Marxist Theory of International Law* (Haymarket Books 2006)

Miles, CA, 'Indeterminacy' in Jean d'Aspremont and Sahib Singh (eds), *Concepts for International Law: Contributions to Disciplinary Thought* (Edward Elgar Publishing 2019)

Muir Watt, H, 'Discours sur les méthodes du droit international privé (des formes juridiques de l'inter-altérité). Cours général de droit international privé' (2018) 389 Collected Courses of the Hague Academy of International Law 363

Mutua, M, 'Savages, Victims and Saviors: The Metaphor of Human Rights' (2001) 42 Harvard International Law Journal 201

Mutua, M, 'What is TWAIL?' (2000) 94 American Society of International Law Proceedings 31

Neff, DC, *Justice Among Nations* (Harvard University Press 2014)

Nelken, D, 'Towards a Sociology of Legal Adaptation' in David Nelken and Johannes Feest (eds), *Adapting Legal Cultures* (Hart Publishing 2001)

Nesi, G, 'Uti Possidetis Doctrine' in Rüdiger Wolfrum (ed), *Max Planck Encyclopedia of Public International Law* (online edn, OUP 2018)

Nollkaemper, A, 'Power and Responsibility in International Law', in Adriana Di Stefano (ed), *Un Diritto Senza Terra? Funzioni E Limiti de Principio Di Territorialità Nel Diritto Internazionale E Dell'Unione Europea/A Lackland Law? Territory, Effectiveness and Jurisdiction in International and European Law* (Giappichelli 2015)

Nourse, V and Shaffer, G, 'Varieties of New Legal Realism: Can a New World Order Prompt a New Legal Theory' (2009) 95 Cornell Law Review 61

Nuzzo, L, 'The Birth of an Imperial Location: Comparative Perspectives on Western Colonialism in China' (2018) 31 Leiden Journal of International Law 569

Nys, E, *Les origines du droit international* (Castaigne 1894).

Obregon, L, 'Empire, Racial Capitalism and International Law: The Case of Manumitted Haiti and the Recognition Debt' (2018) 31 Leiden Journal of International Law 597

Obregón Tarazona, L, 'Writing International Legal History: An Overview' (2015) 7 Monde(s) 95

Oeter, S, 'The Role of Recognition and Non-Recognition with Regard to Secession' in Christian Walter, Antje van Ungern-Sternberg, and Kavus Abuschov (eds), *Self-Determination and Secession in International Law* (OUP 2014)

Onuf, N, *World of Our Making: Rules and Rules in Social Theory and International Relations* (University of South Carolina Press 1989)

Onuf, N, 'The Constitution of International Society' (1994) 5 European Journal of International Law 1

Oppenheim, L, 'The Science of International Law: Its Task and Method' (1908) 2 The American Journal of International Law 313

Oppenheim, L, *International Law*, vol 1 (1st edn, Longmans 1912)

Orakhelashvili, A, *The Interpretation of Acts and Rules in Public International Law* (OUP 2008)

Orakhelashvili, A, 'Statehood, Recognition and the United Nations System: A Unilateral Declaration of Independence in Kosovo' (2009) 12 Max Planck Yearbook of United Nations Law 1

Orford, A, *Reading Humanitarian Intervention* (CUP 2003)

Orford, A, 'Critical Intimacy: Jacques Derrida and the Friendship of Politics' (2005) 6 German Law Journal 31

Orford, A, 'Critical Intimacies: Reading International Law' in Peter Goodrich and others (eds), *Derrida and Legal Philosophy* (Palgrave Macmillan 2008)

Orford, A, 'On International Legal Method' (2013) 1 London Review of International Law 166

Orford, A, 'Scientific Reason and the Discipline of International Law' (2014) 25 European Journal of International Law 369

Orford, A, 'International Law and the Limits of History' in Wouter Werner, Marieke de Hoon, and Alexis Galán (eds), *The Law of International Lawyers: Reading Martti Koskenniemi* (CUP 2015)

Osiander, A, 'Sovereignty, International Relations, and the Westphalian Myth' (2001) 55 International Organization 251

Ost, F, *Du Sinaï au Champ-de-Mars: L'autre et le même au fondement du droit* (Lessius 1999)

Otto, D, 'Resisting the Heteronormative Imaginary of the Nation-state: Rethinking Kinship and Border Protection' in Dianne Otto (ed), *Queering International Law: Possibilities, Alliances, Complicities, Risks* (Routledge 2018).

Özsu, U, 'Legal Form' in Jean d'Aspremont and Sahib Singh (eds), *Concepts for International Law: Contributions to Disciplinary Thought* (Edward Elgar Publishing 2019)

Pahuja, S, 'The Postcoloniality of International Law' (2005) 46 Harvard International Law Journal 459

Pahuja, S, *Decolonising International Law: Development, Economic Growth and the Politics of Universality* (CUP 2011)

Pahuja, S, 'Decolonization and the Eventness of International Law' in Fleur Johns, Richard Joyce, and Sundhya Pahuja (eds), *Events: The Force of International Law* (Routledge 2011)

Papastavridis, E, 'Interpretation of Security Council Resolutions under Chapter VII in the Aftermath of the Iraqi Crisis' (2007) 56 International and Comparative Law Quarterly 83

Parfitt, R, *The Process of International Legal Reproduction: Inequality, Historiography, Resistance* (CUP 2019)

Parfitt, R, 'The Spectre of Sources' (2014) 25 European Journal of International Law 297

Peat, D, *Comparative Reasoning in International Courts and Tribunals* (CUP 2019)

Peat, D and Windsor, M, 'Playing the Game of Interpretation: On Meaning and Metaphor in International Law' in Andrea Bianchi, Daniel Peat, and Matthew Windsor, *Interpretation in International Law* (OUP 2015)

Pellet, A, 'The Opinions of the Badinter Arbitration Committee: A Second Breath for the Self-Determination of Peoples' (1992) 3 European Journal of International Law 178

Pellet, A, 'Article 38' in Andreas Zimmermann and others (eds), *The Statute of the International Court of Justice: A Commentary* (2nd edn, OUP 2012)

Perreau-Saussine, A, 'A Case Study on Jurisprudence as a Source of International Law: Oppenheim's Influence' in Matthew Craven, Malgosia Fitzmaurice, and Maria Vogiatzi (eds), *Time, History and International Law* (Brill 2007)

Peters, A, 'Compensatory Constitutionalism: The Function and Potential of Fundamental International Norms and Structures' (2006) 19 Leiden Journal of International Law 579

Peters, A, 'The Merits of Global Constitutionalism' (2009) 16 Indiana Journal of Global Legal Studies 397

Peters, A, 'Are We Moving towards Constitutionalisation of the World Community' in Antonio Cassese, *Realising Utopia: The Future of International Law* (OUP 2012)

Peters, A, 'Statehood after 1989: "Effectivités" between Legality and Virtuality' in James Crawford and Sarah Nouwen (eds), *Proceedings of the European Society of International Law*, vol 3 (Hart Publishing 2012)

Peters, A, 'The Principle of Uti Possidetis Juris: How Relevant is it for Issues of Secession?' in Christian Walter, Antje van Ungern-Sternberg, and Kavus Abuschov (eds), *Self-Determination and Secession in International Law* (OUP 2014)

Peters, A, 'The Crimean Vote of March 2014 as an Abuse of the Institution of the Territorial Referendum' in Christian Calliess (ed), *Liber Amicorum für Torsten Stein* (Nomos Verlag 2015)

Petersen, N, 'The Role of Consent and Uncertainty in the Formation of Customary International Law' in Brian D Lepard (ed), *Reexamining Customary International Law* (CUP 2017)

Phillimore, R, *Commentaries upon International Law*, 4 vols (William Benning & Son 1854–61)

Pitts, J, 'Empire and Legal Universalism in the Eighteenth Century' (2012) 117(1) American Historical Review 92, 93.

Polanyi, M, *Personal Knowledge: Towards a Post-Critical Philosophy* (The University of Chicago Press 1958)

Postema, G, *Legal Philosophy in the Twentieth Century: The Common Law World* (Springer 2001)

Pufendorf, S, *On the Law of Nature and of Nations* (Charles Henry Oldfather and William Abbott Oldfather trs, Clarendon Press 1934)

Purcell, K, 'Faltering at the Critical Turn to History: "Juridical Thinking" in International Law and Genealogy as History, Critique, and Therapy' (2015) 15 Jean Monnet Working Paper 1

Rajkovic, N, 'Rules, Lawyering, and the Politics of Legality: Critical Sociology and International Law's Rule' (2014) 27 Leiden Journal of International Law 331

Rasulov, A, 'From Apology to Utopia and the Inner Life of International Law' (2016) 29 Leiden Journal of International Law 641

Rasulov, A, 'What is Critique? Notes Towards a Sociology of Disciplinary Heterodoxy in Contemporary International Law' in Jean d'Aspremont and others (eds), *International Law as a Profession* (CUP 2017)

Rasulov, A, 'Imperialism', in Jean d'Aspremont and Sahib Singh (eds), *Concepts for International Law: Contributions to Disciplinary Thought* (Edward Elgar Publishing 2019)

Raustalia, K, 'Form and Substance in International Agreements' (2005) 99 American Journal of International Law 581

Raz, J, *The Authority of Law: Essays on Law and Morality* (Clarendon Press 1983)

Rech, W, 'International Law, Empire, and the Relative Indeterminacy of Narrative' in Martti Koskenniemi, Walter Rech, and Manuel Jiménez Fonseca (eds), *International Law and Empire: Historical Explorations* (OUP 2017)

Rech, W, 'Ideology' in Jean d'Aspremont and Sahib Singh (eds), *Concepts for International Law. Contributions to Disciplinary Thought* (Edward Elgar Publishing 2019)

Reisman, WM, 'The View from the New Haven School of International Law' (1992) 86 Proceedings of the ASIL Annual Meeting 118

Reisman, WM, Wiessner, S, and Willard, A, 'The New Haven School: A Brief Introduction' (2007) 32 Yale Journal of International Law 576

Reus-Smit, C, 'Politics and International Legal Obligation' (2003) 9 European Journal of International Law 591

Reus-Smit, C, 'The Politics of International Law' in Christian Reus-Smit, *The Politics of International Law* (CUP 2004)

Reuter, P, 'Traités et transactions: Réflexions sur l'identification de certains engagements conventionnels' in *International Law at the Time of Its Codification. Essays in Honour of Roberto Ago* (Giuffrè 1987)

Reuter, P, *Introduction au Droit des Traités* (3rd edn, Presses Universitaires de France 1995)

Ridi, N, 'The Shape and Structure of the "Usable Past": An Empirical Analysis of the Use of Precedent in International Adjudication' (2019) 10 Journal of International Dispute Settlement 200

Ridi, N, 'Doing Things with International Precedents: The Use and Authority of Previous Decisions in International Adjudication' (PhD thesis, King's College London) (on file with the author)

Riegl, M and Bohumil, D (eds), *Unrecognized States and Secession in the 21st Century* (Springer 2017)

Roberts, A, *Is International Law International?* (OUP 2017)

Roberts, A, 'Is International Law International? Continuing the Conversation' (EJIL: Talk!, 9 February 2018) accessed 24 May 2021.

Roberts, A and others, 'Conceptualizing Comparative International Law' in Anthea Roberts and others (eds), *Comparative International Law* (OUP 2018)

Rodell, F, 'Goodbye to Law Reviews' (1936) 23 Virginia Law Review 38

Rolin, H, 'Notice sur Ernest Nys: bibliographie' (1951) 4 Revue de l'Université de Bruxelles 349

Roth, B, 'Secessions, Coups and the International Rule of Law: Assessing the Decline of the Effective Control Doctrine' (2010) 11 Melbourne Journal of International Law 1

Rousseau, C, *Principes généraux du droit international public*, vol 1 (Pedone 1944)

Salmon, J, 'Notice Ernest Nys' (2007) 9 Nouvelle biographie nationale 283

Salmond, JW, *First Principles of Jurisprudence* (Stevens and Haynes 1893)

Salmond, JW, *Jurisprudence: or the Theory of the Law* (7th edn, Sweet and Maxwell 1924)

Salmon P, *An Event, Perhaps* (Verso 2020)

Scarfi, JP, *The Hidden History of International Law in the Americas: Empire and Legal Networks* (OUP 2017)

Schachter, O, 'The Invisible College of International Lawyers' (1977) 72 Northwestern University Law Review 217

Schachter, O, 'The Twilight Existence of Nonbinding International Agreements' (1977) 71 American Journal of International Law 296

Schermers, H and Blokker, N, *International Institutional Law* (6th edn, Martinus Nijhoff Publishers 2018)

Schlag, P, '"Le Hors de Texte, C'est Moi": The Politics of Form and the Domestication of Deconstruction' (1990) 11 Cardozo Law Review 1631

Schlag, P, 'Normativity and the Politics of Form' (1991) 139 University of Pennsylvania Law Review 801

Schlag, P, 'Law as the Continuation of God by Other Means' (1997) 85 California Law Review 427

Schlag, P, 'The Empty Circles of Liberal Justification' (1997) 96 Michigan Law Review 1

Schlag, P, 'My Dinner at Langdell's' (2004) 52 Buffalo Law Review 851

Schmalenbach, K, 'Article 2' in Oliver Dörr and Kirsten Schmalenbach (eds), *Vienna Convention on the Law of Treaties: A Commentary* (Springer 2012)

Schmitt, C, *Politische Theologie: Vier Kapitel zur Lehre von der Souveränität* (Duncker und Humblot 1979)

Seidl-Hohenveldern, I, 'Hierarchy of Treaties' in Jan Klabbers and René Lefeber (eds), *Essays on the Law of Treaties: A Collection of Essays in Honour of Bert Vierdag* (Martinus Nijhoff Publishers 1998)

Shaffer, G, 'A New Legal Realism: Method in International Economic Law Scholarship' in Colin B Picker, Isabella Bunn and Douglas Arner (eds), *International Economic Law: The State and Future of the Discipline* (Hart Publishing 2008)

Shaffer, G and Ginsburg, T, 'The Empirical Turn in International Legal Scholarship' (2012) 106 American Journal of International Law 1

Shaw, MN, 'The Heritage of States: The Principle of Uti Possidetis Juris Today' (1996) 67 British Yearbook of International Law 75

Shaw, MN, 'Peoples, Territorialism and Boundaries' (1997) 3 European Journal of International Law 478

Simma, B and Paulus, AL, 'The Responsibility of Individuals for Human Rights Abuses in Internal Conflicts: A Positivist View' (1999) 93 American Journal of International Law 302

Simpson, G, *Great Powers and Outlaw States: Unequal Sovereigns in Their International Legal Order* (CUP 2004)

Simpson, G, 'The Sentimental Life of International Law' (2015) 3 London Review of International Law 3

Singh, S, 'International Law as a Technical Discipline: Critical Perspectives on the Narrative Structure of a Theory' in Jean d'Aspremont, *Formalism and the Sources of International Law* (OUP 2013)

Singh, S, 'International Legal Positivism and New Approaches to International Law' in Jörg Kammerhofer and Jean d'Aspremont (eds), *International Legal Positivism in a Post-Modern World* (CUP 2014)

Sloterdijk, P, *Critique of Cynical Reason* (University of Minnesota 1987)

Sofaer, A, 'Adjudication in the International Court of Justice: Progress through Realism' (1989) 44 Rec. A.B. City N.Y. 462

Sorel, J-M, 'Article 31' in Pierre Klein and Oliver Corten, *Les Conventions de Vienne sur le Droit des Traités: Commentaire article par article* (Bruylant 2006)

Southgate, B, 'Postmodernism' in Aviezer Tucker (ed), *A Companion to the Philosophy of History and Historiography* (Wiley-Blackwell 2011)

Steiner, G, *After Babel: Aspects of Language and Translation* (OUP 1975)

Steiner, G, *Errata: An Examined Life* (Weidenfeld and Nicholson 1997)

Stern, B, 'The Obligation to Make Reparation' in James Crawford and others (eds), *The Law of International Responsibility* (OUP 2010)

Stern, B, 'Custom at the Heart of International Law' (2001) 11 Duke Journal of Comparative and International Law 89

Straumann, B, '"Ancient Caesarean Lawyers" in a State of Nature: Roman Tradition and Natural Rights in Hugo Grotius's "De iure praedae"' (2006) 34 Political Theory 328

Strupp, K, *Eléments du droit international public* (Rousseau & Co 1927)

Svarverud, R, *International Law as World Order in late Imperial China: Translation, Reception and Discourse. 1847–1911* (Brill 2007)

Talmon, S, 'The Duty Not to "Recognize As Lawful" a Situation Created by the Illegal Use of Force or Other Serious Breaches of a Jus Cogens Obligation: An Obligation Without Real Substance?' in Christian Tomuschat and Jean-Marc Thouvenin (eds), *The Fundamental Rules of the International Legal Order: Jus Cogens and Obligations Erga Omnes* (Martinus Nijhoff Publishers 2006)

Tamanaha, B, *A General Jurisprudence of Law and Society* (OUP 2001)

Tancredi, A, 'A Normative "Due Process" in the Creation of States through Secession' in Marcelo Kohen (ed), *Secession: International Law Perspectives* (CUP 2006)

Tang, C-H, 'China-Europe' in Anne Peters and Bardo Fassbender (eds), *The Oxford Handbook of the History of International Law* (OUP 2012)

Tasioulas, J, 'Custom, Jus Cogens, and Human Rights' in Curtis Bradley (ed), *Custom's Future: International Law in a Changing World* (CUP 2016)

Tasioulas, J, 'Opinio Juris and the Genesis of Custom: A Solution to the "Paradox"' (2007) 26 Australian Yearbook of International Law 199

Thirlway, H, *The Sources of International Law* (OUP, 2014)

Thirlway, H, 'Professor Baxter's Legacy: Still Paradoxical?' (2017) 6 ESIL Reflection

Thirlway, H, *The Sources of International Law* (2nd edn, OUP 2019)

Thürer, D and Burri, T, 'Self-Determination' in Rüdiger Wolfrum (ed), *Max Planck Encyclopedia of Public International Law* (online edn, OUP 2008)

Thurschwell, A, 'Specters and Scholars: Derrida and the Tragedy of Political Thought' (2005) 6 German Law Journal 8

Tomuschat, C, 'Self-Determination in a Post-Colonial World' in Christian Tomuschat (ed), *Modern Law of Self-Determination* (Martinus Nijhoff Publishers 1993)

Tomuschat, C, 'Secession and Self-Determination' in Marcelo Kohen (ed), *Secession: International Law Perspectives* (CUP 2006)

Toury, G, *Descriptive Translation Studies and Beyond* (Benjamins 1995)

Triepel, H, *Völkerrecht und Landesrecht* (Scientia Verlag 1899)

Tunç Utebay, S, *Justice en tant que loi, justice au-delà de la loi. Hobbes, Derrida et les Critical Legal Studies* (L'Harmattan 2017)

Tunkin, G, *Theory of International Law* (HUP 1974)

Turp, D, 'Le droit de sécession en droit international public' (1982) 20 Canadian Yearbook of International Law 24

Tzouvala, N, *Capitalism as Civilisation: A History of International Law* (CUP 2020)

Vagts, DF, 'Treaty Interpretation and the New American Ways of Law Reading' (1993) 4 European Journal of International Law 472

van Hoof, GJH, *Rethinking the Sources of International Law* (Kluwer Publishing 1983)

Venzke, I, *How Interpretation Makes International Law: On Semantic Change and Normative Twists* (OUP 2012)

Venzke, I, 'Contemporary Theories and International Lawmaking' in Catherine Brölmann and Yannick Radi (eds), *Research Handbook on the Theory and Practice of International Lawmaking* (Edward Elgar Publishing 2016)

Venzke, I, 'Cracking the Frame? On the Prospects of Change in a World of Struggle' (2016) 27 European Journal of International Law 831

Venzke, I, 'International Law as an Argumentative Practice: On Wohlrapp's The Concept of Argument' (2016) 7 Transnational Legal Theory 9

Venzke, I and Heller, KJ, *Contingency in International Law: On the Possibility of Different Legal Histories* (OUP 2021)

Verdier, P-H and Voeten, E, 'How Does Customary International Law Change? The Case of State Immunity' (2015) 59 International Studies Quarterly 209

Verhoeven, J, 'Considérations sur ce qui est commun. Cours général de droit international public' (2002) 334 Collected Courses of the Hague Academy of International Law 109

Veyne, P, *Les Grecs ont-ils cru à leurs mythes? Essai sur l'imagination constituante* (Seuil 1983)

Vidmar, J, 'Remedial Secession in International Law: Theory and (Lack of) Practice' (2010) 6 St Antony's International Review 37

Vidmar, J, 'Explaining the Legal Effects of Recognition' (2012) 61 International and Comparative Law Quarterly 361

Vidmar, J, *Democratic Statehood in International Law* (Hart Publishing 2013)

Vidmar, J, 'Territorial Integrity and the Doctrine of Statehood' (2013) 44 George Washington International Law Review 101

Vidmar, J, 'The Annexation of Crimea and the Boundaries of the Will of the People' (2015) 16 German Law Journal 365

Vidmar, J, 'The Concept of the State and its Right of Existence' (2015) 4 Cambridge Journal of International and Comparative Law 547

Villiger, ME, *Customary International Law and Treaties: A Study of their Interactions and Interrelations with Special Consideration of the 1969 Vienna Convention on the Law of Treaties* (Martinus Nijhoff Publishers 1985)

Vinuales, JE, 'On Legal Inquiry' in Denis Alland and others (eds), *Unity and Diversity of International Law: Essays in Honour of Professor Pierre-Marie Dupuy* (Martinus Nijhoff Publishers 2014)

Virally, M, 'Sur la notion d'accord' in Emanuel Diez (ed), *Festschrift für Rudolf Bindschedler* (Staempfli & Cie 1980)

von Bernstorff, J, *The Public International Law Theory of Hans Kelsen: Believing in Universal Law* (CUP 2010)

von Martens, GF, *Précis du droit des gens moderne de l'Europe fondé sur les traités et l'usage* (Dieterich 1789)

Waibel, M, 'Demystifying the Art of Interpretation' (2011) 22 European Journal of International Law 571

Walter, C and von Ungern-Sternberg, A, 'Self-Determination and Secession in International Law: Perspectives and Trends with Particular Focus on the Commonwealth of Independent States' in Christian Walter, Antje van Ungern-Sternberg, and Kavus Abuschov (eds), *Self-Determination and Secession in International Law* (OUP 2014)

Watts, A, 'The International Rule of Law' (1993) 36 *German Yearbook of International Law* 15

Weil, P, 'Le droit international en quête de son identité' (1992) 237 Collected Courses of the Hague Academy of International Law 139

Weisburd, AM, 'Customary International Law: The Problem of Treaties' (1988) 21 Vanderbilt Journal of Transnational Law 1

Weisburd, AM, *Failings of the International Court of Justice* (OUP 2016)

Weller, D, 'The International Response to the Dissolution of the Socialist Federal Republic of Yugoslavia' (1992) 86 American Journal of International Law 569

Werner, M and Zimmermann, B, 'Beyond Comparison: Histoire Croisée and the Challenge of Reflexivity' (2006) 45 History and Theory 30

Westlake, J, *International Law* (The University Press 1904)

Wheaton, H, *Elements of International Law* (Carey, Lea & Blanchard 1836)

Wheaton, H, *Histoire des Progrès du Droit des Gens en Europe et en Amérique Depuis la Paix de Westphalie jusqu'à nos Jours* (Brockhaus 1841)

Wheaton, H, *A History of the Law of Nations in Europe and America from the Earliest Times to the Treaty of Washington* (Gould, Banks & Co 1845)

Wijffels, A, 'Early-Modern Scholarship on International Law' in Alexander Orakhelashvili (ed), *Research Handbook on the Theory and History of International Law* (Edward Elgar Publishing 2011)

Wilson, R, *Theodor Adorno* (Routledge 2007)

Windsor, M, 'Narrative Kill or Capture: Unreliable Narration in International Law' (2015) 28 Leiden Journal of International Law 743

Winter, SL, *A Clearing in the Forest: Law, Life and Mind* (The University of Chicago Press 2001)

Wolff, C, *Law of Nations Treated According to a Scientific Method* (Joseph H Drake tr, Clarendon Press 1934)

Woolsey, TD, *Introduction to the Study of International Law* (4th edn, Scribnerm Amstrong & Co 1877)

Xifaras, M, 'Théorie des personnages juridiques' (2017) 2 Revue française de droit administratif 275

Zarbiyev, F, *Le discours interprétatif en droit international: une approche critique et généalogique* (PhD thesis, Geneva Graduate Institute of International and Development Studies 2009)

Zarbiyev, F, *Le discours interprétatif en droit international* (Bruylant 2015)

Index

Printed and bound by CPI Group (UK) Ltd, Croydon, CR0 4YY

09/06/2025

14685770-0004